EQUAL PAY FOR COMPARABLE WORTH

The Working Woman's Issue of the Eighties

Frances C. Hutner

PRAEGER SPECIAL STUDIES • PRAEGER SCIENTIFIC

New York • Philadelphia • Eastbourne, UK
Toronto • Hong Kong • Tokyo • Sydney

Library of Congress Cataloging-in-Publication Data

Hutner, Frances C.
 Equal pay for comparable worth.

   Bibliography: p.
   Includes index.
   1.   Equal pay for equal work—United States.
 2.   Equal pay for equal work—United States—Case studies.
 3.   Equal pay for equal work.   I.   Title
 HD6061.2.U6H86   1986   331.4'21'0973   85-19427
 ISBN 0-03-062873-3 (alk. paper)

Published in 1986 by Praeger Publishers

CBS Educational and Professional Publishing, a Division of CBS Inc.
521 Fifth Avenue, New York, NY 10175 USA

© 1986 by Frances C. Hutner

6789 052 987654321

Printed in the United States of America on acid-free paper

INTERNATIONAL OFFICES

Orders from outside the United States should be sent to the appropriate address listed below. Orders from areas not listed below should be placed through CBS International Publishing, 383 Madison Ave., New York, NY 10175 USA

Australia, New Zealand
Holt Saunders, Pty. Ltd., 9 Waltham St., Artarmon, N.S.W. 2064, Sydney, Australia

Canada
Holt, Rinehart & Winston of Canada, 55 Horner Ave., Toronto, Ontario, Canada M8Z 4X6

Europe, the Middle East, & Africa
Holt Saunders, Ltd., 1 St. Anne's Road, Eastbourne, East Sussex, England BN21 3UN

Japan
Holt Saunders, Ltd., Ichibancho Central Building, 22-1 Ichibancho, 3rd Floor, Chiyodaku, Tokyo, Japan

Hong Kong, Southeast Asia
Holt Saunders Asia, Ltd., 10 Fl, Intercontinental Plaza, 94 Granville Road, Tsim Sha Tsui East, Kowloon, Hong Kong

Manuscript submissions should be sent to the Editorial Director, Praeger Publishers, 521 Fifth Avenue, New York, NY 10175 USA

To Elizabeth, Louise, and Nancy

PREFACE

The unprecedented increase in the last two decades in the numbers of women working at paid labor in the industrialized countries has given great impetus to the struggle for pay equity. As more and more women support themselves and their families and look forward with concern to what they are going to live on in their old age, they see sex-based wage discrimination as a serious problem. Growing numbers of the poor are women—young and old—and the children of women who are heads of households.

The opposition to comparable worth has its concerns as well. Employers fear higher labor costs. Taxpayers worry about higher taxes. Some economists and politicians and lawyers threaten that higher wages for women will cause more female unemployment. Some jurists worry that the government will get heavily involved in the business of setting wages and think this is wrong. Some conservative women support the "feminine mystique" mythology and argue that it is right for women workers to earn less than men for work of comparable value. To the extent that status is tied to pay, some people feel threatened by a rise in female pay and status. Most threatening to many is the fact that getting rid of sex-based wage discrimination means increasing the working woman's share of national income.

The pay equity issue is, therefore, an important one. But despite its importance, the policy of equal pay for comparable worth is poorly understood. My purpose in this book is to help people understand the issue and the arguments for and against it and to illustrate how it can eliminate sex discrimination in pay.

The first section of the book is introductory. It discusses the varied and controversial legal and economic interpretations of the comparable worth concept and the possibility and problems of measuring "worth" by using job evaluation techniques. Next, the history of comparable worth policy both here and abroad is described, emphasizing that the policy has a considerable record of use in the United States, Europe, Australia, and Canada.

Case studies of attempts to secure equal pay for jobs of comparable worth make up the major part of the book. For information about these cases I have interviewed people directly involved in them. As much as possible I have let these people speak for themselves.

The first study is the lively and informative story of the efforts of a union, Local 101 of the American Federation of State, County and Municipal Employees (AFSCME), to bargain collectively with the city of San Jose for comparable worth. In this case clerical workers and librarians, two typically female occupations, provided the impetus for pay equity and succeeded in getting the policy under way with the support and help of male union members—but only after a strike.

The second is a study of the experience of blue-collar women workers in a light bulb factory in Trenton, New Jersey, who sought pay equity from their employer, Westinghouse Electric Corporation. It is a model of a sex-segregated work force, where women employees were paid less than male employees working at jobs comparable or lower in value according to the employer's own job evaluation system. The women finally sued Westinghouse and won a landmark third circuit court of appeals decision. This decision interpreted Title VII of the 1964 Civil Rights Act as protecting women against sex-based wage discrimination even if they were not working at the same jobs as men.

The third is the Denver nurses' case. Nursing is a prototype of the female occupation that has high requirements for training, skill, and responsibility, as well as difficult working conditions, yet is paid substantially less than male occupations with comparable or lesser requirements. The nurses lost their case, but in the long process of working on it they made many people keenly aware of the issue. It was a dramatic confrontation: the women in blue and white against the city of Denver as the confused, apparently well-intentioned employer, and an eccentric, aggressively conservative judge. It was also a lesson in the politics of justice.

The fourth is the story of how women in Washington State and the Washington Federation of State Employees, a local AFSCME union, have worked for more than a decade for pay equity. They were the first to coin the term "comparable worth," and the state made the first formal comparable worth study in this country. Such studies have since been done or are under way in some 18 other states and in many more local government jurisdictions.

The most important legacy of this effort, however, is the 1983 district court decision in the sex-based wage discrimination case the union brought against the state. This decision found the state guilty of discrimination and ordered prompt implementation of pay equity for state employees and back pay for the affected class of some 15,000 employees in predominantly female jobs. The district court's opinion encouraged the supporters of pay equity to continue their efforts to organize women workers, to bargain for pay equity, and to litigate where necessary to achieve it. It shocked many employers into examining their own pay structures. And it increased the efforts of opponents to pay equity to question its validity as a policy and to fight it when it appeared in litigation.

The state appealed the decision to the ninth circuit court of appeals. In September 1985 the appeals court overturned the district court's ruling in a decision which cheered pay equity opponents. The union plans to ask either for *en banc* review of the ruling by the appeals court—review by about half of the appeals justices in the case of the ninth circuit—or for review by the U.S. Supreme Court. The case may, however, be settled out of court before the appeals process is completed. In July 1985, at the request of the governor, the Washington state legislature earmarked $42 million in its budget for a possible out-of-court settlement of the case. And in August 1985, shortly before the appeals court ruling, Governor Gardner and the union agreed to start settlement negotiations. They are continuing these negotiations despite the ninth circuit court's reversal of the district court decision.

The last chapter brings the story of comparable worth policy up to date. It discusses the successful strike for comparable worth at Yale. It describes how unions and management at American Telephone and Telegraph have developed a nonsexist job evaluation plan for measuring the comparable worth of jobs. It discusses the significant progress that state and local governments are making in studying and implementing comparable worth policy. And it briefly describes recent pay equity litigation.

This book addresses several audiences. The first is made up of 50 million women workers. They and their families have an obvious stake in a policy designed to get rid of sex-based wage discrimination. Speaking at the 1979 National Conference on Pay Equity, Eleanor Holmes Norton, who was then the chair of the Equal Employment Opportunity Commission, called comparable worth the working woman's issue of the 1980s. She pointed out, however, that "the average woman has not even heard of the comparable worth issue."

Women's advocates form another audience. A variety of organizations—unions, women's associations, legal defense groups, and federal and state government agencies—have women's issues as a sole or important interest.

The book will be helpful in explaining pay equity theory and practice to students in the large and growing number of women's studies programs as well as in courses on economic principles and labor economics. It will be helpful, also, to both public and private employers and their organizations. Finally, it will inform professional counsellors of women, who are frequently confronted with problems reflecting both the economic and psychological aspects of pay inequity.

I would like to acknowledge with gratitude the support of the Griffis Foundation for the research involved in this project. This support was essential to the success of the interviewing process. I would also like to thank the Princeton Research Forum for their help in supervising the grant and for the advice and encouragement they have provided.

I am deeply grateful to the people who talked to me about their experiences. They were unfailingly generous with their time. They made the project a most rewarding personal experience for me.

I am also grateful to the people who helped me with their advice and criticisms and comments. I learned a great deal from both the supporters and the critics of comparable worth.

I would like to thank Lynda Sharp, my editor at Praeger Publishers, for encouraging me at every stage of the project.

I am most grateful to Dan and Nancy Hutner for teaching me how to use the computer for writing and record keeping and for advising and calming me when it presented dismaying problems. I am deeply indebted to Nancy for her excellent editorial work and even more, for all of the other help and counsel and comfort she has given me.

Finally, I would like to thank my husband, Simeon Hutner, for his unstinting and thoughtful support and encouragement and for his always sensible and informed advice.

CONTENTS

Contents

1

EQUAL PAY FOR COMPARABLE WORTH: "A Can Chock-Full of Worms?"

The nurses of Denver complained that although they did responsible, highly skilled, and often hazardous work they were paid less by the city than men in such all male occupations as sign painter, tree trimmer, and tire serviceman. Blue-collar women assembling light bulbs for the Westinghouse Electric Corporation in Trenton, New Jersey, were paid less than the lowest paid, unskilled men who swept the company's floors.

Working women's advocates point out that most women still work in low-paying, traditionally female occupations. Although the Equal Pay Act of 1963 stipulates equal pay for equal work, this legislation is ineffective when equal work, in practice, means the same work, and most women are not doing the same work as men. The women's advocates say that employers pay their women employees working in female jobs less than they pay their male employees working at men's jobs with similar requirements for education, skill, responsibility, and working conditions. The advocates argue that although the women's jobs are of comparable value to the employer, the women are paid less because they are women, and that this is sex discrimination. They back a policy of equal pay for comparable worth, or equal pay for work of equivalent value, as an essential means for raising women's average earnings.

Indeed, "comparable worth" has become a principal goal of the working women's movement. As Eleanor Holmes Norton, chair of the Equal Employment Opportunity Commission in the Carter administration, said at the 1979 National Conference on Pay Equity, "For the average woman who works—who is increasingly the average woman—I do believe this is the issue of the 1980s." She added, "This is a true sleeping giant. The average woman has come to understand equal pay for equal work, but I think the average woman has not even heard of the comparable worth issue."

1

Organized employers, on the other hand, have repeatedly voiced their unqualified opposition to a policy of equal pay for comparable worth. For example, at the April 1980 hearings held by the Equal Employment Opportunity Commission on the subject of job segregation and wage discrimination, men from the National Association of Manufacturers, the Chamber of Commerce, the Business Roundtable, and the National Public Employers Labor Relations Association all spoke out strongly against the policy. Moreover, trade associations and major corporations, among them General Electric, General Motors, Exxon, Sears, and Prudential Insurance, have joined forces in a Washington, D.C.–based organization called the Equal Employment Advisory Council. The council has spent a good deal of time and money opposing equal pay for comparable worth.

The government agencies that have been concerned with this issue have come out on both sides of the policy. Congress charged the Equal Employment Opportunity Commission with the task of implementing affirmative action as public policy. Under Eleanor Holmes Norton's direction, the EEOC seemed well-disposed to comparable worth and commissioned a two-year study by the National Academy of Sciences on the feasibility of using job evaluation techniques to measure comparable worth. The agency also held hearings on the related problems of wage discrimination and job segregation. But before the EEOC had developed guidelines on using comparable worth to determine pay discrimination, the Reagan administration took office. The current EEOC, under the conservative guidance of Clarence Thomas, is not pursuing this task.

In fact, the Reagan administration has shown increasing hostility to pay equity and to affirmative action as well. The Department of Labor's Office of Federal Contract Compliance Programs (OFFCP) is responsible for enforcing Executive Order 11246, forbidding discrimination in employment by federal contractors and requiring them to adopt affirmative action policies in hiring, promotion, compensation, and training for women and minorities. The Reagan administration has rejected Carter administration proposals mandating comparable worth for federal contractors, which would have put the OFFCP in the forefront of pay equity enforcement, and has severely limited OFFCP affirmative action activities. The EEOC has also reduced its affirmative action enforcement activities and is currently studying revision of EEOC guidelines to reduce reliance on statistical evidence of discrimination.

Furthermore, Reagan has made the U.S. Civil Rights Commission, formerly a bipartisan, independent agency, into a mouthpiece for the administration's conservative civil rights policies. "This is probably the looniest idea since Looney Tunes came on the screen," Clarence Pendleton, chair of the U.S. Commission on Civil Rights, said about comparable worth at a November 1984 news conference. Linda Chavez, staff director of the commission, also expressed strong opposition to pay equity policy.

After Judge Tanner's 1983 finding in the *AFSCME v. Washington State* case that the state had discriminated against its women employees in compensation, William Bradford Reynolds, assistant attorney general for civil rights, attacked the decision and said that the federal government might file a friend of the court brief or even seek to become an intervenor on the side of Washington State in the appeals court review. Shortly before the 1984 presidential election, the administration backed off on filing or intervening. According to *The New York Times,* however, during the campaign White House economist William Niskanen called comparable worth "a truly crazy proposal," and presidential press secretary Larry Speakes said that President Reagan considered it "nebulous at best."

In two early appeals court decisions on pay equity under Title VII of the Civil Rights Act—*Christensen* v. *State of Iowa* (Eighth Circuit, 1977) and *Lemons* v. *City and County of Denver* (Tenth Circuit, 1980)—the courts interpreted the act as being limited to equal pay for equal work cases by the Bennett Amendment. Two subsequent appeals court decisions—*IUE* v. *Westinghouse Electric Corporation* (Third Circuit, 1980) and *County of Washington* v. *Gunther* (Ninth Circuit, 1979)—and the Supreme Court decision in the *Gunther* appeal all found that sex-based wage discrimination complaints are not limited by the Bennett Amendment to equal work cases. These decisions have kept the door open for plaintiffs to bring pay equity suits.

The district court decision in *AFSCME* v. *State of Washington* (1983) was a stunning victory for those who oppose sex-based wage discrimination. Opponents of pay equity, however, view the July 1984 ninth circuit court of appeals opinion in *Spaulding* v. *University of Washington* as an important rebuttal to this district court decision and a legal aid in their fight against equal pay for comparable worth. They have been further cheered by the September 1985 reversal of the district court decision in *AFSCME* v. *State of Washington* by the ninth circuit court of appeals. The union plans to ask for review of the appeals court ruling by a larger group of ninth circuit court justices or by the U.S. Supreme Court.

Why, in 1981, did a *Wall Street Journal* editor write, "The notion that there ought to be equal pay for comparable worth is a can chock-full of worms"? Why, in a 1980 book on comparable worth, did Cornell University professor of industrial relations George Hildebrand call the concept a "notion" that "involves sheer rhetoric alone," lacking in "operational meaning"?[1] Can this be the same policy that the head of the EEOC named as the major issue facing working women today? That a distinguished committee of the National Academy of Sciences spent two years studying? That union organizations like the American Federation of State, County and Municipal Employees, the International Union of Electrical

Workers, and the Coalition of Labor Union Women have made a priority issue in their representation of women workers?

In an interview with the Bureau of National Affairs, Eleanor Holmes Norton described comparable worth as "infinitely more complex," having "implications well beyond anything else confronted" under Title VII of the Civil Rights Act of 1964. She described it as "the most difficult issue ever" to arrive "under the statute," and "the only truly large issue remaining in flux" under equal employment law.[2] But the issue's complexity and difficulty, by themselves, do not make it "a can of worms," or "sheer rhetoric alone." The "implications well beyond anything else confronted" under Title VII have brought it both strong support from women's advocates and name-calling opposition from employer groups and conservative journalists and economists.

What is this complex and controversial issue? What does the concept "equal pay for comparable worth" mean? What is the problem that this policy is supposed to correct? Why has this type of pay equity policy been taken so seriously by organizations of women workers, by employers, by the courts, and by government?

The Problem: "No Noah's Ark"

"Well, you have all heard the occupational system is no Noah's Ark. A male and female get separated at the port of embarkation." In this way Helen Hacker, professor of sociology at Adelphi University, introduced her testimony on job segregation and wage discrimination before the EEOC at their 1980 hearings.[3] The facts that she referred to are well documented. Women workers are concentrated in a few occupations, and these occupations are predominantly, and sometimes entirely, female. "I would like to suggest," Professor Hacker said,

> that sex represents a master or perhaps I should say mistress status, that influences all the expectations about the behavior of women and what is their proper role, and further that the mere fact of job segregation implies the possibility that wages have been discriminatorily depressed. By that we mean that if the jobs now filled almost exclusively by minority groups, including women, were instead to be occupied by dominant group members, these jobs would command a higher wage or salary.

Hacker's contention is that, by and large, women work in sex-segregated jobs and these jobs are lower paid than men's jobs, in part, at least, because they are women's jobs. She explains, for example, that the greater power and prestige of the dominant group, white males, "enables them to define the value position of particular work and occupations in the economy in such a way that the kinds of work done by them are higher in the hierarchy than work performed by minority group members." The lower status of women and other minorities is justified by stereotypes, devised by the dominant groups, that posit "a natural order in society which allocates individuals to statuses appropriate to their defining characteristic, whether it be race, ethnicity or sex."

She adds,

> A telling example of . . . how the characteristics of the worker influence the job is seen in the case of the job of bank teller. Before World War II this job was exclusively the preserve of white men. When the job became feminized, teller's pay did not keep pace with other predominantly male jobs, nor serve as it had before as a step toward bank officers.

Lending credence to Professor Hacker's sociological analysis about the dominant group, which she defines as "one which is able to control power, both economic and political . . .," is the fact that the same sex segregation of jobs and sex-based pay inequity exist in other developed countries and in the developing countries as well.[4]

But modern-day, mainstream labor economists have not been willing to accept sociological analyses attributing pay inequity to male dominance, patriarchy, female biology, and the like without subjecting the phenomenon to economic analysis. Consequently, they have exhaustively studied the possible causes for sex inequity in earnings. One factor, for example, might presumably be relative educational levels. But women's average educational levels are, in fact, as high as men's. Furthermore, women receive a much smaller payoff on their education. For example, women who have completed four years of college typically earn less than men who have only completed eighth grade.

Is length and continuity of service in the labor force a factor in explaining the low pay ratio? This is undoubtedly an influence, but its importance is small, simply because women's earnings do not rise much with age and experience. Length of service in dead-end jobs does not produce substantially higher earnings for older workers. In the apparel industry, for instance, women have shown great attachment to their jobs but have experienced little upward mobility, much less than men. The assumption that women will drop out of the labor force for considerable periods of time does, however, provide employers with a reason for shunting them into jobs where there is little prospect for future advancement.

Are higher rates of absenteeism and turnover an important cause of pay disparity? Research findings do not bear this out. On the contrary, Patricia Cayo Sexton, in her Department of Labor monograph, *Women and Work,* suggests the interesting hypothesis that "women's earnings suffer because they remain committed, steady, able workers, even when wage and promotional incentives are low . . . The problem, then, is not that women are less committed workers than men, but that they may be too committed and undemanding, and therefore less able to increase their compensation."[5] Supporting this view is the fact that, although the majority of women workers are not covered by union contracts, those that are average a third higher earnings than their nonunion counterparts.

On the other hand, full-time women workers do work fewer hours per week than men. They do earn less overtime. And they are less likely to be multiple job holders. All of these factors lower women's average earnings.

But economists have not been able to account for all of the female-male pay gap, even after examining differences in education and training, job tenure, absenteeism, and hours of work and after considering other possible factors. Despite their best analytical efforts, an unexplained "residual" of pay difference between women and men remains. The unexplained residual ranges from 20 percent of the pay gap in some studies to 40 percent in others. Many researchers attribute this residual to economic discrimination.

Economists define discrimination as occurring when two workers of commensurate ability and productivity receive different average returns for their work. This may happen because the two workers are paid different wages for the same work. More often it occurs because the two people work at different jobs paying different wages and having different benefits. And so economic analysis brings us back to the "no Noah's Ark" explanation. By far the most important cause of women's lower relative earnings is that they are trapped in low-paying, female occupational ghettos.[6]

Throughout its final report on its four-year study of "equal pay for work of equal value," the National Academy of Sciences committee provides carefully measured but nevertheless strong support for this conclusion by reiterating its finding that "it appears that the sex composition of occupations, independent of other occupational characteristics and of average personal characteristics, has a strong effect on the earnings of incumbents."[7] And again, ". . . the studies of earnings differences that use job characteristics as explanatory variables . . . do confirm . . . the importance of job segregation by sex in explaining the difference in earnings between men and women."[8] In the report's concluding section the committee writes:

[S]everal types of evidence support our judgment that it is also true in many instances that jobs held mainly by women and minorities pay less at least in part *because* they are held mainly by women and minorities. . . . The evidence is not complete or conclusive, but the consistency of the results in many different job categories and in several different types of studies, the size of the pay differentials (even after worker and job characteristics have been taken into account), and the lack of evidence for alternative explanations strongly suggest that wage discrimination is widespread.[9]

This wage discrimination problem is a serious one. Some 53 percent of the adult women in the country are now in the labor force. In 1979, 45 percent of these working women were single heads of households—separated, divorced, widowed, or never married—the sole support of themselves and their families. An additional 29 percent were married to husbands who made less than $15,000 a year. In 1982, women alone maintained one out of every six of America's 61 million families. Clearly, the majority of women work because they must. How much they earn matters.

Poverty is undoubtedly the worst result of women's low earnings; poverty for women and for their families. The *Monthly Labor Review* reports that in 1979, "persons in families maintained by women with no husband present, had a poverty rate of 30 percent, compared with persons in families maintained by men which had a poverty rate of only 6 percent."[10] The same publication explains,

As has long been the case, families maintained by women are characterized by very low earnings. . . . [In 1981] median weekly earnings of the 5.9 million families maintained by women with wage and salary workers were only about half those of married couples. The low earnings reflect both the small proportion of such families having two workers or more, as well as the generally low earnings of women who maintain their own families.[11]

In 1981, 72 percent of the poor people over 65 were women. Half of the women over 65, living alone, have poverty or near-poverty incomes of $5,000 or less. Even though more women are in the labor force now, poor working women cannot provide for a decent old age. A *New York Times* article predicted the consequences of women's low earnings: by the year 2000, all of the poor would be female. The article called this "the feminization of poverty."[12]

The occupational system is, indeed, no Noah's Ark. Although the sexes board separately and work in separate compartments, should earnings be affected significantly by the sex of the worker? Can women working in separate job compartments claim sex discrimination on the grounds of unequal pay for work of comparable worth? What is comparable worth? Is it "sheer rhetoric alone" or can it be measured and thus gain "operational meaning?" To answer these questions, we will turn first to what economists of various persuasions say comparable worth is—and is not.

Defining Comparable Worth: Economists Disagree

The newspapers inform us daily that agreement among economists is hard to come by, at least on issues with a strong political content. Therefore it should come as no surprise that their views differ, as their politics do, on the issue of comparable worth, with its threat, or promise, of radical changes in existing income distribution. Whether the economic analysis precedes or follows the political analysis is not clear.

The broad division among economists is between the free-market, orthodox, neoclassical group, on the one hand, and the groups that emphasize the importance of other economic, political, and social institutions in influencing the outcome of economic processes, on the other. The neoclassical economist tells us that wages are set in the competitive marketplace by the operation of the laws of supply and demand. The employer's demand for labor is determined by the "marginal productivity" of that labor, that is, by an added unit of labor's contribution to the value of the output of the employer's firm. Profit-maximizing employers figure out how much value additional work will add to their operation, and that value determines how much they are willing to pay—of course they'd be happy to pay less, but in the long run, in a competitive market, they won't and can't profitably pay more.

The supply of labor is determined by the quantity and quality of labor offered employers in the labor market. If there is a large supply of labor offered for a particular job, then the value added to output by the marginal, or last, unit of labor offered will be lower than if there were a small supply of labor relative to the employer demand for it. Or if the quality of the labor offered is low, for example in its educational or skill levels, or its health, or its potential for training, then again the long-run added value of output will be lower than for an added unit of higher-quality labor.

In both these cases, the neoclassical economist would say that the marginal productivity of the labor offered is low, and therefore the wages the employer is able and willing to pay are low. Or, as Oxford economist

J.R. Hicks put it, low wage labor is "often badly paid, not because it gets less than it is worth, but because it is worth so appallingly little."[13] This, then, is the heart of the argument that free-market economists make when women's advocates point to the low average full-time earnings of women compared to men. To echo Hicks, according to the neoclassical economist, if women earn less it's because their work is worth less.

Neoclassical economic theory admits the possibility of economic discrimination but views it as a temporary phenomenon. The workings of the marketplace will tend to eliminate discrimination because competing, profit-seeking employers will bid against each other for the cheap, underpaid labor and will up its price to the level of what it's worth. And workers will move to the jobs that reward them best for their ability and productivity. This process will work, even in the case of monopsony, that is, an imperfectly competitive market with one buyer of labor and many sellers. The employer's "monopsonistic exploitation" of the workers will, in the long run, be reduced or eliminated if workers are willing and able to move to other jobs and if firms are encouraged by the addition to profits from labor exploitation to compete with the monopsonist. Thus Adam Smith's "higgling and bargaining" in the competitive labor marketplace will lead, in time, to market wages that reflect each worker's comparable worth.

Is this really the way labor markets work? Many economists think not. For example, Cambridge economist Frank Wilkinson writes, "The orthodox, neoclassical view rests on the proposition that the worker is paid his worth. . . ." He explains that "this is brought about by well-behaved production functions (. . . diminishing returns to factor input) and perfect labour markets. . . ." But, he continues,

> Despite the enormous importance given to the market in conventional labour economics there is absolutely no evidence that the atomistic labour market has ever been the general rule. The notion of a perfect market is derived from utilitarian philosophy rather than reality. Labour markets have always been structured. . . . Moreover, those parts of the labour market where workers are continually thrown into competition have generally been those typified by low pay and the most degrading working conditions.[14]

Although the critics of neoclassical, or "conventional," labor economics differ among themselves in their theories of how wages are determined, they all emphasize the importance of social and political institutions in affecting wage determination. They agree that the economic institutions that characterize labor markets are not those described in the free-market, neoclassical model. And they agree that "segmentation" of labor markets is the characteristic result of the working of the institutions that their theories variously describe. "Segmentation" is defined by Wilkinson as "different wages for workers of equal efficiency."[15] A second labor market analyst points out that this outcome is the product of segmentation seen as a process—a process he describes as "the compartmentalisation and isolation of different groups of participants in the labour market" and that he likens to the concepts of "non-competing groups," "balkanization," and "apartheid."[16] This process is the "no Noah's Ark" phenomenon described earlier. The result, "different wages for workers of equal efficiency," is the nub of the comparable worth issue.

Why does this process of channeling women into segregated job slots occur, both in initial job assignments and in promotion, or nonpromotion, from entry level jobs? One reason is that the employer saves money by paying women less than comparably qualified men. The electrical industry case is a good example of this. In fact, all of the cases of pay inequity described later have money saving as a prime motive. Since the passage of the Equal Pay Act in 1963, employers have had to separate women's jobs from men's to avoid violating the act.

A second, and powerful, reason for this segmentation is tradition. Women have traditionally acted in nurturing, supporting roles; as mothers, wives, nurses, comforters, doers of "menial" housekeeping tasks. Therefore these are the roles they are assigned in the workplace. Inasmuch as women's work has always been considered less important than men's work and has often been unpaid, the market simply reflects historical attitudes. Furthermore, just as many whites benefited, or thought they benefited, from the slavery of blacks, so many men benefit, or think they benefit, from keeping women in nurturant, low-paid roles.

A third explanation for female job segregation is what economists call "statistical discrimination." Employers treat each woman, without regard to her individual characteristics, as if she had the qualities they attribute to women as a class. For example, they may believe the conventional wisdom that women are more likely to be absent, more likely to be temporary workers, typically secondary family wage earners, always in danger of becoming pregnant, more often ill—and therefore they channel women into the secondary labor market where jobs are typically dead end and low paying.

The broad group of critics of orthodox labor market theory, which I have lumped together, breaks down into four principal categories: critics of marginal productivity analysis, segmented (or dual) labor market theorists, institutional economists, and radical economists. The groups overlap. Most, for example, would agree in criticizing marginal productivity analysis, the analytic method central to neoclassical labor market theory.

The critics of marginal productivity analysis argue that business people, the economists' "entrepreneurs," do *not* use marginal analysis in making business decisions. They do *not* calculate marginal quantities that may be difficult, if not impossible, to ascertain. They do *not* balance marginal productivity and marginal cost in hiring factors of production. They do *not* use marginal revenue and marginal cost to determine output and price decisions. These latter decisions are made, the critics claim, on the basis of a desired markup over average cost and on such considerations as market-share goals. As far as personnel decisions are concerned, marginal productivity critics would concede that the ability and productivity of a worker are important but would claim no close correlation between these and an employee's average remuneration or her or his job assignment. They would see this as especially true for large firms where wages, benefits, promotions, and training decisions are made in a labor market internal to the firm.

The segmented, or dual, labor market theorists, from whom I have quoted extensively, stress that perfect competition does not operate in labor markets to place people in jobs according to their potential and actual abilities. And it does not result in rewarding people according to their productive contributions. They describe a segmented labor market, which, they say, "fails to treat its participants evenhandedly, in that it accords significantly different opportunities and rewards to otherwise comparable people."[17]

They call the failure to provide equal opportunities to otherwise comparable people "pre-market segmentation." This results in the differences in "human capital investment" made famous by economist Gary Becker.[18] Some economists and business men have used human capital differences to explain female-male earnings differentials. But, as we have seen, substantial earnings differentials persist even after differences in human capital have been considered. Women workers, on the average, have a much lower return on their education, training, and years of experience than male workers.

The major emphasis of these economists is, however, on "in-market segmentation." They define this as occurring "when individuals of similar achieved productive potential receive markedly different access to employment or job rewards, including both pay rates and opportunities for training, experience and pay increases."[19] They see this as a persistent problem, not one that disappears "in the long run." They consider it a serious problem because, they say, "a segmented market acquires an active role in the generation of inequality and low pay."[20]

Some economists in this group stress the dual nature of segmented markets. They describe the labor market as having a primary and a secondary sector. The primary sector provides good jobs with well-defined training and promotion steps in internal-to-the-firm labor markets, good working conditions, and stable employment. The secondary, external labor market is characterized by unskilled jobs, little opportunity for job training, few promotion possibilities, poor working conditions, and unstable employment. Typical women's jobs are apt to have the secondary labor market attributes of poor opportunities for on-the-job training and promotion.

Institutional economists, beginning in the late nineteenth century with sociologist-economist Thorstein Veblen and labor economist John R. Commons, have criticized the "economic man" concept of rational, profit-maximizing business enterprisers and calculating, utility-maximizing workers and consumers. They emphasize the importance of psychological motivations, which are not economic and are often not even rational in economic terms. They also stress the role that social and legal institutions play in economic decision making. Veblen, for example, coined the phrase "conspicuous consumption" and emphasized status seeking as a motive for economic action. He pointed out how an interest in making money could lead to monopoly and the production of inferior, high-priced goods, rather than to competition and the making of inexpensive, quality goods, as the orthodox economists had assumed it would. Commons analyzed the way in which the legal foundations of capitalism affected how the economy worked and the results it produced. More recent institutional economists have criticized the use of marginal productivity analysis as a method for justifying the status quo of discrimination by the haves against the have-nots.

Radical economists, while agreeing with much of the criticism by these groups, differ principally in the degree to which they emphasize the political, or power, aspects of human behavior. They analyze discrimination as a question of power. The Marxists see it in terms of the historical class conflict, stressing the desire of the capitalists to retain power. One way to do this is to create conflict in the working class. Another is to maintain the "reserve army of the unemployed." Both methods involve segmentation—rewarding workers unequally, keeping them in noncompeting groups—as well as exploiting workers by paying them less than the value of their work. Radical feminists also equate discrimination with power—male power—and with patriarchy.

In summary, then, conventional labor economists see the comparable worth of a worker as being correctly determined by supply and demand in the marketplace. They view attempts to define worth by any other means as sheer rhetoric and without operational meaning. They think that such attempts would result in "economic chaos" and "a hopeless bureaucratic muddle."

Many labor economists do not agree. Each school of thought emphasizes particular forces in the wage-setting process. But all the critics agree that the market wage-setting process does not result in wages that closely reflect the productive contribution of the woman worker to an employer's business. By and large they find that women work in women's jobs and are paid women's wages. According to their analysis, this situation will persist, without correction by the free market, unless some outside agent like a union or a governmental division intervenes in the wage-setting process.

The Legal View: Pandora's Box?

When the Supreme Court handed down its five-to-four decision in the case of *County of Washington* v. *Gunther* in June 1981, the conservative press mourned that the Court had opened a Pandora's box filled with human ills. Working women's advocates, on the other hand, saw the box in its later mythical version as full of blessings and were greatly relieved because the Court had let out of the box the possibility of claiming sex discrimination in pay based on comparable worth grounds. An adverse decision would have made it impossible to pursue these claims under existing law.

Two federal laws and an executive order dealt, and deal, with sex discrimination in compensation. The Equal Employment Opportunity Commission (EEOC), an independent federal agency, enforces both laws. The Office of Federal Contract Compliance (OFCCP), part of the Department of Labor, administers the executive order, 11246, as amended.

The first law is the Equal Pay Act of 1963, an amendment to the Fair Labor Standards Act of 1938. The Equal Pay Act requires that employers pay the same wage to men and women workers doing equal work. The act defines "equal work" as "jobs the performance of which requires equal skill, effort and responsibility, and which are performed under similar working conditions." The courts have interpreted this to mean that jobs should be "substantially identical," though they may have different titles, such as janitor and maid, or nurse's aide and orderly.[21] The act provides employers with four affirmative defenses for payments that are not equal—seniority, merit, differences in quantity or quality of production, and "a differential based on any other factor other than sex."

The second law is Title VII of the Civil Rights Act of 1964, as amended by the Bennett Amendment. Title VII is a much broader law than the Equal Pay Act. It prohibits not only discrimination in compensation, but also all types of discrimination in the terms of employment. It includes discrimination based on race, color, religion, and national origin as well as sex discrimination. Legislative history indicates that a strong opponent of civil rights, Representative Howard W. Smith of Virginia, chairman of the House Rules Committee, added sex discrimination to the law late in the game in the hope that this addition would cause Congress to vote it down. The Bennett Amendment to Title VII deals only with sex differences in pay and states that an employer may pay men and women differing amounts "if such differentiation is authorized by the provisions of [the Equal Pay Act]."

Executive Order 11246 makes discrimination by federal contractors with more than 50 employees, or with contracts of more than $50,000, illegal. Before the Reagan administration, the OFCCP considered that the order covered comparable worth cases as well as those involving equal work. Working women's advocates then saw it as a promising road to comparable worth.

Before the Supreme Court's *Gunther* decision in 1981, the overriding legal issue was whether Title VII covered a "segregated job structure where women are paid less for work that is different from that of male employees, but is of comparable value to the employer."[22] Some courts, and many employers' lawyers, argued that the Bennett Amendment restricted Title VII to the equal pay for equal work standards of the Equal Pay Act. The landmark *Gunther* decision established that Title VII is not limited to the equal work standards of the Equal Pay Act. But the Court pointed out that its decision was a narrow one and declared that it was not ruling on the issue of comparable worth.

Thus the Court left a number of important questions unanswered. What are the grounds for making a prima facie case of sex-based wage discrimination when an employer's women employees are not doing the same work as male employees? How can the plaintiff establish comparability of jobs? Can job evaluation prove comparability? Must the plaintiff prove intentional discrimination? What are acceptable pay differentials "based on any other factor other than sex"? Are market wages, which typically reflect sex discrimination, one of these "factors other than sex"? Can employer policies that appear sex neutral but that, in fact, have a "disparate impact" on women workers be grounds for finding sex-based wage discrimination? Can the male-female comparisons be companywide or are they restricted, like Equal Pay Act cases, to employees in the same establishment of a company? Post-*Gunther*, case-by-case decisions are making law on these issues.

Since the Reagan administration took office in 1980, federal progress on pay equity issues has ground to a halt. In fact, the movement, where there has been any, has been backward. Private litigation, however, has taken up some of the slack. Working women's advocates are aiming at step-by-step development of case law on the questions left open by the Supreme Court in the *Gunther* decision. Their strategy is to proceed cautiously on narrowly defined issues and to avoid confronting judges with big economic questions they feel they cannot decide.

Job Evaluation: "Apples and Pumpkins and Cans of Worms?"

In 1977, Governor Dixy Lee Ray cancelled a funding request for comparable worth pay reform for state government employees in the state of Washington. She argued that the job evaluation study by the well-known firm of Norman D. Willis and Associates, on which the reform was based, compared "apples and pumpkins and cans of worms and they are not comparable." With this colorful language she dismissed the Willis study, which had been commissioned by Ray's predecessor, and which was "hailed as a national landmark study . . . the first public sector attempt to use point factor job evaluation technology for the expressed purpose of comparing jobs traditionally held by women with jobs traditionally held by men, and analyzing the potential disparity between them."[23]

The Willis study had found clear evidence of pay inequity. It showed that "overall . . . women received about 20 percent lower pay than men for comparable work."[24] It concluded, "Any action to achieve internally equitable salary relationships between men's and women's classifications would involve a significant modification of or departure from, the present salary setting method."[25]

In 1976 the study was updated. An interagency group monitoring this update emphasized:

> of particular concern has been the relationship of clerical job classes, since they represent the highest concentration of women in the state government. . . . Job classes predominantly filled by men continue to be paid at a higher rate, currently averaging $245 per month or 36 percent higher than clerical job classes of *similar point value*. In addition, the percentage rate of increases granted to jobs predominantly filled by men continues to exceed that of those filled by women. In the sample job classes, the three year percentage increase for clerical positions averaged 13.4 percent while that for job classes predominantly filled by men averaged 21.6 percent.[26]

Among the factors cited by Taber and Remick as obstacles to implementing the Washington State study were "the husky price tag," the effect on private sector pay scales, and the trauma of change.[27] They concluded that "while more and more persons are becoming aware of the concept [of comparable worth], and even support it in principle, few persons in power are committed to make implementation of comparable worth a reality."[28]

Perhaps these obstacles were, in fact, what bothered Governor Ray about the Willis study. Despite her cynicism, job evaluation is a technique for doing exactly what she said it couldn't do: that is, comparing the worth of dissimilar jobs. It has been used successfully by the federal government to determine pay scales by classifying and ranking jobs since the U.S. Civil Service Commission first set up a formal job evaluation system in 1871.[29] "Its use in the private sector became widespread" during World War II, as industry responded to War Labor Board restrictions on all wage increases except those correcting "demonstrated inequities in wage structures."[30]

Job evaluation is a method of ranking, or ordering, jobs according to their value to the employer. Its purpose is to provide a system for comparing "dissimilar work . . . to determine appropriate wage levels."[31] The result of the evaluation process is a hierarchy of job values, a model reflecting the relative worth of jobs in a governmental unit, a plant, or a firm.

There are a variety of types of job evaluation systems, ranging from the simplest ranking procedures used in many small firms to the more complicated methods based on points, or scores, awarded to "compensable factors," used by large employers. Typical compensable factors are the skill and training requirements of the job, its working conditions, its physical and mental effort demands, and the amount of responsibility for people and materials that it requires. In the more sophisticated systems, job evaluation involves describing each job in terms of "compensable factors," then ranking the jobs on the basis of this job content, and, finally, tying the resulting job grades into a wage structure. According to one authority, "A basic tenet of job evaluation is that it is the job, not the worker, that is evaluated and rated."[32] Job content determines pay grades for each job. Worker characteristics—seniority, merit, productivity—determine the individual worker's pay, within each job grade.

A critical part of the process, from the pay equity point of view, is assessing the compensable factors without sex bias. For example, when working conditions are evaluated, more weight is frequently given to the rigors of male jobs, such as dirt and noise, than to that of female jobs, such as the stress of dealing with difficult bosses or clients, or the eye and back strain of working at word processors. More points may be given to typically male jobs that bring in money, like sales, than to female jobs dealing with people, like customer service. Furthermore, if, when dollar values are assigned to the compensable factors, market values for typically female jobs are used as benchmarks for female jobs in the establishment, then discrimination in the marketplace is simply carried over to the firm.

Job evaluation is important to comparable worth policy for three reasons. First, as the National Academy of Sciences study states, "The conventional job evaluation procedure and its modifications . . . determine earnings entirely on the basis of a weighted sum of compensable factors. In this sense they are all versions of a comparable worth approach."[33] Winn Newman, a labor attorney who has represented the International Union of Electrical Workers, the American Federation of State, County and Municipal Employees (AFSCME), and other unions in pay equity cases, also makes the point that determining comparable worth by some type of job evaluating procedure is a common practice. He cites as examples collective bargaining determination of wage scales and the work of arbitrators in determining relative wages in pay disputes.[34] These statements refute the argument that comparing the worth of different jobs is not possible because it is like comparing "apples and pumpkins and cans of worms."

The second reason that job evaluation is important for comparable worth policy is that it often results in legitimizing a discriminatory pay structure. Employers can use it, and have used it, to rationalize pay discrimination. This may be done with the intent to discriminate. But it can also simply be the result of formalizing existing pay scales that contain historical elements of discrimination. Basing benchmark wages and compensable factor weights on market rates also perpetuates existing discrimination. Finally, to the extent that the evaluation process is judgmental and not objective, the bias of the evaluators can result in discriminatory pay structures.

Undoubtedly the most important feature of job evaluation for comparable worth policy is, however, its potential for providing a means of detecting pay discrimination and a method for eliminating it. Determining nondiscriminatory pay scales is central to achieving pay equity, whether by litigation, by collective bargaining, or by individual negotiation. Job evaluation can do this if it can solve the sticky problem of defining comparable worth, that is, of determining the relative values of dissimilar jobs to the employer without being influenced by the sex of the jobholder.

Is job evaluation up to this task? Marsh W. Bates, partner in a leading management consulting firm, Hay Associates, is optimistic. He states that the thorough analyses of jobs done by Hay often show that "jobs traditionally occupied by women pay less per unit of job content than male-dominated jobs do. . . . In general, there will not be enough job evaluation differences to explain male-female pay differentials. . . ." Therefore, he labels job evaluations "the absolute friend of comparable worth advocates."[35]

Daniel Leach, former vice chair of the EEOC, pursues this vein further when he describes job evaluation as "vulnerable." He says that employers are "in control—they can choose or not choose to adopt job evaluation systems. And if they choose one that can be shown to be irrational or based upon premises that are so old as to demonstrate that they were predicated upon sex discriminatory elements, then they may expose themselves to substantial liability [under Title VII]."[36]

Can job evaluation eliminate sex bias in setting up a wage structure? Can it eliminate the bias introduced into current systems by using market rates as benchmarks, and by the subjective judgments of evaluators? A number of authorities believe that it can.[37] Their suggestions include: using white male wages for determining benchmarks and point values; using objective rather than subjective compensable factors wherever possible; using statistical procedures that minimize discrimination in choosing factor weights; using one job evaluation system for an entire establishment to facilitate comparison between sex segregated job groups; including representatives of all groups of employees involved in setting up the system; validating the importance of factors selected; and continuously auditing the performance of a system in use.

For comparable worth advocates, job evaluation is both a threat and a promise. A threat, because as presently used it typically rationalizes and solidifies sex discrimination in pay systems. A promise, because it offers a way of measuring the relative value of jobs that are not identical. Moreover, it may provide the only evidence acceptable to the courts as proof of sex discrimination in pay.

Summary

Yes, equal pay for comparable worth *is* a can chock full of worms. Economists disagree about whether the concept has meaning, and, if it does, how to measure worth. Legislators, lawyers, and judges are similarly divided. Working women's advocates cite case after case of sex discrimination in pay, cases that they see and know to exist. They label the academic and legal questioning a smokescreen to hide the problem. Believers in the validity and the importance of the concept offer job evaluation as a workable technique for measuring the comparable worth of dissimilar jobs. They recognize, however, the problems that have made it a tool for rationalizing, not eliminating, discrimination.

The heart of the comparable worth issue is equity in income distribution. It is a political as well as an economic question. Are women being paid what they are worth? Is the value of their contribution to the output of the economic system greater than their reward for working? Are women workers receiving their fair share of the nation's output of goods and services? As more and more women enter the labor force, pay equity becomes an increasingly important question, not only to them and their families, but also to their employers, to the consumers of their services, and to their male fellow workers as well.

Notes

1. E. Robert Livernash, ed., *Comparable Worth: Issues and Alternatives* (Washington, D.C.: Equal Employment Advisory Council, 1980), p. 83.

2. Bureau of National Affairs, *The Comparable Worth Issue: A BNA Special Report* (Washington, D.C., 1981), p. 49.

3. U.S. Equal Employment Opportunity Commission, *Hearings on Job Segregation and Wage Discrimination* (Washington, D.C., April 28–30, 1980), p. 164.

4. *Hearings,* p. 165.

5. Patricia Cayo Sexton, *Women and Work,* R and D Monograph 46 (Washington, D.C.: U.S. Department of Labor, Employment and Training Administration, 1977), p. 67.

6. For economists' definitions of discrimination see Glen C. Cain, "The Challenge of Segmented Labor Market Theories to Orthodox Theory: A Survey," *Journal of Economic Literature* 14 (1976): 1215–57. See also Lloyd C. Reynolds, *Labor Economics and Labor Relations,* 7th ed. (Englewood Cliffs, N.J.: Prentice-Hall, 1978).

7. Donald J. Treiman and Heidi I. Hartmann, eds., *Women, Work, and Wages: Equal Pay for Jobs of Equal Value* (Washington, D.C.: National Academy Press, 1981), pp. 30–31.

8. Ibid., pp. 38–39.

9. Ibid., p. 93.

10. U.S. Department of Labor, Bureau of Labor Statistics, *Monthly Labor Review* (August 1982): 53.

11. Ibid., p. 47.

12. *The New York Times,* July 29, 1982. Statistics on the aged are from WEAL, *Washington Report* 11 (June–July 1982).

13. J.R. Hicks, *The Theory of Wages,* 2nd ed. (New York: St. Martin's Press, 1963), p. 82.

14. Frank Wilkinson, ed., *The Dynamics of Labor Market Segmentation* (New York: Academic Press, 1981), pp. ix–x.

15. Ibid., p. x.

16. Paul Ryan, "Segmentation, Duality and the Internal Labour Market," in *The Dynamics of Labor Market Segmentation,* ed. Frank Wilkinson (New York: Academic Press, 1981), p. 4.

17. Ibid.

18. Gary Becker, *Human Capital* (New York: Columbia University Press, for the National Bureau of Economic Research, 1st ed., 1964, 2nd ed., 1975).

19. Wilkinson, *Labour Market Segmentation,* p. 5.

20. Ibid., p. 6.

21. Treiman and Hartman, *Women, Work, and Wages,* p. 4.

22. Margaret L. Moses, "Pay Equity: Status of Litigation Efforts," in *Preliminary Memorandum on Pay Equity,* ed. Nancy Perlman (Albany, N.Y.: Center for Women in Government, 1980), p. 6.

23. Gisela Taber and Helen Remick, "Beyond Equal Pay for Equal Work: Comparable Worth in the State of Washington," paper prepared for Conference

on Equal Pay and Equal Opportunity Policy for Women in Europe, Canada, and the United States, Wellesley College, May 1–4, 1978.

24. Ibid., p. 9.

25. Ibid.

26. Ibid., p. 11, italics added.

27. Ibid., p. 13.

28. Ibid., p. 14.

29. See Donald Treiman, *Job Evaluation: An Analytic Review* (Washington, D.C.: National Research Council, National Academy of Sciences, 1979), p. 1.

30. Ibid.

31. Suzanne E. Meeker, "Equal Pay, Comparable Work, and Job Evaluation," *Yale Law Journal* 90 (1981): 674.

32. Treiman, *Job Evaluation,* p. 1.

33. NAS, *Women, Work, and Wages,* p. 88.

34. Winn Newman, *Hearings,* U.S. House of Representatives, September 16, 1982, pp. 150–51.

35. Bureau of National Affairs, *The Comparable Worth Issue,* p. 44.

36. Ibid., p. 53.

37. See, for example, David Thomsen, Director, Compensation Institute, *Nondiscriminatory Salary Report: Survey and Model* (Los Angeles: Compensation Institute, 1979); Helen Remick, "Strategies for Creating Sound, Bias-Free Job Evaluation Plans," in *Job Evaluation and EEO: The Emerging Issues,* IRC Colloquium, Atlanta, Georgia, September 14–15, 1978; Marvin G. Dertien, Manager of Compensation and Benefits, Salt River Project, Phoenix, Arizona, "The Accuracy of Job Evaluation Plans," *Personnel Journal* (July 1981): 566–70.

2

PAY EQUITY IN THE
UNITED STATES:
The History

"Mr. President, after many years of yearning by members of the fair sex in this country, and after very careful study by the appropriate committees of Congress, last year Congress passed the so-called Equal Pay Act, which became effective only yesterday." This is Senator Bennett speaking on the Senate floor, introducing his controversial Bennett Amendment to the Civil Rights Act of 1964.

The "fair sex" have indeed "yearned for many years" for equity with men in pay, not only in the United States but in all the advanced industrial countries. One reason they have "yearned" is because there were, and are, so many of them. There are so many of them because they need the income that comes from paid labor. They are not working for fun, for pin money, or to fill the days after the nest empties. They are working because of economic pressure—the pressure of being a single head of household with children to support; the pressure of being single, widowed, or divorced; the pressure of being married to a low-income or unemployed man; the pressure of inflation.

These pressures are reflected in the unprecedented increase, after 1950, in the proportion of all adult women who have gone out of the home to work in the paid labor force in the United States, Western Europe, Australia, and Canada. Furthermore, as the labor force participation rates of men have fallen, in these and the other so-called advanced industrial democracies, the share of women in the total work force has risen impressively. If these trends continue, women will soon equal men in their rate of participation in the labor force.[1]

Economic pressures are also shown by the dramatic change in the demographic characteristics of working women. In the days before World War II, women in these countries who worked outside the home were typically single and young. By their early twenties, most were married and had dropped out of the labor force, either by choice or by company or governmental rule, never to return. During World War II, middle-aged married women began working for industry, business, and the government in substantial numbers, as the need for labor forced employers and unions to change their antifeminist attitudes. In the 1950s, middle-aged married women continued to enter the labor force in significant numbers. Perhaps the most dramatic demographic change of all occurred in the 1960s, and particularly the 1970s, when young married women, often mothers of preschool-age children, flouted the social strictures against working for pay. As a result, women have made up around two thirds of the addition to the work force in the developed economies since 1960.

The circumstances surrounding the "yearning" of these women for pay equity are common to the Western European, North American, and Australian industrialized economies. They are not new. In all of these countries women typically work, and have worked, at segregated women's work and for women's wages. Indeed, until the last decade or two, in most of these countries even women who performed the same jobs as men worked at lower, women's, wages.[2] In the case of women working in the same "male occupations" as men, Australian wage tribunals were an exception to the rule and gave women the male wage. "On the assumption that females were not, in general, as efficient as males, this principle was designed to prevent females from making inroads into male occupations."[3] Everywhere, it seems, women's work is concentrated in a few occupational groups: clerical work; the lower status in professional ranks, such as elementary school teaching, library work, nursing; services like waitress, beautician; the lower ranks of retail sales; and operatives in labor-intensive manufacturing like textiles, the garment industry, electronics. "Men's work," on the other hand, is widely spread across the spectrum of industrial, professional, and service jobs. Everywhere, it seems, women's work has lower status and gets less pay and fewer benefits than men's, considering its requirements of skill and responsibility and its working conditions. For women to whom work is a necessity, these things matter.

One remedy for the problem of the female-male wage gap is to open up male occupations to women and to encourage women to train for and enter these fields. This affirmative action strategy is constantly put forth by opponents of comparable worth policy as the proper means to upgrade female work, at least in the United States. A cynic might suggest that the reason comparable worth opponents here support it may well be because so far it hasn't affected the wage gap. To be sure, women in the United States have entered some formerly male occupations, notably law, medicine, business administration, accounting, and engineering. But by and large, American women still work at women's work, and still earn, on average, three fifths as much as American men.

Why is it so hard to get women spread across the whole range of occupations? Part of this can be explained by tradition in training and counseling girls and young women. Part results from the prejudices of employers, based on stereotypes about the characteristics of female workers. Part is due to the economic advantage to employers of segregating women employees and then paying them less than men. Part is doubtless due to the opposition of male workers, perhaps most clearly seen in the male craft unions. Part is due to the difficulty in enforcing antidiscrimination laws. And history shows that part results from the fact that when women start to have a substantial presence in an occupation, its status is lowered, its pay falls, and men leave it.

It is at least arguable, however, that affirmative action—getting women into nonfemale occupations and into the higher levels of all occupations—is the best long-run solution to pay inequity. But the long-run looks to be very long indeed, and in the meantime many working women want to be paid equitably for the work they now do.

Pay Equity in the United States:
"After Many Years of Yearning"

What the "members of the fair sex" in the United States wanted, at least those that made their wants known in the many years of yearning that Senator Bennett referred to in 1964, was equal pay for work of comparable value. What Congress gave them, when it passed the Equal Pay Act of 1963, was equal pay for equal work, that is, work that is "substantially identical" to men's. This was certainly an important gain, because even those women who were doing the same work as men were typically paid less, on the theory that they did not have to support a household and that their work effort was in some way inferior to men's. But the act did not reach the majority of working women who were in sex-segregated jobs. Nevertheless, women's advocates considered half a loaf far better than none, and they had had none for a long time. As Dorothy Haener, an official of the United Auto Workers, points out,

> In order to get the legislation enacted in 1963 the compromise was made accepting the severely limited language of "equal pay for work requiring equal skill, effort and responsibilities done under similar working conditions in the same establishment," etc. It was a compromise that had to be made in order to get any legislation at all after over 17 years of effort.[4]

The history of the effort to secure federal legislation requiring equal pay for comparable worth goes back at least to World War II. Supreme

Court Justice Rehnquist summed it up succinctly in a footnote to his 1981 dissent in the case of *County of Washington* v. *Gunther,* writing, "Comparable work was not a new idea. During World War II the regulations of the National War Labor Board (NWLB) required equal pay for 'comparable work.' Under these regulations, the Board made job evaluations to determine whether pay inequities existed within a plant between dissimilar jobs.[5] As a result, in every Congress since 1945 bills had been introduced mandating equal pay for 'comparable work.' "[6]

President Roosevelt set up the National War Labor Board to help management and labor settle disputes in the wartime no strike–no lockout environment. Wartime wages were frozen, except for cases of "gross inequities or to aid in the effective prosecution of the war."[7] As a result, according to labor economist Herbert R. Northrup, then a senior hearing officer at the War Labor Board, "The WLB was faced with the enormous task of stabilizing wages and settling labor disputes throughout the country. . . . Many of the bargaining relationships were new, the bargaining participants inexperienced, and the wage systems more chaotic than rationalized." Moreover, he points out, the change to production of war materials "necessarily involved new processes that required different levels of knowledge, effort, and skills and, consequently, different wage levels and relationships. Finally, of course, thousands of workers were not only new to their jobs but had never before worked in an industrial plant."[8] Faced with these huge problems of determining equitable intraplant wage structures satisfactory to both labor and management, while at the same time preventing wage inflation, the Board turned "to job evaluation and related wage classification programs as a necessary tool. . . ." Professor Northrup concludes, "The National War Labor Board of World War II gave job evaluation and related internal wage classification systems in collective bargaining a tremendous boost."[9]

This experience certainly indicates that despite the criticisms noted in Chapter 1, job evaluation is a tool that can be used cooperatively by workers and management to set up wage structures satisfactory to both groups. If job evaluation and related wage classification systems could straighten out the chaotic wage systems and handle the problems of setting new "wage levels and relationships" for "new processes that required different levels of knowledge, effort, and skills," which Professor Northrup describes from his first-hand experience, should they not be able to deal with the problems of relating the value of sex-segregated jobs? Why, then, have industry representatives stated so strongly that job evaluation is not up to this task?

Professor Northrup's discussion of the spread of job evaluation plans in the post–World War II period suggests one explanation; that management may prefer to keep job evaluation as a tool primarily for its own use. He asserts that, in the United States, industry has dominated the introduction and management of the plans. He indicates that, according to "an outstanding work on the subject" various industry groups have seen them as an industry

> device both to improve company wage structures and wage administra-
> tion and to maintain management control of the wage structure under
> collective bargaining. . . . Job evaluation was used by management partly
> to deter or prevent unionization, partly to rationalize its wage scales
> prior to unionization . . . and partly to stabilize the wage structure and
> eliminate continuous bargaining over particular rates after unioniza-
> tion.[10]

Wartime wage regulation made clear the extent of sex inequity in compensation and thereby gave the NWLB a problem it never thoroughly resolved. As the war effort grew, encouraging women to take jobs became a national necessity. As historian William Henry Chafe points out, this was a quick and radical change from government and industry policies of the 1930s designed to discourage and, in many cases, to prohibit married women and all women over 35 from holding paid jobs.[11] The federal campaign to effect this 180-degree turn in social policy included a directive by the War Manpower Commission to employers "to hire and train women 'on a basis of equality with men,' to 'remove all barriers to the employment of women in any occupation for which they are or can be fitted,' and to use 'every method available' to ensure women's complete acceptance."[12]

But, as Chafe describes, "the gap between promise and performance" in these government efforts "was perhaps best illustrated in those areas where women continued to receive less pay than men." He declares, "the government could not be faulted on its formal commitment to equal wages. The War Manpower Commission had repeatedly urged a uniform pay scale for men and women, and in a series of decisions handed down in the fall of 1942, the National War Labor Board (NWLB) appeared to give substance to the WMC's policy."[13] He cites the Brown and Sharp Manufacturing case, in which the NWLB "rejected the company's practice of paying women 20 percent less than men for the same work and endorsed the principle of equal pay 'for female employees who in comparable jobs produce work of the same quantity and quality as that performed by men.' "[14] In subsequent equal pay for equal work decisions, however, he notes that the board weakened its policy by allowing industry escape loopholes. A favorite was reclassifying women's work, giving it a different name than the same male job, or categorizing it as "light and repetitive" instead of "skilled".[15] This tactic of job reclassification has continued to be a popular response to equal pay for equal work enforcement both here and in other countries.

"The worst form of discrimination against female workers" according to Chafe, occurred in the pay for "women's jobs"—the comparable worth situation. "No class of work exhibited more profound prejudice. . . . At the root of the disparity was the pervasive assumption that any job historically filled by women had less intrinsic value than a comparable position held by men. The premise prevailed even where 'objective' evaluations showed a woman's occupation to require more skill than a man's."[16] He goes on to discuss a wartime General Electric case. The company's job evaluation plan gave the job of janitor 36 points and that of inspector 68. It paid the janitor, a male, 12 cents an hour more than the inspector, a female. When asked why, "the company asserted that the point totals were not comparable, since men's work and women's work were classified separately."[17] Chafe comments, "That was precisely the problem, however. Men and women were arbitrarily assigned to separate labor categories on the basis of sex rather than skill, and it was presumed that women deserved less pay than men."[18]

Chafe assigns some of the responsibility for perpetuating sex segregation to the unions. Even the new industrial unions, he reports, "frequently insisted that females be grouped together in distinct job classifications" and bargained for contracts limiting women's union membership and their seniority on the job to the war period. He cites a clause in a 1944 United Auto Workers contract stating that "men and women shall be divided into separate, non-interchangeable occupational groups unless otherwise negotiated locally."[19] Unions did demand equal pay for women who replaced men in men's jobs, but Chafe indicates that their concern was more for protecting the returning soldier's wage scales than with ensuring equitable pay for women workers.

Despite the government's "gap between promise and performance," the wartime experience with paid work encouraged many women in the postwar years to ignore the "feminine mystique," which extolled the suddenly rediscovered virtues of domesticity, and to remain in, or join, the labor force. The feminine mystique history in this country calls to mind the German experience of the 1930s and 1940s. When it served the purpose of relieving unemployment, Hitler encouraged women to remain in the home with his "kinder, kueche, kirche" ideology. But when preparations for war and war itself caused severe labor shortages, all sorts of paid labor became proper and patriotic for women.

Women Take Action: The Equal Pay Act

Because of their heightened awareness of the gap, women workers in this country and their advocates pressed demands for pay equity persistently in the postwar period. As their numbers grew, the pressure increased.

The Women's Department of the United Auto Workers was one of the most strongly supportive organizations in the equal pay for comparable worth cause. Dorothy Haener, international representative, Women's Department, UAW, was one of its active workers. She and Caroline Davis, director of the UAW Women's Department, both served on the National Equal Pay Committee. Members of the Equal Pay Committee included the UAW Women's Department, the National Council of Church Women, the National Council of Catholic Women, the National Council of Negro Women, the Business and Professional Women, and the League of Women Voters.

This committee, Haener told me, "tried to coordinate what effort it could to get the [equal pay for comparable worth] legislation, and, of course, that legislation was introduced in every session of Congress for over seventeen years. . . . One time we brought in a whole group of women just to lobby and to contact the congressmen and senators to vote for it—we did do that sort of thing. And then, of course, we testified repeatedly, over and over again. I testified on a number of occasions, both before the House and the Senate Labor Committee." In addition to the women's organizations, "most of the labor unions were in support of it. But some of them, you know, supported it more verbally than they did in actual fact."

And who was opposed to equal pay? "Opposed, of course," Dorothy Haener answers, "were the Chamber of Commerce and the National Association of Manufacturers. And the various corporations—the glass companies were usually down there in full force to testify against it and the electrical companies were very opposed to it. "So," she concludes, "it was a clear-cut case of anyone who stood to lose money because they had to pay women the same as men, was down there testifying against it."

Thus the pulling and hauling went on. Although the Truman, Eisenhower, and Kennedy administrations all gave pay equity their support, Congress took nearly 20 years to resolve its disagreements over the policy. Finally, in 1963, after lengthy congressional debate starting in 1962, Congress passed what we know as the Equal Pay Act, as an amendment to the Fair Labor Standards Act of 1938.

As Supreme Court Justice Rehnquist noted, the kind of equity sought during all these years was equal pay for work of comparable value, or, as we have called it, equal pay for comparable worth. The first bills taken up by the House in 1962 did, in fact, require employers to pay equal wages for "work of comparable character on jobs the performance of which requires comparable skills."[20] The Kennedy administration strongly backed comparable worth. Secretary of Labor Arthur Goldberg told the subcommittee, "I am not impressed when the argument is made that it is difficult or impossible to determine work that is comparable."[21] He argued that industry could do this by using its existing job evaluation techniques. Also supporting comparable worth were many of the unions and, of course, the women's organizations already mentioned.

Predictably, organized employers vigorously opposed the idea of comparability. The National Association of Manufacturers expressed grave concern about the use of comparable worth, arguing that the concept was "so general and vague as to give an administrator a grant of power which could destroy the sound wage structure which many industrial companies have worked for years to perfect."[22] The U.S. Chamber of Commerce agreed. Industry's concern prevailed. Representative St. George proposed an amendment to the pay act substituting "equal" for "comparable." Other representatives supported her aim of limiting the discretion of the Labor Department over business's wage policy.

"It became very evident that it was not going to get enacted unless we did some compromising," Dorothy Haener says. So the final version of the Equal Pay Act specified "equal" work. Representative Goodell, its sponsor, explained, "When the House changed the word 'comparable' to 'equal' the clear intention was to narrow the whole concept. We went from 'comparable' to 'equal' meaning that the jobs involved should be virtually identical, that is they would be very much alike or closely related to each other."[23] The bill defined "equal work" in job evaluation terms of "equal skill, effort and responsibility and . . . performed under similar working conditions," and provided exceptions for unequal compensation for reasons of "merit, seniority, quality and quantity of production, and any other factor other than sex."

Another compromise made by the advocates of equal pay was to accept enforcement of the act by the Wage and Hour Division of the Labor Department. Earlier drafts had specified a separate enforcement agency. "This compromise proved to be a blessing," says Dorothy Haener, "because the enforcement procedures of the Wage and Hour Division did prove to be very successful in the courts. Betsy Margolin was in charge of that. She was very selective in choosing cases in areas where she thought the courts would be sympathetic. And as a result she did succeed in building up very good case law."

Alice H. Cook, professor emeritus of labor economics at Cornell University, agrees. In her study of the working mother in nine countries, she states, "Most observers of the enforcement of American laws in this area agree that the best administration has been that of equal pay under the Fair Labor Standards Administration with its large experienced staff of enforcement officers located in branch offices throughout the country." She quotes a former Labor Department associate solicitor as saying, "If women in the 1960s had to rely totally on Title VII to blot out sex discrimination in the workplace, virtually nothing would have been accomplished. . . ."[24] Following President Carter's administrative reorganization plan, however, the Equal Pay Act has been administered by the EEOC. But this is an EEOC with greater powers than it had in the 1960s.

Pay equity supporters found that they had made a more damaging compromise in limiting coverage of the act to women covered by the Fair Labor Standards Act. This meant, according to Haener, that the original bill covered fewer than half of the women working in the labor force. Later amendments have, however, extended the act's coverage.

Despite these compromises, Dorothy Haener emphasizes the importance of the act. When asked why she feels that the Equal Pay Act was so important, even though it was not a comparable worth act, she replies, "It was important because, up until that time, everyone had argued that there *was* no discrimination." But, she points out, when cases like *Wheaton Glass* came to court and were decided, the "terrible abuse and the kind of inequities that were going on became obvious." Furthermore, she adds, even for some time after the passage of the Civil Rights Act in 1964, "the only thing we really had going for us, that was really documenting and proving some of the discrimination, was the 1963 Equal Pay Act. That," she concluded, "was the rationale. That and the amount of money that was found due under it." She says that, during the Labor Department's administration of the act, the courts awarded a total of $2 billion to working women. "And this went primarily to lower-income women to whom 12 or 15 cents an hour meant a lot." Furthermore, she adds, some of the Equal Pay Act decisions are proving useful in the present comparable worth effort—for example, decisions based on the way companies use job evaluation in assessing jobs.

Looking at the Equal Pay Act from today's perspective, many women's advocates do more criticizing than praising. They point out that, as we have seen, many women are not doing "equal work," so the law doesn't affect them. They say the law encourages employers to segregate women to avoid "equal work" situations, thus making the problem worse, not better. They also feel, according to Haener, that the Wage and Hour Division could have administered the act more strongly, particularly in the area of insurance and pensions.

"But those of us who fought on this battle from the beginning, you know, and understood what we were up against, knew that for that time that we were going through, we were really accomplishing a great deal. It's very easy to look back ten years later and say, 'Well, if they had just issued a directive saying this instead of saying that, things would have moved much more quickly.' " She continues, "The point is, ten years ago you couldn't have done that. So, you know, it's kind of sad to me to see the anger that some of them show toward the 1963 Equal Pay Act because it didn't achieve equal pay for comparable worth. Well, there was no way it was going to do that. We had lost the ability to make that argument under the law, because of the language we had accepted. . . ."

Doubtless everyone would agree that the Equal Pay Act has benefited working women in cases where it has discouraged or eliminated pay
inequity for equal work. The benefits have been substantial because the
violations have, unfortunately, been considerable. But what about the
nurses, the librarians, the secretaries, the retail clerks, the elementary
school teachers, the electronics assemblers, and all the other women who
are *not* doing "equal" work? If any of them believe they are being discriminated against in pay, what can they do about it?

Title VII: "Accidental Result of
Political Maneuvering"

It would be cheering to women's advocates now to think that Congress belatedly recognized the extent of this problem and therefore set
about correcting it in Title VII of the 1964 Civil Rights Act. But unrecon-
structed history tells us differently. The initial goal of the Civil Rights Act
was to end discrimination against blacks. The House did not include prohibition of sex discrimination in Title VII until almost the end of floor debate on the bill. And then it was added by the bill's chief foe, Representative Howard Smith of Virginia. Whatever the motive, "the sex provisions
of Title VII can be viewed more as an accidental result of political maneuv-
ering than as a clear expression of congressional intent to bring equal job
opportunities to women."[25]

The House passed the act and it went to the floor of the Senate. As a
result of Senate concern about the relationship between the sex discrimination provisions of Title VII and those of the Equal Pay Act, Senator Bennett proposed an amendment to resolve this issue. His amendment, accepted by both Senate and House, provides "that an employer may dif-
ferentiate upon the basis of sex in determining compensation if 'such differentiation is authorized' by the Equal Pay Act."[26] But what does this
mean? Does it mean that women workers cannot claim sex discrimination
under Title VII unless it fits the Equal Pay Act criterion of equal pay for
equal work? Or does it simply state that the employer's four affirmative
defenses for paying unequal wages in the Equal Pay Act—"merit, seniority, quantity and quality of work, or any other factor other than sex"—also
apply to sex discrimination claims brought under the Civil Rights Act?

How the courts would decide this issue has been critical to working
women. Limiting sex discrimination in pay under Title VII to Equal Pay
Act standards would effectively make it impossible to claim sex discrimination for comparable but not equal work. Male groups protected by Title
VII from discrimination in compensation because of race, religion, color,
or national origin are not held to equal work standards. Would the courts
decide that the standard for women workers should be more restrictive
than for these male protected workers?

As case law developed, the courts came down on both sides of this issue. The EEOC, the agency administering Title VII, shifted from its initially restrictive, equal work standard to a broader interpretation of the law. Meanwhile, over and over again, both proponents and opponents of comparable worth debated the "true" meaning of the Bennett Amendment. Finally, in 1981, the Supreme Court handed down a five-to-four decision in the case of *Gunther* v. *the County of Washington,* ruling that claims of sex discrimination in compensation were *not* limited to equal work situations. The Court's decision did not directly address the comparable worth issue. But the door for such claims was left open.

Were women's advocates active in getting the prohibition of sex discrimination added to the Civil Rights Act? "No, the National Equal Pay Committee had nothing to do with that," Dorothy Haener responded, when I asked her this question. "As a matter of fact, you see, the tragedy is that the whole enforcement of the 1964 Civil Rights Law just sort of hung on the efforts of a couple of international unions and NOW, which was newly formed and pushed to get the law. But basically the majority of the groups that were associated with the Equal Pay Committee refused to do anything to get the 1964 Civil Rights law enforced." She explained that "some of us felt that there was a relationship now between the two laws and we ought to push to get them both enforced. We tried to get a motion passed to have the National Committee on Equal Pay go on record as taking on the project of supporting the 1964 Civil Rights Law. But the best we could do was to get the committee to send out a questionnaire polling the committee members as to whether they were willing to do that. The majority of them refused."

Did they refuse because they felt they had done all that needed to be done? "No, no," Dorothy Haener replied, "they refused because, you see, all of the women's organizations on the committee, with the exception of the business and professional women's groups, all of them were opposed to having the 1964 Civil Rights Law enforced in regard to sex because they felt it would wipe off the so-called protective laws." She explained that the UAW Women's Department "had been involved in it long enough by then, in terms of the work we did, that we knew the laws were not protecting the women. They were just being used to discriminate against them. But," she added, "it's a tragedy that it was such a long-fought battle." She pointed out that when Caroline Davis, of the UAW, urged the Kennedy Commission on the Status of Women "to look into what these laws were doing to women, they refused even to do that."

When I commented that I had not seen this part of the history of the Civil Rights Act in any books I had read, she replied, "Well, it's well hidden—you see, many of these organizations are now very embarrassed about their position and so it's the kind of thing that you don't rub their face in, I guess it's what you'd call it. But," she added, "sometimes I think that for the sake of the kinds of things that I now see going on, in terms of, oh, using toxic substances and using other rationales to keep women out of jobs again, it really is a story that I think ought to be told. It really ought to be told."

But this is history. Since those early years of the 1964 Civil Rights Act, women's groups, except for those of the far right, have seen the importance of the act for working women. Furthermore, many of these groups have united in support of equal pay for comparable worth by forming a new national coalition, the National Committee on Pay Equity, an organization devoted to achieving this goal. They believe that this *is* the issue of the 1980s. They believe, as Dorothy Haener states, that "it's an issue that's not going to go away. Women are going to continue to press for it." They are concerned, as she is, "that there will be efforts to water down their anger and to find ways to circumvent them. But," she adds, "I think women are getting smart enough now that they do understand and that they aren't going to let that happen to them." She repeats, "I've been saying for a couple of years now that this *is* the issue of the eighties. And," she concludes, "you know, it *is* a nice time to be alive, for me. In terms of what women are accomplishing, it is a beautiful time."

Notes

1. For statistics for OECD countries, see Organisation for Economic Cooperation and Development, *Women and Employment* (Paris, 1980), Table 1, p. 22.

2. For statistics and discussion on women's wages and job segregation, see OECD, *Women and Employment,* pp. 29–33.

3. R.G. Gregory and R.C. Duncan, "Segmented Labor Market Theories and the Australian Experience of Equal Pay for Women," *Journal of Post-Keynesian Economics* 3 (Spring 1981): 407.

4. Joy Ann Grune, ed., *Manual on Pay Equity* (Washington, D.C.: Committee on Pay Equity, 1980), p. 66.

5. Justice Rehnquist asked the reader to see 28 *War Lab. Rep.* 666 (1945).

6. *County of Washington, Oregon, et al.* v. *Gunther et al.* No. 80-429, June 8, 1981, reprinted in Bureau of National Affairs, *The Comparable Worth Issue: A BNA Special Report* (Washington, D.C., 1981), p. 70, n. 1.

7. National War Labor Board, *Termination Report* (1945) 1: 8–9, cited in Equal Employment Advisory Council, *Comparable Worth: Issues and Alternatives* (Washington, D.C., 1980), p. 205.

8. EEAC, *Comparable Worth,* p. 111.

9. Ibid.

10. Summer Slichter, James J. Healy, and E. Robert Livernash, *Union Policies and Industrial Management* (Washington, D.C.: The Brookings Institution, 1960), p. 561.

11. See, for example, William H. Chafe, *The American Woman* (New York: Oxford University Press, 1972), p. 146.

12. Ibid., p. 148.

13. Ibid., p. 154.

14. Ibid., pp. 154–55.

15. Ibid., p. 156.

16. Ibid., p. 157.

17. Ibid.

18. Ibid.

19. Ibid.

20. *Hearings Before the Select Subcommittee of Labor of the House Committee on Education and Labor on H.R. 8898, 10266, Part I,* 87th Cong., 2d Sess., 1962, pp. 2–10, reported in EEAC, *Comparable Worth,* p. 213.

21. *1962 House Hearings,* p. 17, in EEAC, *Comparable Worth,* p. 213.

22. *1962 House Hearings,* p. 166, in EEAC, *Comparable Worth,* p. 214.

23. Quoted from 109 *Cong. Rec.* 9197, in EEAC, *Comparable Worth,* p. 219.

24. Alice H. Cook, *The Working Mother,* rev. ed. (New York: New York State School of Industrial and Labor Relations, Cornell University, 1978), p. 27.

25. Quoted from Miller, 51 *Min. L. Rev.* at 880, by Williams and McDowell, in EEAC, *Comparable Worth,* p. 226. The bill prohibits discrimination in all aspects of employment on the basis of race, color, religion, country of national origin, and sex.

26. Bureau of National Affairs, *Special Report,* p. 5.

3

PAY EQUITY ABROAD:
Europe, Australia, and Canada

Is it a beautiful time for women in other industrialized countries? No doubt young women there, as well as here, would question how much women have accomplished and are accomplishing. But to those with long memories, the distance women have come and the outlook for where they are going may well seem encouraging. As we shall see, the history of pay equity abroad shows both substantial achievements and a long way still to go.

Equal pay for comparable worth policy is actually being implemented in Australia and Canada. In this section we will review the international history of pay equity briefly and then look at what is going on in these two countries—the accomplishments, the problems, the effects on women and the economy. This gives us a chance to check the record and see whether American critics' predictions that the policy would produce economic chaos seem likely to come true. We can also learn something about how pay equity affects working women's earnings and employment.

The Australian policy has affected women's wages across the board and has been implemented over a short period of time. Therefore it is particularly instructive about the effects of such a thoroughgoing change in a capitalist economy. The Canadian example, on the other hand, is limited to workers subject to federal regulation—about 10 to 11 percent of the labor force—plus workers in Quebec Province. It proceeds on a case-by-case basis. This more gradual introduction of pay equity may more closely resemble the possible future course of comparable worth policy in the States.

The story of pay equity policy, both here and abroad, emphasizes the fact that pay equity *has* a history. As Ronnie Ratner explains in "The Policy and the Problem,"

> The goal of "equal pay" was first articulated by three distinct groups in the late nineteenth and early twentieth centuries: by the socialist movement in its striving to realize equality generally, . . . [by] trade unions, whether socialist or pragmatic, who viewed with consternation and alarm the increasing number of women in all kinds of employment, . . . [and by] middle class women's rights movements, shocked at conditions of their working class sisters, whom they saw caught between "white slavery" and "wage slavery."[1]

In her multinational study of equal pay, Alice Cook points out that pay equity "periodically surfaced as an issue in various countries, most notably during World War I," but that it "did not become a serious political demand until World War II, when certain countries, including the United States, passed regulations that women receive equal pay for equal work." She attributes the war and postwar progress to "sustained political lobbying . . . on the part of [a] small group of women activists and their trade unions."[2] This is reminiscent of Dorothy Haener's description of the pay equity efforts of American women's groups and trade unions in the 1940s, 1950s, and 1960s. Alice Cook's study points out that the unions were motivated to demand equal pay by a desire to protect their own (male) wage rates and jobs rather than by an ideological commitment to "equal treatment for women."[3]

As a result of these lobbying efforts, the International Labor Organisation (ILO) in 1951 and the organizers of the European Economic Community (EEC) in 1961 both adopted equal pay measures. ILO Convention 100 required signing nations to "ensure the application to all workers of the principle of equal remuneration for men and women workers *for work of equal value*" (italics added). Significantly, this clause stated a principle of comparable worth rather than one of "the same or substantially similar work."

The 1961 Treaty of Rome setting up the European Economic Community specified in Article 119, however, that "each Member State shall . . . ensure and . . . maintain the application of the principle that men and women should receive equal pay *for equal work*" (italics added). The meaning of "equal work" proved uncertain. So the Council of European Communities delayed implementation of Article 119 for more than a decade while the EEC European Commission studied the problem of female-male wage disparity and investigated the operative meaning of equal work and equal pay.

Finally, in 1975, the council adopted a directive on equal pay implementing Article 119. The directive said that the "equal pay for equal work" requirement in Article 119 of the Treaty of Rome means equal pay "for the same work or for work to which equal value is attributed." The directive added, "In particular, where a job classification system is used for determining pay, it must be based on the same criteria for both men and women and so drawn up as to exclude any discrimination on grounds of sex."[4]

In her analysis of Article 119, Janice R. Bellace, assistant professor of legal studies and management at the Wharton School, University of Pennsylvania, concludes,

> It is clear from the Commission's 1979 report that it views the equal pay directive as mandating equal pay for work of comparable worth. . . . The Commission states that a narrow interpretation of the directive's equal pay guarantee "would completely negate" the directive, "the aim of which . . . is to broaden the concept of "same work" to that of "work of equal value."[5]

A second important requirement of the directive was its stipulation that job evaluation systems, where used, must be nondiscriminatory. This clause took aim at an acute problem, the use of job classification systems to perpetuate sex discrimination in pay. We will run into this situation in the American cases we examine. It is endemic and epidemic in job evaluation setups.

In Germany, for example, the Supreme Labor Court, in 1955, forbade employers to base pay scales on sex on the grounds that this violated constitutional guarantees of equality. It was customary there, as indeed it was in every industrial country, to pay women "women's wages," which were a fraction—three fifths to three fourths—of the male wage for the same work. After the court order employers evaded this prohibition, with apparent understanding from the male-dominated unions, by expanding the number of categories in their job classification systems and rating jobs as "light" or "heavy" work. Women workers were put into the "light" classes and these, not surprisingly, were at the bottom of the pay scale. Spurred on by women workers' complaints, a Social Democratic labor minister finally initiated a study of the problem. After a delay of a number of years, these pressures resulted in some movement toward reform in the job-rating system. Both the EEC directive and the studies made by the German government, by our own National Academy of Sciences, and by others have illuminated this difficulty of sex discrimination in rating jobs. But the problem is still widespread.[6]

The ILO, as well as the EEC, acted in 1975, recognizing International Women's Year by amplifying its Convention 100 with a "Declaration on Equality of Opportunity and Treatment of Women Workers." This declaration required, among other things, that

> Special measures shall be taken to ensure equal remuneration for work of equal value for women also in occupations in which women predomi-

nate and to measure the relative value of their work with full regard to the qualities essential to performing the job.

Special measures shall be taken to raise the level of women's wages as compared with that of men's and to eradicate the causes of lower average earnings for women possessing the same or similar qualifications or doing the same work or work of equal value.[7]

Thus, by the mid-1970s, the initiatives of the ILO and the EEC, begun in the 1950s and early 1960s to promote equality for women in pay and opportunity, had finally gotten up steam. But, as Francis Blanchard, director-general of the ILO, later put it, "progress is 'slow on the ground', so to speak."[8] It was 1978 before the EEC directive on equal pay went into effect. And in its 1979 report on technical compliance of the member states with the directive, the European Commission was "highly critical."[9] So critical, in fact, that it began "infringement proceedings" against all of the community countries except Ireland and Italy for failure to have taken even the first step of adopting the type of equal pay legislation required by the directive. Bellace reports that "the United Kingdom, Denmark and Germany were considered to be prime targets of this proceeding, because their lack of compliance was of a patently substantive nature."[10] The pressure has had its effect and these and the other delinquent community members have since begun the process of complying with the EEC equal pay policy.

In a 1982 interview, the ILO director-general asserted that "the world is far from having achieved the goal of equality." He concluded that "promoting further progress towards this goal by all the means at its disposal must therefore continue to be a basic objective in the ILO's work as regards all groups who are victims of discrimination and, among these, as regards women in particular." The new assistant director-general of the ILO, Antoinette Beguin, added, "Everywhere, sex discrimination and sex segregation in the labour market will continue to be a major concern, with their linkages upstream to unequal access to education and training and downstream to unequal pay and low remuneration." Beguin sees this, however, as a program for "many years," because "women workers' problems are so deeply rooted in the socio-economic and cultural context. . . ."[11]

Despite the obstinate nature of "women workers' problems," the 1970s did see some real gains in narrowing the gap between women's and men's average earnings in a number of countries. In 1980, the Organisation for Economic Cooperation and Development (OECD) reported "substantial gains for women" for the period from 1968 to 1977 in 10 of the 19 countries it studied.[12]

Australia appears to have made the largest gains of any non-Communist country to date. Two Australian economists, R.C. Duncan and

R.G. Gregory, have studied the Australian experience exhaustively. This is an instructive example of comparable worth policy in action. After scrutinizing the Australian case we will conclude our historical review with a look at how equal pay for work of equal value has worked in Canada.

The Australian Experience

What happened in Australia? In the 18-year period from 1950 to 1968, the full-time earnings of Australian women had steadily averaged around 58 percent of those of Australian men—a wage gap similar to ours in the United States. Yet, only 7 years later, Australian women's earnings had jumped to 76 percent of men's—a whopping 31 percent relative increase. What caused this dramatic change?[13]

What happened was an "equal pay for work of equal value" policy introduced by the Australian Federal Wage Tribunal in 1972 on the heels of an "equal pay for equal work" decision made in 1969. Adopting the equal value, or comparable worth, principle had a major impact on women's earnings because most Australian women do not do the same work as men. As one analyst says, "In Australia there are two labour markets—a female labour market and a male labour market. There is an extreme degree of segregation between the female and the male labour markets and this segregation appears not to have diminished during the past 60 years."[14]

Australian economist R.C. Duncan explains that, in Australia, minimum wages are set "for almost all categories of workers" by a

> complex system of wage tribunals, both State and Federal. . . . The wage-setting process involves hearings before a semi-judicial body which accepts representations from unions, employer associations and governments. . . . There are several thousand minimum wage awards, aligned to the different occupational descriptions. . . . The tribunals have trained evaluators who carry out job evaluation studies both for *comparative purposes* or where it is argued the *job itself has changed.*

He points out that unions and management can, and do, negotiate wages at levels above the minimum awards.[15]

According to Duncan, the wage tribunals classify occupations as mainly male or female. They award a male occupation a wage calculated to support a man and his wife and children "living in a civilized community." In figuring the female minimum wage rate, they decide what the male rate would be, if the occupation were, in fact, male. Until 1975, they made the women's rate a percentage of the hypothetical male rate. They arrived at this percentage by considering the amount necessary to support a single woman.

Before the Second World War, they set the women's rates at 54 percent of "the equivalent male rate, i.e. as if a male were employed in that job."[16] In 1950, both the federal and the states' wage tribunals raised the percentage to 75 percent. And in 1969, they began to allow equal pay for equal work for the one fifth of the women workers who worked in "male occupations" and were considered to be doing the same work as men. But the other four fifths of the women in the labor force were understandably unhappy with their minimum wage awards of 75 percent of the male rates when women in "male occupations" were being awarded 100 percent. Therefore, in 1972, the Federal Wage Tribunal "followed a number of state government initiatives" and adopted the comparable worth principle of "equal pay for work of equal value" for all women workers.[17] They put this into effect in three stages over three years. Thus, by 1975, the minimum wage for women in occupations labeled "female" equaled the minimum wage award that a man would receive if he worked in that occupation. Or, in other words, the percentage award for female minimum wage rates had risen to 100 percent from the pre–World War II 54 percent and the postwar 75 percent.

In his talk to the National Committee on Pay Equity, R.C. Duncan commented that the "apples and oranges" argument so common in the States—that you can't compare jobs that aren't the same—has never been an argument in Australia. He explained that "even back at the beginning of the century, they were doing these wage determinations saying what was a man's wage and then turning around and saying we'll set the woman's wage as such and such, in relation to a man's."

In response to a question about the politics of the process, he said that the wage-setting system is "something that no one disputes." After the 1972 wage decision, he explained, "All the courts had to reevaluate all the minimums on the basis of comparable worth. . . . They had to go through thousands of them. . . . Nobody disagreed. . . . Male workers can't disagree because that job has been evaluated as if they were working in it, so for them, it can't be put too high."[18]

Did implementing comparable worth in Australia create economic chaos by disrupting the entire economic system, as Judge Winner, in the case of *Lemons* v. *the City and County of Denver*, predicted? Did "the notion that there ought to be equal pay for work of comparable value" turn out to be "a can chock-full of worms" and "a deep conceptual mire," as a *Wall Street Journal* editor said it would?[19]

As we have noted, Gregory and Duncan said that the "conceptual mire" was nonexistent in a country that had been calculating relative wages for 80 or 90 years. But what of the economic effects? Their research found, for example, that women's earnings rose 31 percent compared to men's in the 7 years from 1968 to 1975, thus exactly matching the change in the ratio of female-male minimum wage awards. They found, also, that the ratio of women's earnings to men's continued at about the same level from 1975 to 1981, despite fluctuations in the economy. They concluded "that the equal-pay decisions have stuck with respect to earnings, and moreover, that minimum wage awards are the primary determinant of movements in total earnings [in the Australian case]."[20]

Were the effects of this quick and large rise in minimum wage rates and earnings, resulting from institutional decisions of the government rather than from the operation of supply and demand in the "free" labor market, as drastic and unacceptable as American critics have predicted? Duncan and Gregory investigated the effects of wage increases for women workers on women's employment, on income distribution, and on prices. The Australian analysis is uniquely valuable in giving us some insight into these questions.

As far as female employment was concerned, they found "that there was very little reduction." During the period when women's relative earnings rose 31 percent, their employment "grew by 42 percent, while that of males rose by 14 percent. At the same time, their measured unemployment rate fell relative to males."[21] Duncan explains that the job segregation that confines women "to lower-paying occupations . . . protects their employment when their wages are increased relative to males *within* these occupations and between male and female intensive occupations."[22] Furthermore, he adds, "it should be remembered that the equal-pay decisions have taken place during a period of extraordinary growth in female employment . . . generated by the services and government sectors. . . . In effect, almost all employment [growth] in the 1970s in Australia was growth in female employment."[23] Female-intensive manufacturing industries did suffer in the 1970s. But Gregory and Duncan find this is largely due to "the across-the-board tariff reduction of 25 percent on manufactured imports, and the declining competitiveness of Australia's labor-intensive manufacturing industry."[24]

What about the effects on income distribution? These two scholars find that "between 1964 and 1976 the *share* of the total community wage bill paid to the female workforce rose from *18 percent to 28 percent*." They compare this 10 percent rise to the 2 percent increase in women's share of the wage bill from 1950 to 1964. They estimate that the rise in wages contributed about 6 percent of the growth in women's share, while the growth in women's employment added 4 percent. They conclude that "*as a group* females gained considerably from equal pay."[25]

But if women gained, who lost? These researchers estimate that the share of adult males fell 10 percent from 1964 to 1976 with about half of this reduction due to a fall in relative wages. And teenagers lost slightly, largely due to a relative decline in their employment.[26]

Furthermore, they estimate that consumers bore part of the cost of the increase in women's wages through an increase in prices. According to their "best judgment . . . the equal pay decision contributed about one-third to one-half of the 10 percent inflation rate of the period."[27]

In concluding his talk, Duncan stressed that, despite continued occupational segregation in Australia, equal pay for work of comparable value had achieved a striking increase in women's income share. He pointed out that the favorable economic and political climate had made "the implementation of equal pay *over such a short period* . . . less painful socially than it may be at a time like the present." He added, "The bright spot from your perspective is that it has been done in Australia, it does stick and its consequences, as far as we can tell, are not nearly so bad as its adversaries would have us believe."[28]

In judging the Australian experience we should stress once more that this has been a case of applying comparable worth policy throughout the economy. This makes Duncan's conclusion that it is a feasible policy even more impressive, and certainly more encouraging to the policy's supporters. In contrast, the comparable worth initiatives that we will discuss in Canada as well as the efforts in the United States are limited to a case-by-case basis, affecting a minute part of the nations' workforces at any one time. Their economic effects, both gains and costs, will, therefore, be equally limited. In the light of the Australian experience, it is hard to see how they can produce economic chaos.

The Canadian Picture

Introducing "a bold new element into the long struggle Canadian women have waged to get equality in the work force," the Canadian Parliament, in 1977, adopted the Canadian Human Rights Act. The "bold new element" was the

> provision for equal pay for work of equal value. No longer could employers get away with paying women less by hiving them off . . . in different classifications from men. Now women would be entitled to the same rewards as men whenever they used skills as great, had to make the same effort to do their jobs, exercised as much responsibility and worked under equivalent conditions.[29]

At the same time Parliament set up a Canadian Human Rights Commission to administer the act.

The Human Rights Act replaced a federal law of 1956, amended in 1967, mandating equal pay for women and men doing the same or substantially similar work. In a paper explaining the methodology and principles for applying the comparable worth sections of the new act, the Canadian Human Rights Commission asserted:

> "Equal pay for equal work" . . . proved ineffective . . . in solving the problem of wage disparities between men and women. Its very narrow interpretation, requiring two jobs to be identical before they could be compared, accentuated systematic job categorization and the formation of ghettos of so-called female occupations (nursing, secretarial science and the like) and male occupations (electronics, truck driving and so forth). Once certain types of requirements or duties specific to particular categories were introduced into job evaluation systems, the principle of equal pay for equal work could be ignored, since the jobs held by men and by women were different and could not be compared.
>
> Sexist job categorization and the gap between men's and women's salaries therefore both increased considerably, as the following statistics from 1978 Statistics Canada Reports show. . . .[30]

The commission's working paper also emphasizes with statistics the importance of the pay gap to Canadian working women. Nearly half of adult women in Canada were in the labor force in 1977, an increase of about 30 percent since 1960. In contrast, labor force participation of the population as a whole grew only 9 percent. But, the paper stresses, "although nearly 50 percent of working women support a family, 61 percent of women who work receive less than $6,000 a year, compared to 28 percent of men." Not surprisingly, families headed by women workers are much more likely to live in poverty than families headed by male wage earners.

The commission concludes:

> These statistics underline the need to come to grips with the employment systems which have enshrined such compartmentalization of job opportunities for women. There are two separate but complementary approaches to this problem, namely the principle of equal employment opportunities . . . and the principle of equal pay for work of equal value, which involves compensation and job evaluation.
>
> The latter approach was introduced by the International Labour Organization in 1951, in the Convention de Rome. . . . Canada signed the Convention . . . in 1972 and altered its legislation in 1977. Section 11 of the Canadian Human Rights Act is designed to eliminate job ghettos and push for a reappraisal of existing compensation and job evaluation systems in organizations under federal jurisdiction.[31]

But Canada is very much a federation of provinces, and the authority of the 1977 federal act extends only to federal government employees and to the employees of private companies chartered or regulated by the federal government, such as the transportation industry, banks, and the media. So only about 11 percent of the nation's employees come under the act. Nevertheless, the companies affected are among Canada's largest, and action taken by, or against, them sets a noteworthy example for smaller businesses.

The provinces had begun enacting equal pay for *equal work* laws in the early 1950s. By the early 1970s, all but Quebec had legislation requiring equal pay for *the same or substantially similar* work. Quebec may have dragged its feet, but more likely it was a question of needing more time. Quebec is an important center of Canadian business, industry, and finance. It has a working population that is 40 percent female and has a mix of races and religions as well as ages. Therefore its Charter of Human Rights had plenty of affirmative action considerations, in addition to pay equity, to deal with. When it did act in 1975, it passed a broad and comprehensive Charter of Human Rights and Liberties that included provision for a comparable worth type of pay equity. It predated the federal act by two years.

The Quebec Charter stated the principle, in its article 19, of "à travail équivalent, salaire égal, sans discrimination"—equal pay, without discrimination, for *equivalent* work. No other province has such an equivalent work, or what we would term comparable worth, law. Because of Quebec's economic prominence and its different cultural and legal background, its experience provides us with an interesting contrast to that of the federal government.

Before discussing Quebec, however, let's turn to the national scene and look at how the federal Canadian Human Rights Act, with its roots in English institutions, has worked. The comparable worth provisions of the act's Section 11 are simply put:

(1) It is a discriminatory practice for an employer to establish or maintain differences in wages between male and female employees employed in the same establishment who are performing work of equal value.

(2) In assessing the value of work performed by employees employed in the same establishment, the criterion to be applied is the composite of the skill, effort and responsibility required in the performance of the work and the conditions under which the work is performed.

Section 11 sanctions wage differences when these are permitted by the guidelines of the Human Rights Commission. It prevents employers from setting up separate establishments solely to maintain female-male wage differences.

For a first-hand analysis of how the commission implements the act, I interviewed Claude Bernier, a compensation specialist, who is director of the equal pay section of the Canadian Human Rights Commission. The commission's function is to interpret and apply the provisions of Section 11 of the act in such a way as to "ensure that prejudice based on sex is not a factor in the determination of wages. . . ."[32] Their most important job, in comparing the equity of pay for dissimilar work, is to determine the value of the work, "the value being determined on the basis of approved criteria, *without the wage market or negotiated wage rates being taken into account.*"[33]

To do this, the commission has developed "Equal Wages Guidelines." The guidelines define "skill," "effort," "responsibility," and "working conditions" as the criteria used in assessing "value of work." The guidelines also describe the characteristics the commission considers in defining an "establishment," the unit within which work is being compared. And they explain the "reasonable factors," that is, the exceptions that employers can use to justify differences in wages among employees doing work of equal value.

In describing how the commission functions, Claude Bernier said that cases begin primarily in response to complaints of either workers or their unions. "Although we know of cases of pay discrimination and we would like to initiate action ourselves, we simply do not have the resources," she explained, adding, "I have only two people working with me for the whole country."

She pointed out, however, that the cases she handles involve large employers. They are cases of what she terms "systemic discrimination." "We are talking about classification and compensation systems. And as soon as you deal with these kinds of systems, you are likely to deal with categories of people who are identified in the system as doing equivalent work. And that is the interesting thing about these cases. With one case you can touch thousands of people." She added, "This is our approach at the commission. Although we may not handle many cases at one time, we pick those which affect as many people as possible."

A second part of the commission strategy is to involve the unions in the process. Bernier explained that the organizations under the federal jurisdiction are large ones and most of them are unionized. "We try to convince the parties at the bargaining table to include the pay equity changes in the collective agreement." This is done, she explained, "to make sure that three years from now we will not come back to the previous situation." The commission also finds it less costly and more effective to negotiate settlements without going to the stage of litigation before an industrial tribunal. It has been successful in doing this in almost all of its cases.

When a complaint comes to the commission, it investigates it to substantiate whether or not the claim of discrimination is justified. Here the guidelines come into play. Are the classes of workers being compared working "in the same establishment"? Is their work, while dissimilar, "of equal value"? Do any of the legitimate employer defenses apply?

"Equal value" is a major problem. What does it mean? How do you measure it? Bernier said, "We *did* dismiss cases, because after the investigation we found the jobs were *not* of equal value, and we *did* compare jobs which were *very* different. So we've been able to indicate that it *is* possible to compare jobs which are dissimilar. And that is a big accomplishment."

How does the commission determine that jobs are, or are not, of equal value? "We use job evaluation techniques. We use job evaluation plans," Bernier replied. "And what we do," she explained, "is cross-examine ourselves. We have three different job evaluation plans because these job evaluation schemes can be biased themselves. And it's difficult to have a plan that we can say is not discriminatory. It depends on the people interpreting and applying the plan."

"So what we've done," she continued, "is that we have three different plans and we cross-check ourselves with the various plans." She explained that it was very important for the commission to be sure that its findings were proper. In cases that they dismissed because they found the jobs did *not* have equal value, she said, "the complainants could have sued us if we were wrong." Or, in cases they pursued because the commission found that dissimilar jobs *did* have equal value, "the respondents could have sued." But, she added, "in each of these cases, the evidence and the documentation that we had was good enough that people were convinced that the evaluation was properly done and the result was acceptable. Which was another major achievement."

In its "Employer Guide," the commission defines the "value of work" as "the value which the work performed by an employee in a given establishment represents in relation to the value of the work of another employee, or a group of employees, the value being determined on the basis of approved criteria, without the wage market or negotiated wage rates being taken into account."[34] In its "Methodology and Principles for Applying S.11," the commission stresses that "the value of a job must be defined in terms of the value to the employer, of the work accomplished, rather than solely on the basis of labour market conditions."[35]

In the light of these definitions, I asked Bernier whether the commission referred at all to the market in their evaluations. She replied, "Yes, we do refer to the market in certain very specific circumstances." She reminded me that originally the commission had prescribed seven "reasonable factors" justifying differences in wages. These are merit, seniority, red circling of a position (where the position of an employee is re-evaluated and down-graded, and the wages of that employee are temporarily fixed until the wages appropriate to the position equal or exceed that employee's wages), a rehabilitation assignment, a demotion pay procedure, phased-in wage reductions related to demotion pay, and a temporary training position in a nonsexist employee development program.

"Last year," she said, "we issued two new guidelines, one of which referred to the outside market, very carefully worded, because we found that in certain circumstances we had to take into consideration the market supply and demand. But in order for the respondent to show that the lack of supply in a certain category of job *does* justify paying these people a higher salary in order to attract them, the onus is on them to show that, first of all, they have done everything they could for a certain period of time to try to attract people to these jobs and there was nobody available in the market at the rate of pay they were paying. The second thing," she continued, "is that they have to find, within their organization, a third group which is mainly male-dominated, and show that the overpaid group is overpaid in relation to a male group as well as to a female group." In this way, the commission tries to prevent "transferring the bias of the market into the organization without questioning it." Bernier thinks, however, that in Canada's present depressed economic situation the problem of scarce labor is not likely to occur.

The first important complaint settled by the commission was that of *Leona Mollis* v. *the Treasury Board*. This case involved six nurses working in two federal penitentiaries in the Atlantic provinces. The Treasury Board was their employer. According to the commission's "Summary of Decisions," health care in these prisons had originally been provided solely by male "technicians," or "care officers," who "did not have the training or qualifications of nurses." The government decided to bring in nurses "to provide [prisoners] with professional nursing care," and the nurses "worked side by side with the male technicians, performing the same tasks."

"However," the summary points out, "the technicians' job descriptions were much more imposing than the nurses" and were twice as long, so that it appeared on paper that they had more responsible positions." In addition, the men, who were not professionals, belonged to a different union than the nurses, who "are members of the Professional Institute of the Public Services of Canada." The male technicians' trade agreement "established significantly higher rates of pay."

After receiving the complaint of Leona Mollis, one of the nurses, the Canadian Human Rights Commission investigated. The commission found that, despite the more elaborate male job descriptions, "the nurses and the technicians were performing the same jobs. The only differences were that the nurses were better qualified and the men were better paid."

So this case, which initially seemed to be a comparable worth case, turned out to be, in fact, an unequal pay for equal work case. The commission negotiated a settlement involving both pay raises and back pay for the nurses. This was agreed to by the complainant, the nurses' union, and the Treasury Board. The government also agreed to review its pay for nurses in other federal health care centers.[36]

The case of *Public Service Alliance of Canada* v. *the Treasury Board* became the first settlement involving classes of workers doing dissimilar work. Public Service Alliance of Canada, a union of nonprofessional federal employees, had filed a complaint for the Library Services group, 66 percent of whom were women, claiming that these 470 librarians did work of equal value to that of the mainly male Historical Research group, but were being paid less.

The employer used different job evaluation plans for valuing the jobs in each group. Neither plan was useful for comparisons between the groups. So the commission modified a private-sector plan that was acceptable to both the union and the employer. It employed sampling methods and statistical techniques to make the comparisons between the large number of positions and pay levels in the two groups.

The investigation showed that the librarians were indeed being paid less than the historical researchers for jobs of equal value. The settlement negotiated between the parties provided for pay adjustments, retroactive to March 1, 1978, the effective date of the Human Rights Act. These totaled $2.3 million. The continuing cost of the settlement is about $900,000 a year.[37] This case showed the feasibility of making "equal value of work" comparisons between dissimilar jobs. Apparently all the groups concerned—the commission, the librarians and their union, and the Treasury—agreed with the validity of the result.

Claude Bernier noted, "Some of the settlements have had some interesting repercussions on other companies and employers." She cited the librarians' case just described. She explained that the settlement "did influence the market for librarians in Ottawa, since most of the librarians in Ottawa work for the federal government. Because of the impact of the decision on the market, the librarians working for other organizations in Ottawa have been able to negotiate, at the bargaining table, salary increases to get to the same level as the librarians working for the federal government."

"Interesting repercussions" will doubtless result from the recent settlement of one of the largest cases yet undertaken by the commission. Public Service Alliance of Canada filed a complaint against the Treasury

Board on behalf of employees in the federal food, laundry, and miscellaneous personnel services. The majority of workers in these three subgroups, 2,300 of a total 3,300, were women. The remaining four federal support worker subgroups—messenger, custodial, building, and stores—totaling another 8,800 workers, were mainly male.

According to Rita Cadieux, deputy chief commissioner of the Human Rights Commission, the board's own "classification system establishes that at any given level [of work] regardless of occupational grouping, all general services employees are performing work of equal value." The Treasury Board "acknowledged . . . that all CS sub-groups perform work of equal value."[38] Despite this, "within each [geographical] zone and at each level, the seven groups were each paid at a different rate."[39] The three largely female groups were all paid less than the four male-dominated groups. After investigation, the commission found the complaint substantiated.

Negotiations for settlement were difficult. The Treasury Board proposed a compromise that would have raised wages in the female-dominated groups somewhat, but would have continued a situation where many workers were being paid unequal wages for equal work. The commission found this unacceptable and contrary to the intent of Section 11 of the Canadian Human Rights Act. It appointed a tribunal to hear the case. Explaining this action, the chief commissioner, Gordon Fairweather, said, "The settlement of this complaint must not dilute the principle of equal pay for work of equal value. Equal must be equal, not almost equal."[40] The union also rejected the proposal.

The case appeared headed for litigation. But before hearings began, the Treasury Board decided to accept an agreement that "dissolved the sub-groups involved in this complaint, introduced a new single common pay plan for the general services group and established a new rate structure from which all previous differential in pay based on sex has been eliminated."[41] The agreement also provided for back pay. The settlement was large—$19 million in back pay and an increase of about $12 million a year in the payroll of the 3,300 people in the low-paid groups. Reports of the case stress that 1,000 of the workers benefiting from the agreement were men.

With the commission's encouragement, the union and the board modified the collective bargaining agreement to include the pay rate and structure changes. As Bernier said, using the bargaining process is part of the commission's enforcement strategy. "The union will be making sure that the collective agreement will always reflect the change, you see."

When I asked Bernier whether these decisions had an influence on employers other than those directly affected, she replied by citing the instance of "one respondent, a large bank, which decided on its own that it would be better for them, and less expensive for them, to comply before they had a complaint against them." She explained, "We offer a consultant service to respondents who would like to comply voluntarily. We are trying to convince employers slowly to come to us and ask us for some advice. If they want to look at their system, we will provide them with some technical advice. Then they can make sure that they are in compliance with the act and avoid having any complaints." She added, "We are having more and more employers who found out, after having had a few complaints against them, that this was disrupting. So they decided that they would look at their system before having more complaints."

One of these, the large bank she had mentioned, decided to do a total review of the classification and compensation system in their organization. "They did consult with us, all along the process, although they employed a consulting firm to do the review. But we were called upon at various steps in the assessment and change of the system to give some advice. In this way, they could make sure that their system would be in compliance with the act."

Bernier stressed that "we are trying as much as we can to emphasize these sorts of things, because we have so few resources. If we tried to work out something on a one-to-one basis, it would take years to achieve anything. So we are trying to use the bargaining process and the unions as much as we can, and also provide technical advice and services. We have very knowledgeable people who have good credibility with the various organizations dealing with us, and it seems to pay off." Of the 43 complaints received by the commission in its first four years since March 1978, 35 have been substantiated, and 7 of these have been settled. Only one has been taken to the Federal Court of Appeals.

I concluded the interview with Claude Bernier by asking for her forecast for the future of equal pay for work of equal value in Canada. She replied that last year there was "a lot of lobbying to eliminate the equal value concept from the legislation because of the big settlement we were getting. But," she continued, "we went through that without any problem and it is something that I think will never come back. And I think that it is good. It is something which is not in question any more. However," she added, "with the economic situation the way it is right now, I doubt very much that there will be any other legislation in Canada which will be amended to include the concept for the next three or four years."

She also did not foresee any increased action by the federal commission in the way of initiating complaints in big cases because of the commission's lack of resources. "We can hardly deal with the work load we have, with the complaints we receive right now. And so there is no way we can initiate. I have two people to deal with equal pay for the whole country. And I don't think that the government is very keen on giving me a lot more at this time."

"À Travail Équivalent, Salaire Égal, Sans Discrimination"

"Equal pay for equivalent work, without discrimination"—this is the title of the *cahier* published by the Quebec Human Rights Commission in 1980. In the *cahier*, the commission aims "to establish the bases and the method of applying Article 19" of the Quebec Charter of Human Rights. The provincial government enacted the charter in 1975. The Human Rights Commission began administering it in 1976. It was amended in 1983 to include affirmative action policies and to prohibit discrimination on the basis of age.

As the commission's *cahier* points out, the scope of the Quebec charter is vast. At the heart of its economic provisions is the broadly stated right of every worker to "just and reasonable" conditions of work. The charter spells out the meaning of this right by prohibiting discrimination in all aspects of the employment process and contract, on the basis of sex, race, color, age, sexual orientation, family status, religion, political convictions, language, ethnic or national origin, social condition, or physical handicaps.[42]

Article 19 of the charter applies the broad principle of nondiscrimination in work to the particular issue of equality in pay. According to Article 19, "Every employer must, without discrimination, grant equal salary or wages to their employees who perform equivalent work in the same place."

It provides, however, that "there is no discrimination if a difference in salary or wages is based on experience, seniority, length of service, merit, output or overtime, if these criteria apply to all employees."

The commission's *cahier* explains that promoting a policy of equal pay for equivalent work is an integral part of a general policy of equality in employment. It says that the equal pay policy

> attacks that situation where categories of workers are concentrated in a limited number of jobs which are among the least well paid. More specifically, it attacks that situation where the inequalities of remuneration are not justified because the jobs held, although different, have the same value as others which are better paid, and are mainly held by another category of employee.[43]

In his foreword, René Hurtubise, president of the commission, emphasizes the importance of Article 19:

> In the continuing fight against discrimination, this article ranks in the forefront by proclaiming a basic policy of *equality of treatment for equi-*

valent work. It is inspired by the policies outlined by the International Labor Office since 1919 and it places Quebec in the avant-garde of the struggle for the recognition and the exercise, in full equality, of the rights and liberties of the individual.

Hurtubise continues, "Indeed, this concept of equivalent work moves beyond that of equal work and of work which is substantially the same: it permits the comparison of different tasks for the purpose of measuring their degree of equivalence. In Canada," he adds, "only the federal legislation—article 11 of the Canadian law on human rights—has, since 1977, had the same provision."

I found the same sense of accomplishment and pride reflected in the comments of Muriel Garon, assistant director of research for the Quebec Human Rights Commission, when I interviewed her about the commission's work in administering Article 19. She was recommended to me as "the expert on this question."[44]

When asked "Why has Quebec done more than the other Canadian provinces in dealing with the pay equity problem?" she replied, "Our charter is written in a different style. Our civil code is French. It's the French approach. It's a much broader approach." She added, "Our charter was one of the last ones to be adopted in Canada, so we probably had time to see what was going on. But," she continued, "the spirit is different. The British approach, or the Anglo-Saxon approach, is much more precise. It tries to foresee all the specific situations and exceptions. Ours is a human rights code which is very close to the United Nations code. It defines big principles that we have to interpret. So, the spirit is very different."

"Is it more efficient?" she asked rhetorically. "I don't know. We have to deal with big things. Our hands are filled with all types of cases. So, are we more efficient when we try to take on so much? I don't know. But," she concluded, "we *have* been efficient as far as cases under the equal pay section are concerned. We *have* been efficient."

She went on to explain the success of the equal pay section, "The phrasing 'equal pay for equivalent work' has been very satisfactory for this type of case. The approach of this phrasing can deal with the type of problem that emerges from our society." She contrasted this with the Equal Pay Act in the United States, which cannot address the pay equity problem arising from the typical situation of sex-segregated occupations where women and men are not doing "the same or substantially similar work."

She said that Quebec was interested in making their human rights law "the best law in Canada. . . . Our law has given us possibilities which other provinces envy." She observed that in Ontario "they have been really fighting to have a phrasing in their law which would be similar to ours." I had heard this also from Mary Cornish, an Ottawa lawyer who is active in the women's movement in Ontario. Cornish stressed the strong employer opposition there to comparable worth. She saw no hope of passage of such legislation in Ontario in the near future.

When I asked Muriel Garon how Article 19 of the Quebec Human Rights Law actually worked, she replied that the Quebec approach was similar to the federal approach. But she explained that the Quebec "population" was different. The federal commission deals mainly with large employers, while Quebec deals with all kinds of companies and more frequently with small companies than with large ones. She said they had handled about 35 "equal pay for equivalent work" cases, a caseload similar to that of the federal commission. She estimated that about 2,000 women had been directly affected by the decisions and that many others had been indirectly affected. She explained that most of the cases were not simple pay equity cases, but also involved other types of employment discrimination.

As for procedures, she said that, except for their first case against the tobacco companies, all the cases developed from employee complaints. The commission found that it didn't have the time or resources to initiate cases. "It just takes too much energy." The complaints "came in so rapidly" that it had to "deal with them day by day." She regretted that they hadn't been able to select and develop the "good cases." The commission has been seriously understaffed, she explained, especially since the legislature added the handicapped to the groups protected by the legislation. This brought a heavy load of work, but the legislature did not raise the commission's funds or personnel commensurately.

Contrary to the trends elsewhere in Canada, however, the Quebec legislature recently approved a larger budget for the commission. "We are swimming against the current," Garon commented. "But we had accumulated so much delay in handling our cases that it was evident that we were not big enough. Now we are about to hire new personnel. So we think that we will be able to start doing things more seriously."

The key question, of course, is always how to determine that there is sex discrimination in pay when comparing jobs that aren't the same, or substantially the same. How do you determine that unlike jobs have equivalent value?

The Quebec commission's *cahier* describes a number of cases it has settled and then summarizes the methods used in these cases.

As one observes, the evaluation of the equivalence of tasks has been carried out in certain cases by using the evaluation system already in use in the industry. In other cases it has been considered necessary to introduce a non-discriminatory system of job evaluation to measure the tasks. In other cases, particularly those which concern the same, or substantially the same jobs, the establishment of this identity, or similarity, has been made by simple observation. The results obtained in all these ways, up until the present, show that effecting the disappearance of discriminatory salary differences between equivalent employments is a realizable thing.

The *cahier* adds, "the number of dossiers bearing on these questions is going to increase."[45]

Muriel Garon's experience extends the *cahier*'s discussion. In my talk with her she pointed out that the commission deals largely with small companies and "most of the time they don't have an evaluation system. So we have to make a job study. But we don't have one specific system, since, as you know, for different cases, you cannot use the same type of evaluation system. It depends largely on the type of work. So," she explained, "we make systematic job studies."

She continued, "We have an example, a type of system, which has been defined as nondiscriminatory. We compare a company's job evaluation system with our example as far as point distribution and the rating of mostly female characteristics like dexterity and attention versus mostly male characteristics like physical strength are concerned. So this is one area where we are very careful." She added, "Many of the cases, of course, are equal work cases that don't require a job study. Our law requires equal pay for work of equivalent value and this, of course, includes equal work as the most simple case."

How do market values affect the commission's evaluation of the worth of jobs? The *cahier* devotes a section to this topic. It states:

The study of . . . evaluation systems shows that they have been conceived with the aim of systematizing remuneration plans, not transforming them. The technique employed for this consists of finding methods for determining points and weights which permit arriving at as close an approximation as possible to the salary scales already in existence in the workplace.

The *cahier* states that "this approach does not imply any corrective aim: on the contrary, it contributes to reproducing the pre-existing conditions of the market." It asserts that it is "unnecessary to repeat that these conditions are profoundly branded by the history of discrimination of which minorities and women have been the object and of which one of the consequences has been making their work cheap." Therefore, the *cahier* continues, the Human Rights Commission rejects "the argument that the laws of the market justify salary differences between certain categories of workers when the differences are the result of the effects of discrimination."[46]

The commission's *cahier* concludes that there is a "panoply of instruments" available that has been "developed precisely for the end of evaluating and comparing groups of jobs." These instruments "are not perfect" and they "harbour numerous possibilities of bias." But the commission's analysis finds that they are useful tools for measuring value objectively. They involve both an internal analysis and comparisons of a particular job evaluation scheme with other systems. And, the *cahier* says, "The Human Rights Commission intends to continue to refine and validate these instruments, working with cases which are submitted to it or with those which it chooses to undertake on its own initiative." It concludes, "The transformation of the notion of equal work into that of equivalent work is indeed essential if one wishes to give full meaning to the principle of equality of remuneration."[47]

Muriel Garon reiterated the commission's position that it does not allow an employer to use a low value of women's labor in the marketplace to justify paying low wages to women in the firm. Then she added, "We would never allow an employer to pay women less because women will accept less. Nor would we allow this even when they signed a collective agreement. The argument that women accepted less in an informal or formal way wouldn't be accepted." She commented, however, that it is often difficult to compare the equivalence of the value of typically female, "ghetto" types of jobs with typically male jobs in small companies with few positions and no evaluation systems.

In response to a question about the case of male labor in short supply whose pay is high due to market scarcity, she replied that the commission had not developed a formal guideline covering this situation because it has "not confronted cases where we needed that." She explained that the commission does allow higher wages for merit. Inasmuch as it is usually the highly qualified groups of workers who are scarce, she said that the employers may be able to justify higher wages for them on these grounds. Also, if the employer can prove that there is real scarcity the commission would accept that. The problem would come, she said, when scarcity stopped and men were still being paid at higher levels than women because they came in during a period of scarcity.

The Quebec commission's methods of settling a case resemble those of the federal commission. It emphasizes mediation rather than litigation. And it sees the role of the unions and other organizations representing the workers as "absolutely central."[48] It believes that these methods have been effective, in practice, in achieving good settlements.

When I asked Muriel Garon what she considered to have been key, or landmark, equivalent value cases, she mentioned first the cases brought against companies in large industries—tobacco, liquor, glass, paper. These she stressed because of the importance of companies in big industries as examples. "I think that our investigation into the tobacco industry, even though we didn't go as far as we wanted to go, was a strong example. And," she added, "it was not only an example but it shook the whole tobacco industry. That's why I think—I'm only a researcher—that we should choose cases like that in order to have more influence. Our main influence shouldn't be in terms of inquiries but in terms of examples which would bring people to negotiate themselves, afterwards."

Then she explained that key, or landmark, could be defined "in terms of the possibilities which are approached" and went on to describe a case she considered "a very important case theoretically, and as an example, also." It was important because it involved comparisons between very different jobs.

This was the case of a Quebec North Shore paper company. The company had an evaluation system

> which applied both to people working in the office and people working in the field. So we could compare receptionists doing office work to surveyor's assistants doing more manual work. This is the case where the difference between the jobs is greatest. It was a case we liked very much because of that. It showed that it is not impossible to compare things which are very different, because evaluation systems *are* really good enough to compare very different types of jobs. In this case the employer could not question our decisions because we used his own evaluation scheme. It was an easy case and a good example of the type of case that can be carried on under our law.

The commission's *cahier* also describes cases it has settled involving the evaluation of unlike jobs. One of these, for example, concerns Industries Valcartier, where over 200 women workers were integrated into an evaluation system from which they had been excluded. The women's

> tasks consisted, for example, of inserting powder into empty cartridge cases, while the men, working also at the same level of production, assembled guns and moved empty cartridge cases. The equivalence of these tasks having been demonstrated by the application of an evaluation system, the women obtained about $120,000 in retroactive pay and the eradication of the wage difference for the future.[49]

So far, then, the Quebec commission, unlike the federal commission, has dealt mainly with work of equivalent value situations involving factory workers. It expects that in the near future it may tackle a complicated case involving a number of different female professions and a number of different unions and some jobs that are highly skilled—one more like several of the federal cases. But this has not come in yet, and the commission's representatives could not discuss it.

When I asked Muriel Garon about the future, she replied first that, with the recent increase in funds, the commission planned to undertake more "positive action programs"—more initiation of cases and more programs to inform the public about the human rights charter and the commission's work. She thought that opposition from employers had been reduced recently, but she pointed out that the complaints were also reduced. "In a recession period," she explained, "jobs are scarce, and people are afraid to lose their jobs, so they don't use the possibility to make complaints to the commission the way they did before. People are trying to *cut* salaries. So we are in a period in which we have less cases coming in. We really think this is due to the recession.

"So, in the short period, I think that we will have to change our approach. We are too small and we'll always be too small to settle all cases that come in. We'll have to choose cases that act as examples, or test cases, in terms of our inquiries. We have to rely on the population to do most of the job, because we're not able to. And we'll have to invest much more into the prevention, education, and publicity program."

Summary

The foreign history of the equal pay for comparable worth issue, particularly the experience of Australia, Canada, and Quebec, shows that such a policy is not only workable but that it is working. The Australian case shows that even an across-the-board introduction of the policy does not produce economic chaos and that it does have a significant effect on the share of income going to women workers—which doubtless helps explain the opposition to it, here and elsewhere.

The Canadian experience, at both the federal level and the provincial level in Quebec, illustrates the possibilities as well as the problems of gradual, low-key introduction of the policy. Our situation, in the States, is more akin to that of Canada and Quebec than to that of Australia, but we can learn from them all.

Notes

1. Ronnie Ratner, ed., *Equal Employment Policy for Women* (Philadelphia: Temple University Press, 1980), p. 29. The quote is from an unpublished manu-

script of January 1975 by Alice Cook, titled "Equal Pay: A Multi-National History and Comparison," pp. 7–8.

2. Ratner, *Equal Employment Policy,* pp. 29–30.

3. Ibid., p. 30.

4. Janice R. Bellace, "A Foreign Perspective," in E. Robert Livernash, ed., *Comparable Worth: A Symposium on the Issues and Alternatives,* 2nd ed. (Washington, D.C.: Equal Employment Advisory Council, 1984), p. 143.

5. Ibid., p. 145.

6. The discussion of the German experience is based on the work of Alice H. Cook, "Collective Bargaining as a Strategy for Achieving Equal Opportunity and Equal Pay: Sweden and Germany," pp. 5–9, paper prepared for the Wellesley Conference on Equal Pay and Equal Opportunity Policy for Women, Wellesley College Center for Research on Women, 1978.

7. International Labour Office, "Declaration on Equality of Opportunity and Treatment of Women Workers," *Women Workers and Society: International Perspectives* 202 (1976), cited in Laura N. Gasaway, "Comparable Worth: A Post-*Gunther* Overview," *Georgetown Law Journal* 69 (1981): 1150.

8. International Labour Office, *Women at Work* 1 (1982): 29.

9. Bellace, "A Foreign Perspective," p. 144.

10. Ibid.

11. ILO, *Women at Work,* pp. 29–30.

12. Organisation for Economic Cooperation and Development, *Women and Employment: Policies for Equal Opportunities* (Paris: OECD, 1980), pp. 32–33.

13. Much of my information on the Australian experience comes from the work of R.G. Gregory and R.C. Duncan. Duncan was first assistant commissioner at the Industries Assistance Commission in Canberra at the time of their original study. He is now with the World Bank in Washington, D.C. Gregory is senior fellow at the Australian National University.

These two scholars have done an exhaustive study of the Australian experience with "equal pay for work of equal value." Their most recent article is R.G. Gregory and R.C. Duncan, "Segmented Labor Market Theories and the Australian Experience of Equal Pay for Women," *Journal of Post-Keynesian Economics* 3 (Spring 1981): 403–28.

Most recently, I heard R.C. Duncan speak on "Comparable Worth in Australia" at the fourth annual meeting of the National Committee on Pay Equity, Washington, D.C., December 6, 1982. A draft of his talk is available from the committee.

14. Margaret Power, senior tutor, Department of Economics, University of Sydney, "Women's Work Is Never Done—by Men: A Socio-Economic Model of Sex-typing in Occupations," *Journal of Industrial Relations* (September 1975): 225.

15. Duncan, "Comparable Worth in Australia," p. 1.

16. Ibid., p. 2.

17. Ibid., p. 3.

18. Duncan, question period in talk to National Committee on Pay Equity, December 6, 1982.

19. *Wall Street Journal,* July 16, 1981, p. 24.

20. Duncan, "Comparable Worth in Australia," p. 6.

21. Duncan and Gregory, "The Australian Experience," p. 427.

22. Duncan, "Comparable Worth in Australia," p. 6.

23. Ibid., pp. 6–7.

24. Duncan and Gregory, "The Australian Experience," p. 421.

25. Duncan, "Comparable Worth in Australia," p. 7.

26. Ibid.

27. Ibid., p. 8.

28. Ibid.

29. Rita Cadieux, deputy chief commissioner, Canadian Human Rights Commission, *Equal Pay for Work of Equal Value—The Canadian Experience* (Ottawa: Canadian Human Rights Commission, 1982), p. 2.

30. Canadian Human Rights Commission (CHRC), "Methodology and Principles for Applying S. 11," working paper, p. 2.

31. CHRC, "Methodology," pp. 2–3. For a short history of Canadian sex-equality law see Harish C. Jain, "Canadian Legal Approaches to Sex Equality in the Workplace," *Monthly Labor Review* (October 1982): 38–41.

32. Canadian Human Rights Commission, "The Canadian Human Rights Act, Employer Guide" (1981), p. 31.

33. Ibid., p. 28, italics are added. In one type of case market wages are considered. See pp. 94–95.

34. CHRC, "Employer Guide," p. 28.

35. CHRC, "Methodology," p. 3.

36. Canadian Human Rights Commission, "Equal Pay for Work of Equal Value," news releases and excerpts from CHRC's "Summary of Decisions" (May 1982), pp. 2–4.

37. Cadieux, "Equal Pay," p. 19.

38. CHRC, news releases, p. 17.

39. Cadieux, "Equal Pay," p. 21.

40. CHRC, news releases, p. 18.

41. Cadieux, "Equal Pay," p. 26.

42. Commission des Droits de la Personne du Quebec, "À Travail Équivalent, Salaire Égal, sans Discrimination" (1980), p. 12. Hereafter referred to as *Cahier*. This is Article 10 of the Quebec Charter of Human Rights and Freedoms.

43. *Cahier*, p. 13.

44. The recommendation was made by Jacques Bergeron, Quebec Human Rights Commission.

45. *Cahier*, p. 41.

46. *Cahier*, p. 90.

47. *Cahier*, p. 105.

48. *Cahier*, p. 93.

49. *Cahier*, p. 40.

4

COMPARABLE WORTH IN
SAN JOSE:
The Opening of Pandora's Box?

In July 1981, nonmanagement municipal employees in San Jose, California—women and men, blue-collar, clerical, and professional workers—struck successfully for a comparable worth pay adjustment. Severely shaken by this event, a *Wall Street Journal* editor wrote:

> When the nine-day strike by municipal workers in San Jose, Calif., was settled Tuesday, the lid was removed from a Pandora's box and a new approach for setting pay for women has made its escape. Under the innocuous name of "comparable worth," it would abolish the labor market and have everyone's pay set by bureaucrats. . . . If the taxpayers of San Jose choose to hoist themselves with this petard then so be it. But the Supreme Court will some day have to tackle directly this issue of whether equal pay for essentially different jobs can be construed as the intent of Congress.[1]

According to one version of the myth, Pandora's box, along with all its evils for mankind, contained Hope. And certainly the success of the collective bargaining effort for pay equity in San Jose brought hope to many workers both there and elsewhere. It showed how job evaluation techniques could be used to measure inequities in pay scales and to value the comparable worth of work. It demonstrated that male and female union members, working at a variety of occupations, could agree on pay equity as a goal and stick to that goal through the rigors of a strike. It indicated that there are employers with a concern about pay equity. It made clear that collective bargaining can be an effective way of gaining equitable pay and that relying on politically minded government administrators, or on costly litigation, are not the only routes.

Most importantly, San Jose had a national impact. The strike for comparable worth became a media event with nationwide coverage on television's morning and evening news shows, on the radio, and in the press. Suddenly an obscure concept, understood by few and belittled by many businessmen, editors, judges, and economists, became an issue with content and weight. Women and unions awakened to its possibilities. Furthermore, the Supreme Court's *Gunther* decision, in mid-June 1981, just before the San Jose strike, had already strengthened the significance of comparable worth by permitting female plaintiffs to claim sex discrimination in pay even when the work they were doing was not "substantially similar" to that of males. The issue could no longer be disparagingly dismissed.

Why San Jose?

Why San Jose? Why did the first major collective bargaining effort for comparable worth happen here? And the first strike for pay equity? What led the union and the city government to become "pioneers" on "the cutting edge" of pay equity, as one local official put it?

That official, Sally Reed, was deputy city manager at the time of the negotiations and strike. She is now chief executive officer of Santa Clara County's board of supervisors, a powerful board, managing a nearly $900 million budget for social services, criminal justice, and tax assessment and collection. She and two other women control this board with a three-to-two majority.[2]

When I asked her, "Why San Jose?" in a recent interview, she replied, "Clearly, the fact that there were and are so many women in leadership positions in government in this area played some role. It drew attention to what women were doing. Also, I think that this group of women in both administrative and political leadership positions in San Jose were seen as more sensitive and open to an issue like that. And the third thing that I would point out is that the [San Francisco] Bay area, Silicon Valley, is very, very often the first place that things happen. We have a high level of innovation and a high level of education—engineers, inventors come here from all over the country. This is where the action is."

She continued, "It's a melting pot. It's an area that people are moving to all the time. And so there is less structure here. There is a more open mind in general to philosophical issues like this. I think that all these were factors."

Nevertheless, she asserted that "from the beginning the city management believed that the decision to make the Hay job evaluation study, with its emphasis on investigating pay equity for the entire work force, was a very high-risk decision. It was a political decision—it's always hard to say no to a study, in a political process. I think we knew from the beginning that it was very risky and we had grave reservations. It is an issue that is difficult to understand and this tended to make it more explosive. It was clear that we would be on the cutting edge of something we weren't in a position to afford to be on the cutting edge of."

But, as Reed suggested, Santa Clara Valley is an area where innovation is the rule, not the exception. "The city of San Jose is an old Spanish settlement that turned into an agricultural community, which turned into a manufacturing community—first in aerospace—and then turned into a high-tech community," Bill Callahan, business agent for the local municipal employees union until July 1983, told me. "And it is, I guess you might say, the cradle of high-tech."

The valley has the densest concentration of high technology industries in the world, according to the San Jose Chamber of Commerce. A livelier source, Ivan Sharpe, describes it as

> a Buck Rogers wonderland of wizard-inventors, who have made fortunes overnight by creating now commonplace things—digital watches, pocket calculators, video games. . . . One out of every six Ph.D.s in California works in the valley, where more than 1,000 "high-tech" companies such as Apple Computer, Memorex and Advanced Micro Devices pour out ever-shrinking electronic devices that have revolutionized the world.[3]

To a visitor to these companies, the "wizards" that run them all seem to be young. In Silicon Valley's high-tech industries, 30 appears to be middle-aged, while 40 is over the hill and time to retire.

This environment attracts dynamic professional women and encourages them to go into business as well as politics. The women here "who probably have it best are those who started their own companies," Ivan Sharpe says.[4] He goes on to cite an impressive list of these women and their achievements. "What has happened in the valley is a lot more choice," he concludes. In making these choices, women "are helped by the palpable spirit of excitement and innovation that pervades the valley."[5] He points out, however, that women still have a way to go in Silicon Valley before they achieve "complete equality." He quotes Billye Ericksen-Desaigoudar, president and owner of a "$7 million specialty-electronics sales company," who suffered an unfortunate experience with sex discrimination. "You'd better believe it's still a man's world," she told him.[6]

The valley's transformation from agriculture to manufacturing took place in a hurry. "As bull-dozers rumbled over orchards," acreage of agricultural land fell from 80,000 in 1960 to less than 15,000 today.[7] Since

1950, the population of San Jose has increased sevenfold, from around 95,000 to 667,700. The chamber of commerce describes it as the largest city in the Santa Clara Valley, the fourth largest city in California, and the fourteenth largest city in the United States. And it is still growing.[8]

Thanks to high-tech, Santa Clara County is wealthy, ranking "first in the nation in median household effective buying income ($32,336)."[9] "It is a fast-paced, fast-growing community," Bill Callahan says, "with a very high standard of living, and with problems of growth like a shortage of jobs and affordable housing for workers in the area."

When I asked him about the ethnic diversity of the city's population, Callahan replied, "Well, we have a great deal of diversity, but we don't have it in the old eastern breakdown of ethnic boroughs. We have a diverse population but it is homogeneous in the sense that it's not ethnically sectioned. It's because it's so new." (The 1980 census reports that 17.5 percent of Santa Clara County's population is of "Spanish origin." Other minority groups are "Asian and Pacific Islands," 7.7 percent; "Black," 3.4 percent; American Eskimo and Aleut Indians, 0.7 percent; and "Other," 9.7 percent. The "White" group predominates at 78.6 percent of the total.)

"Was there something unique about San Jose that produced a major comparable worth effort here?" I asked, repeating my "why San Jose?" question.

He agreed that there has to be an environment—"something to kindle," as he put it:

> I think that the makeup of the union, at that point in time—and it's pretty much the same now—in terms of leadership, leadership coming out of the library and clerical areas, had an awful lot to do with the direction in which the union went. The personalities of the people involved I think were important, too.
>
> It was an issue that the [city] council was receptive to from a political standpoint. In the mid and late 1970s we were adopting affirmative action plans all over the country, so that the atmosphere was probably conducive to looking at this other issue of discrimination, sex-based wage discrimination. There was receptiveness, awareness, and the commitment on the part of workers and union staff to the issue.
>
> And we saw it as winnable. I think that's most important, too. If you have a mission or a goal, you have to see something out there that may give you a spark of hope. To us, it did not appear to be that difficult. It was just how much and when that became the problems, but not the issue itself.
>
> San Jose was unique in that the people involved all came together at the same time, in the same place and, over a period of two to three years, stayed together on the issue. We also were able to attract a very large and diverse group of support—everything from people who protect the lives

of laboratory animals to traditional women's groups to the Sisters of Notre Dame. I was looking through the files and noticed all of these groups that you would not traditionally see aligned with labor, or with a civil rights cause. They just really came out and supported this issue.

Mike Ferrero, president of the Municipal Employees Federation, Local 101, American Federation of State, County, and Municipal Employees (AFSCME), had a different explanation for the success of the San Jose effort. Engrossed in completing extended negotiations for the current 1983 union contract with the city and weary from the many meetings involved, he nevertheless graciously made time to talk with me and thoughtfully considered my questions.

I don't think it so much had to do with it being California and being San Jose—maybe some of it did. But I think that all of the political ingredients happened to be just right. In 1978 [when the city gave in to union pressure for a pay equity, job evaluation study] we had a woman mayor. We had a female-dominated city council, concerned politically about women's issues. At the same time, we had a clerical work force that was becoming extremely concerned about clerical wages and the lack of upward mobility and just the general plight of women in the workplace. And San Jose was a city like any other city, I think, with a lot of the "good old boy" syndrome and that's the way things were run. So it was really ripe for a political insurgence of those with more radical feminist thoughts.

At the same time AFSCME's business agent was a woman, Maxine Jenkins. One of Maxine's assignments was to organize the clerical work force in city hall. This economic issue was obviously one issue around which she could do that. And so she did a lot of work, attempting to organize the clerical work force into the union, using a number of issues—job-sharing, day-care, career ladders, and pay equity. Then pay equity seemed to just catch fire as an issue. She was pounding away at [city] council when they went into bargaining that year [1978].

The then city manager, Jim Alloway, was talking about wanting to study all of his management classes for some kind of redistribution of salary scales there. I don't think that anybody knows why—I certainly don't, maybe he got tired of listening to Maxine—but during those negotiations, he signed an agreement saying that at the same time that they initiated the study of the management positions, they would also initiate a study of the nonmanagement positions in the city. It was an agreement to study the nonmanagement classifications and particularly to look at any major discrepancies between male and female salaries. That's when Hay Associates came into the picture. And that's also when I became president of the union, just as the study was getting started.

"You work in the library," I commented. "Were the librarians particularly interested in this issue?"

"As professionals with high educational levels," he replied, "the librarians were probably more aware, at the time, of inequities and quickly saw that this whole study process was a mechanism for doing something that they had wanted to see happen for a long time—some basic adjustments moving the librarians' salaries much higher than they had been." He continued:

> I don't think that at the very beginning the manager, the city council, or probably even Maxine recognized that the real effort was not going to come out of the clerical groups but was going to come out of the librarians—the issue wound up providing a vehicle for the librarians and carried everybody else along with it.
>
> The librarians already had fairly good representation within the union in 1978, on the executive board. They had controlled the presidency since 1977 or 1976. At the time that I came in they also elected three or four other members to the executive board and so they became a real power within the union structure at the time of the agreement. The library was already well entrenched within the union and was able to pretty well direct things as they felt they should be directed, in terms of our influence on the study and then, finally, the bargaining.
>
> I think the combination of all of those things had to exist. The librarians, all by themselves, would never have been able to get this issue off the board. The inequity, particularly as it reflected on the clerical workers, had to be there. But once it was set up and operating, I think that the librarians and their ability to make things work and to stick with the process were important—because it took a good two years before that process got to the bargaining table as an issue.

Two of those librarians who had an "ability to make things work and to stick with the process," Patt Curia and Joan Goddard, took me to lunch the day after I talked with Mike Ferrero. Both women had been on the union negotiating team in 1981 and one had been on the evaluation committee. We discussed why the librarians had been and still are so active, disproving the stereotype of librarians as reclusive keepers of books and files, the last people to be interested in unions, collective bargaining, and strikes.

They described the librarians as highly educated, skilled, knowledgeable professionals. As such, they saw them as more aware of their own interests and more cohesive as a group than the city's clerical workers. Furthermore, they stressed, as did Ferrero, the librarians' political abilities and activities. In the recent election for mayor and city council, for example, the librarians were out in the streets, working at the precinct level, to get "their people" elected so as to have a solid political base on the council. They considered this very important to achieving the union's goals in bargaining for the 1983 trade agreement.

And finally, Curia and Goddard pointed to the pay statistics for San Jose and elsewhere, which show a large gap between the salaries of librarians and those of male-dominated professions with comparable qualifications, responsibilities, and working conditions. Therefore, pay inequity is a serious concern for librarians.

In San Jose, for example, the Hay job evaluation showed that "acquisition librarian," a female-dominated occupation, had a job grade rated at 405 Hay points and paid $952 a month. "Senior planner," a male-dominated occupation, also with 405 points and similar office working conditions, paid $1,130 a month, or 18.7 percent more than the librarian.

Moreover, the male "senior planner" job paid 25 percent more than "senior librarian," a female-dominated class with more (493) Hay points and pay of $898. "Senior chemist," a class with both men and women, also had 493 points but had a salary level of $1,119 or 25 percent more than the "senior librarian."

Consequently, it is not surprising to read that "librarians have been in the forefront of the comparable worth issue since 1971, when the first library-based comparable worth study was done at the University of California Berkeley Libraries, which reported that the salaries of librarians were 25 to 27 percent lower than those of other academic nonteaching positions [filled predominantly by men]."[10] The librarians' national organization, the American Library Association, has actively supported comparable worth activities, particularly with its information bulletins and "action guides." And librarians across the country—working mainly for public employers, but also some in private, university employment—have filed class action suits and successfully undertaken bargaining efforts to evaluate jobs, change pay grades, and achieve pay equity increases.

So far, however, librarians have won their most notable success in Canada, in settlement of their 1979 complaint of sex-based wage discrimination against the federal government. They claimed their work was comparable in value to that of the male-dominated group of historical researchers, but that they were paid some $3,000 less a year. The Canadian Human Rights Commission agreed and awarded the librarians $2.3 million in salary equity adjustments and back pay.[11]

In Pandora's Footsteps

For a long time, certainly throughout the happy Golden Age, only men were upon the earth; there were no women. Zeus created these later, in his anger at Prometheus for caring so much for men. . . . He made a great evil for men, a sweet and lovely thing to look upon, in the likeness of a shy maiden, and all the gods gave her gifts. Because of what they gave her they called her "Pandora," which means "the gift of all." When this beautiful disaster had been made, Zeus brought her out and wonder took hold of gods and men when they beheld her. From her, the first woman, comes the race of women, who are an evil to men, with a nature to do evil.

So Edith Hamilton, in her book *Mythology,* recounts one of the Greek myths of the creation of "the world and mankind," told by Hesiod.[12]

She continues, "Another story about Pandora is that the source of all misfortune was not her wicked nature, but only her curiosity." The gods had given her a box full of harmful things and had ordered her not to open it. But "Pandora, like all women, was possessed of a lively curiosity. She *had* to know what was in the box. . . ." So, as we know, Pandora opened the box "and out flew plagues and sorrows for mankind." But the box contained one good thing—hope. "It was the only good the casket held among many evils, and it remains to this day mankind's sole comfort in misfortune."[13]

Hamilton calls Hesiod's Pandora myths "naïve." But, as pronouncements on comparable worth like the *Wall Street Journal*'s or Judge Winner's "economic chaos" comment in the Denver case show, the negative parts of the myths are still current—that women, with all their "yearnings," are an evil influence on "mankind," and that "lively curiosity" and independence are harmful traits when practiced by women.

Over the years, some descendants of Pandora, or, if you will, Eve, have courageously refused to accept the negative stereotypes. They encourage all women to act on their yearnings, to give free rein to their curiosity, and to develop their independence. They aim to keep alive the hope that Pandora loosed on the world.

As we have seen, in recent years San Jose, for a variety of reasons, has had an ample share of these lively and determined women. Maxine Jenkins is one of them. Her name came up repeatedly as I talked to people about the comparable worth effort in San Jose. For example, when Dave Armstrong, personnel administrator for the city, reviewed the history of pay equity in San Jose for me, he explained, "We had a woman, her name was Maxine Jenkins, and she was the business agent for AFSCME . . . she was the one that was behind the whole comparable worth effort here in San Jose." He added that after leaving AFSCME she led the nurses' strike for comparable worth in San Jose's four hospitals. "Comparable worth was really a very important issue for her," he said.

When I called Maxine Jenkins to ask for an appointment for an interview she was in San Diego, working for the California Nurses Association, organizing the nurses on the San Diego campus of the University of California. She was too tied up with this to keep our first appointment. But some months later we met in Santa Clara at the headquarters of the California Nurses Association. Her efforts, and those of others, to organize the nurses on all the state university campuses had been successful. I gathered that she was having a break between organizing efforts, a pause she needed to refuel herself with energy. She seemed happy to take the time to tell me about her work for pay equity.

> Pay equity for women is an issue that I have felt personally since I've been old enough to work as an adult woman trying to make my way in the work world. When I became involved in organizing labor unions, in the mid-1960s, it seemed the natural next course to take. If one was a woman whose field was the labor movement, when so many women needed to be represented, this was just the logical next step.
>
> I was working on the issue of comparable worth as far back as 1970, when, at the University of California at Berkeley, there was a group of dormitory maids employed by the university who made approximately one third of what their male counterparts made. The only distinction between their duties was that the women cleaned up the dormitories and the men cleaned up the office buildings. Well, the women who were maids argued, quite reasonably, I thought, that it was even more difficult to clean the dormitories than it was to clean the office buildings.

Having spent a considerable amount of time in both academic office buildings and in college dormitories, I readily agreed.

"So we went to work on that grievance," she continued.

> It was one of the first ones I know of where we weren't able to approach it on the basis of equal pay for equal work. Some new ground had to be worked. So we said that it was an offshoot of equal pay for equal work. We hadn't yet hit upon the phrase "equal pay for comparable worth," and we had other names for it. But in retrospect, it was in fact a struggle for comparable pay.
>
> We were successful in getting the classifications combined into one for both men and women. Some women were assigned to work in the office buildings and vice versa. So we did get that wiped out. It took us months and we had to mount a public campaign in that year of 1970, but we were able to do it. That was at the tail-end of the antiwar movement, just the beginning of the women's movement, when we were becoming aware of the fact that our agenda was more than just ending the war—we had a lot more things to work on.

Her next assignment after Berkeley was San Francisco. Here she worked for the Service Employees International Union (SEIU), which represented about 5,000 clerical workers, mostly women, who worked for the city. The issue she tackled there was "a piece of legislation being sponsored by the now *mayor* of San Francisco, unfortunately. She's not a real supporter of comparable worth. She's very famous now—Diane Feinstein."

> She sponsored a piece of legislation which went on the ballot. The result of that legislation would have been to freeze all city pay rates, and base them upon whatever was gotten in the private sector. I argued that that would discriminate against women because it would freeze them into a pay rate that was set in an era of sex discrimination and would give them no right to bargain their way out of it.
>
> This created quite a furor in the city. I debated Diane Feinstein on television. We wrote articles in the newspaper. And we again had to mount a public campaign. That was in 1974. There again, it was on the issue of wage discrimination against women.
>
> We beat that back that year. But I subsequently had to leave. And the economy of the city got worse after Proposition 13 passed. My understanding is that a few years later, Feinstein and others did engineer getting that legislation passed, and there is such a formula now in the city of San Francisco. I don't work for that union any more and I don't know what they have been able to do about it.

This was a time, she said, when public employees in the area were becoming unionized and she was working on organizing them. She explained:

> Everywhere, I saw that pay equity was the problem. And everywhere I found that women were skeptical about getting into a union because they had an underlying knowledge that their real needs of pay equity weren't going to be addressed. Although all of this had not been formulated, I knew that. You could see that. So I began to organize on the basis of "Let's get the pay rates for the women up where they belong, to be paid for what they're worth." And our organizing was quite successful.

In 1976, AFSCME, for whom Maxine Jenkins was then working, sent her on a special assignment to the city of San Jose. In their briefing they told her that "there were women, working for the city, who were very unhappy about their pay rates." She emphasized that "that was a spinoff of the public campaign that we had conducted in San Francisco over comparable worth, which shook up the whole area. So there was a fallout. It was almost a continuation of the same campaign. Down here it had really affected the women. They were already in the union, so they put pressure on the union to bring in a business agent that could respond to their special needs, and I was sent in. It was the logical arena for me."

"From that point on," she said, "we took it one step at a time. We did our own study, back before there was a Hay study. It's called 'Women Working,' and the basics of it are still true."

Bill Callahan filled me in on the background of that study. "In 1977," he said, "the union formed a committee. It was a women's caucus, where women, through the union, wanted to develop issues that they felt were primary to women—issues such as child care, career ladders, and bridge classes whereby women could promote from the nonmanagement, nonprofessional classes into professional classes. Bilingual pay was an issue that was expressed then. Safety conditions affecting clerical workers was an issue. And the other issue, an issue with just as much weight at that time, was pay parity, the wage gap." There were nine women on the committee; two librarians, six clerical workers, and one engineering technician.

"And so," Callahan continued, "they set about this task of developing an analysis of those issues and how they related to employees in the city of San Jose. They worked many hours for many months developing this: looking at the city, looking at the job classifications, looking at the history, looking at surrounding agencies and what their practices were in child care and such. The result of all that work was a position paper called 'Women Working: Eliminating Sex Discrimination from the Pay and Personnel Practices of the City of San Jose.' In this position paper the union detailed the pay gap in San Jose. And during that period it became clear that one issue had become a focal point. That was the issue of pay parity— sex-based wage discrimination."

Their report discussed the effects of pay inequity on working women and their families. It then documented the existence and degree of sex discrimination in pay in the city of San Jose for two of the principal nonmanagement, female-dominated occupations, clerical workers and librarians. It pointed out, for example, that an entry-level (male) laborer, with minimum qualifications of an eighth-grade education and six months of experience, earned a biweekly salary of $501. An entry-level (female, typist clerk, however, with minimum qualifications of a high school education, one year of experience, and the ability to type, earned $432.[14]

In what it termed "promotional positions," the report showed that a male occupation, maintenance worker I, with minimum qualifications of "the combined equivalence of an eighth-grade education and one year of construction and maintenance experience," earned $537 biweekly. But a female police records clerk II, required to have "any combination equivalent to graduation from high school and one year of clerical experience in which the major assignment was the entry and retrieval of Police Records and identification information through a full range of automated information systems; or one year of varied experience in entry and retrieval of information through a full range of automated information systems," was paid only $456 biweekly.[15]

"The difference in minimum qualifications relative to pay is startling," the paper's authors commented. "Clearly, something is 'wrong' here."[16] They then went on to show that something was also wrong for librarians, San Jose's "only female-dominated professional series" in the nonmanagement category. Here they found that sex discrimination in pay was not large at the entry level for professional jobs, but that it grew substantially as the level of experience and training and responsibility required went up.[17]

The committee report then discussed the difference between what it termed the "market standard" for setting pay and the "equity standard." It defined the market standard as setting pay rates by "a comparison of pay rates for a particular job in the market area that the employer believes employees are being drawn from." It defined equity standard in comparable-worth terms as "a comparison of differences between jobs in the same agency and paying salaries according to these internal differences."[18]

"The employer, before 1963, could hire women for less than men and did," the position paper pointed out. "The market standard still supports paying women less than men for the *same* job, but *equal pay* for *equal work* is the law, and employers have reluctantly ceased (for the most part) this practice. It took wholesale Federal intervention to halt this gross form of discrimination."

"The more common form of discrimination at present," the report continued, "is stereotyping jobs according to sex and paying less for 'women's jobs' than for 'men's jobs.' Of course employers engage in this practice because the market supports it and it hasn't yet been proved to be against the law." The authors then asserted, "While affirmative action programs that help channel women into jobs traditionally held by men will help expand women's opportunities, they will not measurably affect the pay rates of women's jobs vis à vis men's jobs in the foreseeable future as long as employers are able to use the market standard as a basis for relative salaries." They gave several reasons for making this assertion.[19]

"Sex-biased salaries are now institutionalized in their own right," the committee concluded. "It will therefore take positive action (or *affirmative* action) to change the relative pay rates of jobs that have been historically female dominated." They recommended that the city "depart from the market standard and adopt an equity standard" for determining pay rates in sex-stereotyped jobs.

In supporting this recommendation, the report cited the case of the Carlsbad, California, school district, which, in 1975, adopted an equity standard for setting pay scales. Carlsbad claimed that its system "virtually eliminates the historical pay differentials of those positions normally held by males over those held by females."

"If someone doesn't make the first move," a trustee for the Carlsbad School District said, "this thing could go on another 100 years."

"The first move has been made by certain smaller employers," the San Jose union committee commented, "but history awaits the first move of a major employer. Why," they urged, "can't it be the City of San Jose?"[20]

The union group then proposed four measures "to eliminate discrimination in pay practices." Their proposals were:

1. That the market standard no longer be used where sex stereotypes and discrimination against women is a factor;
2. That librarians and clerical workers of the city of San Jose be paid equally to male-dominated professional classes and semiskilled male-dominated classes, respectively;
3. That the above be effected by scaling rates of pay upward for discriminated classes rather than lowering rates of pay for men's jobs. Lowering the rate of pay to accomplish "equality" is not a legal remedy under the EEOA;
4. That these changes be effected in 1978–79 contract negotiations with the union.[21]

Their position paper also included contract proposals on the other issues that concerned women workers—career ladders, pay for bilingual work, job sharing, flexible work schedules, and child care. But pay equity received most of the study's attention and, as Callahan reported, it was clearly the union committee's main concern. According to Callahan,

In May 1978, the union presented that position paper to the city as part of a comprehensive contract package for negotiations. In June, the voters of California passed the now infamous Proposition 13. And with Proposition 13 came the "bail-out legislation" for the state. Part of the bail-out legislation was the requirement that no city, county, or other local government agency receiving bail-out funds could grant a salary increase in excess of what state employees would receive. And, of course, state employees were receiving zero. So in effect it said you could not give a wage increase to your employees if you were to accept bail-out funds. That issue was contested and was finally ruled on by the California State Supreme Court in April 1979. The court said it was illegal for the state to impose that restriction. And so negotiations, which had stalled in June because of that restriction, resumed in April 1979 with the city.

When we got back to the bargaining table, we did not find any significant movement on the part of the city concerning our proposal on
sex-based wage discrimination or pay parity. What we requested was
that the issue be put to study, that an outside firm be hired to do it, and
that the issue be one limited to *internal* comparison, not to external mar-
ket-place comparison.

During the 1978 to 1979 period of stalled negotiations, however, the
union had been "building our political base," as Maxine Jenkins described
it, "by working our political alliances so that we would support people
who would help the women in the city on this issue. I was the chief
negotiator for the union, in 1979. We got everything else wrapped up—
this was concurrent with a sick-out by the police officers. We were now in
coalition with police officers.

"What really did it," she said, "was all of the pressure, and then
while we were in negotiations we pulled a wildcat sick-out of the women
in City Hall. And I refused to sign a contract until we got the city manager
to agree in writing that he would conduct an outside scientific study in
which we would have the right to participate. And he agreed to that, in
writing. You may have seen that letter, that famous letter."

"You have requested that the city establish a method of setting pay
which differs from the current procedure," City Manager James Alloway
wrote, after first protesting that the city had not intentionally segregated
city jobs into men's and women's jobs, as he thought the union's argument of a sex-based pay gap suggested.

"I am willing to pursue an analysis of the city's salary plan based on
the Hay value system," his letter continued.

With the exception of Police and Fire, this system could be used to establish the internal relationships within the salary plan. The Hay point system is based upon three factors: know how, problem solving and accountability. The weights developed as a part of this system would permit the city to compare salaries with a variety of users of the Hay system
including governmental agencies and private systems.

I will include in the 1979–80 budget proposals to the City Council a
request for funds to initiate the Hay job description and Hay classification system. I will anticipate that the result of this program would provide equitable salaries based on the city's ability to pay.[22]

"We are pleased that you have agreed to pursue an analysis of the
city's salary plan based on a different value system," Maxine Jenkins

wrote back. "However, we have two concerns about your proposal that we hope you will address.

"We are unwilling to accept comparisons with other users of the Hay system as the major determination of salary rates for those classifications where women are the majority," Jenkins asserted, "unless other users of the Hay system have already corrected the bias against women workers that is inherent in any market standard of establishing salaries. We do not wish to change systems only to find ourselves confronted with the same bias in different guise.

"We need remedial action to correct salary rates that were in-stitutionalized in an era when women workers were not expected to earn living wages," she added. "Responsibilities of women workers have changed dramatically in the last decade but discriminatory wages have not improved."[23]

"The second stage of the struggle, our second concern once that agreement was gotten," Jenkins told me,

> was to monitor who did the study and under what conditions. We didn't want to be removed from the process, ourselves. We wanted to be in there, on those committees. When we heard that the Hay people were coming in to do the study, we did some investigation and found out that they had done a few studies before where the outcome had not been favorable to women. By now, the *president* of the union was a feminist, and the *business agent* was a feminist, and we had a *mayor* who was a woman, though maybe not an avid feminist, so we had some favorable things for working for us.
>
> The president of the union and I wrote a letter to the president of Hay—quite a letter—telling him that we understood his company had been chosen to perform this study. We said, "We would like to welcome you here. However, some matters we would like to bring to your atten-tion before you arrive. And that is, that we are aware of the studies you have done in the past. We know they have not had a favorable outcome for women. And a lot is riding on this study."
>
> We mentioned the fact that we were members of a union that was a million strong in the country, with a newspaper that would go out all across the country to public agencies, and that we would be reporting on the conduct and the findings of Hay in the newspaper.

"It was a letter of intimidation," Jenkins concluded, "putting him on notice that we were not fools and were not going to just let them steamroll us. So with that kind of aggressive front and determination, we went into the study." She paused for a moment and then said, with a cheerful, mat-ter-of-fact tone, "And everything else is history."

Notes

1. *Wall Street Journal,* July 16, 1981.

2. Ivan Sharpe, "Is the Future Female?", *Working Woman* (January 1983): 73–77.

3. Sharpe, "Is the Future Female?", p. 74.

4. Ibid., p. 77.

5. Ibid.

6. Ibid.

7. Ibid., p. 74.

8. Economic Development Department, San Jose Chamber of Commerce, *Economic Fact Book—1982–1983* (San Jose), p. 2.

9. Ibid.

10. Comparable Worth Project Newsletter (Winter and Spring 1983), p. 8.

11. Ibid. See also Chapter 3, the sections on Canada.

12. Edith Hamilton, *Mythology* (New York: New American Library, 1969), pp. 63, 70.

13. Ibid., p. 72.

14. Affirmative Action Committee, MEF, Local 101, AFSCME, AFL-CIO, "Women Working: Eliminating Sex Discrimination from the Pay and Personnel Practices of the City of San Jose" (1978), p. 9.

15. Ibid., pp. 9–10.

16. Ibid., p. 10.

17. Ibid., p. 11.

18. Ibid., p. 12.

19. Ibid., p. 13.

20. Ibid., pp. 12–14.

21. Ibid., p. 15.

22. Letter of April 13, 1979, from James A. Alloway, city manager, city of San Jose, to Maxine Jenkins, senior business agent, MEF, AFSCME, Local 101.

23. Letter of Maxine Jenkins to James Alloway, dated April 19, 1979.

5

VICTORY IN SAN JOSE:
History in the Making

In the spring of 1979, the city of San Jose set about making two job evaluation studies for all of its employees, one for management and one for nonmanagement. Did the impetus for the management study come first? Or the union's push for a formal nonmanagement study? Union and city differ on the chronology. The answer to this chicken and egg question is, as usual, uncertain.

What is certain, however, is that the two studies began at the same time and both showed significant sex-based wage discrimination. It is also certain that the city fully implemented a comparable worth plan to correct pay inequity for management classes, but refused to do this for nonmanagement classes. The size of the pay increases for management, the fact that they covered *all* classes that were out of line on the low side, coupled with the pressures of high consumer price inflation rates—11.3 percent in 1979, 13.5 percent in 1980, and 10.4 percent in 1981—are more than enough to explain the urgency of the union's demands for pay equity. Was the cost of comparable worth for nonmanagement classes the only explanation for the city's heel-dragging?

I asked David Armstrong, personnel administrator for the city of San Jose, about the San Jose story and the city's part in it. "We probably should use another term rather than comparable worth", he began, anxious to make plain what he was talking about. "I think that people are getting all fouled up on just exactly what the definition is. What I've found is that what we're really talking about is the 'pay gap' between women-dominated jobs and male-dominated jobs. And I think the other thing we're talking about is 'internal equity.' I've found that to be a little better than 'comparable worth.' People in the profession seem to be able to handle that a lot better," he added.

75

The problem with "comparable worth," I think, is what do you do with those jobs that are up above the job evaluation average line, so to speak? In other words, those jobs like electrician and plant operators, and those kinds of jobs that are critical to operating, say for instance, a city? You can't *drop* them. It looks to me like you still have to pay the market rate, until maybe 25 years from now. For all kinds of reasons. Number one, they're male-dominated classes. Number two, they've had strong unions. Number three, I think a lot of people have just had a preconceived idea about certain kinds of work—that checking books in a library isn't very valuable compared to real men's work, like operating under the hood of a car.

But the problem you have, if you want to go with a straight comparable worth model, is that we can't get electricians now and we're paying them probably twenty percent above the average internal equity kind of line. I have no problem with the concept of comparable worth, it's how you get there.

I think the best way right now is just to identify how big the problem is and then start dealing with those classes that are below your average line and try to move them up. And also, when you're in collective bargaining, to try to keep in mind that when you're dealing with somebody like the operating engineers or the brotherhood of electricians—when they're coming in with their fabulous demands—that you're just extending that gap.

"You don't have a problem, then," I asked, "with the argument you hear so frequently that nurses and librarians and clerical workers are low paid because of supply and demand in the market? And that if they're willing to work for low wages, why not let them?" I explained that this was the argument given me at dinner the night before in Los Angeles, by a retired financial officer of a large conglomerate. "You're saying you should bring these classes up," I added, "without regard to the fact that the market has set lower wages?"

"Well, you know, do you want to be on the leading edge?" he answered. "Or do you want to be dragged into the twenty-first century? If you go and evaluate jobs on a fair and equitable basis, using an objective method, whatever that is—you can select a whole bunch of different methods and I think you'll probably come out plus or minus 10 percent every time, no matter what method you use—then you're not going to be that far off, as far as the value of particular jobs to the organization. And then when you find this tremendous pay gap between jobs, based on *no* objective criteria, only what I choose to think of as discrimination against women—I don't even think that's an argument any longer. I think the individual who was sitting next to you at dinner probably has not examined the issue, because I think that's a given."

The Management Study

After this digression on the meaning and relevance of comparable worth, we returned to talking about how it all started in San Jose. "We originally weren't going to examine this issue," Dave Armstrong said. "That wasn't the main focus of our study. Our focus was to start paying managers, whether you were a woman or man or whatever, on an objective internal basis." He paused while he put up some charts on a wall board. "It's a little dog and pony show that I was doing for a while," he explained.

What was happening is this. We have approximately 300 jobs in the city that are management jobs. (According to Hay Associates, in 1979 the city had 366 positions, or 164 classes of management jobs.[1]) And by law in our state, they can't be affiliated with a union or an outside association. They're paid by the manager deciding what they should get paid, on some kind of criteria, and then going to the council each year and asking for a raise. One of the problems was that the city council wanted some kind of objective criteria as to what kind of money they should get, and whether they were overpaid or underpaid. That was really one problem, how to deal with your management unit that isn't into negotiations, and treat them in an equitable manner.

The other thing that you had here was that a lot of our departments—library and parks and recreation, in particular—felt that their market did not reflect what their real talents were. For instance, the assistant librarian—she had 265 people reporting to her. She had a budget of close to $3 million. She had 26 facilities. She had all the responsibilities of what we would consider, in our organization, to be one of the highest managers in the city. And she was being paid at the same level as an entry-level manager. It was because we were paying market and, in the market, librarians traditionally have been underpaid.

So she was upset. She was saying, "Don't look at me as a librarian, because I don't deal with books that much. I'm dealing conceptually with where the city is going. I'm dealing with human relations kinds of problems. Look at me as a manager, similar to the police chief, or the assistant police chief, or the manager of the airport." Then we had parks and recreation. They were yelling. They really felt like their unique situation wasn't being addressed.

The city manager that we had was James Alloway. And the way city managers start out is down in small cities. He started in New Jersey, and worked his way across the United States.

"Did it take him long to get across?" I asked.

"Yes," he answered, "it took him 20 years. And one of the things that was very successful for him, all the way across the United States, was the fact that he did go for a job evaluation of management jobs and did base pay really on comparable worth or value to the organization. It worked for him in New Jersey. And it worked for him in Dayton, Ohio. So when he got here, and he heard of the problems, and he had experienced going in to the city council with hat in hand, with no objective criteria—he was a very systems-oriented type of manager—he said, 'Well, I'm going to do what I did in those other places.'

"He had had a good experience with Hay Associates, a management consulting firm that works mainly with private organizations. It was his intent, the whole time," Armstrong said, "to have a job evaluation system only for managers. Because he never did think it ever worked for the negotiation situation. Because there it's not what's equitable. And it's not what's fair. And it's not what's objective. It's what you demand. It's a power game, at the bargaining table.

"So he went ahead and he hired Hay." Armstrong paused to put up some exhibits about the consulting firm and its methods of evaluating jobs. "It's an international firm with the third largest consulting business in the world, and they're on the West Coast. So they had a lot of credibility, and the big bottom line there was that everybody saw them as qualified, so they felt good about it.

"The process that we used required first that we do a complete classification study of the whole organization." Armstrong referred to one of his charts. "The reason for that," he explained, "was that you have to have up-to-date specs in order to do an objective analysis. So we went through and did specifications on every management job in the city. And the second part of it is that this job evaluation method is a committee process."

"Did you ever get a chance to read the editorial that the *Wall Street Journal* did on us?" Armstrong interrupted himself to ask me. "It's the same kind of attitude as the man sitting next to you at dinner, right?" he went on. "You see, this scares the business community."

"But I spoke before a management group in Detroit," he said, "mainly people in the automobile industry, and mainly private. And I was really surprised at how willing they were to accept the concept. They had a lot of people who were negotiators.

"I went to the University of Michigan, also, and spoke, and I learned out there," he explained, "that what we're talking about, if you really want to get down to it, is a new orientation, almost a socialistic kind of orientation that this country's not used to. If you want to get really at the roots of it, it's given the employee more say over their particular job and the way they are going to be paid. In other words, the way people were paid originally, in this country, under the capitalist system, was that management said what the people were going to be paid, and they let the market decide it. Well, under this method, this job evaluation method, the whole key to it is a committee process, at least under the Hay process.

"And so," he continued as he turned to another chart, "we brought ten people together from throughout the city—peers. We had a representative from each job area. We had people who were respected in management, that weren't just 'yes' people but who would stand up and be counted. We had people who were experienced in many job classifications. And we had people who were familiar with various parts of the city, that got around, who weren't just locked up in their little areas. These people came together and *they* evaluated the jobs. And you see that's a whole different orientation than we're used to in management. That the *people* would come together and they would evaluate the jobs and say what's fair. Most of the time we would either hire somebody, or we'd do it ourselves. And *we* say what the job's value is. Now you had ten peers throughout the city coming together, getting a consensus as to what the values of those particular jobs were."

Armstrong described how the Hay method evaluates jobs by using three categories of requirements: know-how, problem solving, and accountability. Using his charts for illustration, he went into detail on the factors considered in each category and how point values are assigned to the three categories and then summed. Each job ends up with a certain number of "Hay points," based solely on the requirements of the job, or as Hay calls it, "job content," and not on the characteristics of the particular person holding the job. Then all the jobs can be compared and ranked in terms of their Hay points. During this stage of the evaluation process, "no reference to salary was included in the management decisions at any time," according to Hay Associates' "Executive Summary."[2]

"What we evaluated in the committee meetings," Dave Armstrong continued, giving me an insight into how the Hay process worked in practice, "was the old job specs, if there were any, and we saw how the job evolved over the years. We looked at an organizational chart to see who was reporting and where the relationship was. We took a look at their budget and how it broke down into personnel and nonpersonnel expenditures. We took a look at their goals and their objectives. We took a look at the individual questionnaires that they filled out when we did the specs. And then we also had individuals who were familiar with the jobs—personnel analysts—who came in and sat down and gave us a briefing. We had a telephone there so we could call people and have them answer our questions. And in some cases, we actually called 'time' and had our analyst go back out and get answers to questions that we had about the jobs."

"So you feel that this method does produce an objective evaluation?" I asked.

"Oh, I do," he replied. "The one thing that was amazing to me through the whole thing, even when we got into the nonmanagement jobs, was that it was accepted by both union and management as being valid. The Hay people say that it's probably plus or minus 10 percent in accuracy. In other words, if you were to have 25 committees come together you would probably find an error factor of plus or minus 10 percent. That's been their experience.

"Then," he continued, "what they do with this is that they come up with a hierarchy of points. Here's ours," he said, and he put up another chart. "The first fellow on this one is the assistant city manager. Here is the know-how. Here is the problem solving. Here is the accountability. Here are the total points.

"What we did next was—" he paused as he posted another chart, "Well, we don't live in a vacuum. So, what the Hay method really does is make a kind of a balance between internal equity and external market comparison. So here's where the market comes into play. Because we have to know what a Hay point is, how much it should be paid. In our case, we compared with the 14 largest California jurisdictions and we took 28 benchmark classes that we felt we could compare with in at least some of those agencies. What we were really trying to do was not compare, for instance a librarian with a librarian. We were comparing, say, 585 Hay points. So we were looking for bench classes that would not be skewed. For instance, one of the bench classes wouldn't be the librarians. We were already aware, from our own department, that librarians were down. We were looking for jobs that were right with the trend line, an average-type job."

"So you were taking mostly male jobs, I guess," I said.

"Sure," Armstrong replied, "you know when you're talking about management, you're talking about mostly male jobs, right? We are underrepresented in our management unit with women. So," he went on, "basically what we were trying to do was to pick a job for benchmark that was pretty close in evaluation points and was pretty close in salary, and was right on what we call the trend line."

"Here's the trend line, right here," he said, pointing to a graph drawn on the blackboard. "I was just explaining it to somebody. Down at the bottom you have a scale showing the total points assigned to each job. And on the side you have the scale of salaries. And what you do is, you make a scattergram plotting job content points and salaries for each management job. And then you draw a best-fit line. That's your trend line, a line fitted to the plots on the scattergram so that about half the jobs are above the line and half the jobs below.

"The other thing that we looked at," he added, "was a plus or minus 10 percent cone around it. The reason for that is because of the error factor. Any job that is outside of that cone, more than 10 percent away from the trend line, really is a problem. And then we went outside the city and did a Hay point comparison of how we related to the rest of the world."

"You got the dollar value of the Hay point by this method of surveying 28 benchmark jobs in 14 other jurisdictions and taking an average of how those jurisdictions paid the benchmark jobs?" I asked, reviewing the process to make sure I had it straight.

"Right," Armstrong answered.

"And you had points assigned to those jobs so you could say a point is worth so much?"

"Yes," he said. "We had a little formula that we ran and then we would know what a point would be paid.

"One change occurred because at the time we had a very, very high turnover in managers. So the council had a salary policy of paying the mean of the upper two thirds of salaries in the 14 largest jurisdictions in California, so that our people wouldn't leave. So we really kind of paid up here," he said, pointing to an area above the trend line. "I think we only salary-stabilized about five management jobs in the whole city. Everybody else came up.

"And the Hay recommendations were a 9.5 percent general increase, because we hadn't had a raise in about two years. The *average* raise for a manager was 14.7 percent, 9.5 percent of that the general, and the other 5.2 percent the equity adjustment. Now that's an average. Some classes were salary stabilized. And classes in the parks and recreation department experienced 30 percent raises. Classes in the library, 30 percent raises. Other classes, for instance, in the airport, or personnel, or in the budget office, they got only the 9.5 percent general increase. They did not get an equity adjustment.

"One unfortunate thing did happen last year," he added. "As a result of city financial problems, the manager felt that our managers should hold the line for six months and not accept their raise. The union did get their raise. They got their raise in July and we got ours in January. This created a lot of problems with the managers. A number of them formed a bargaining unit. They're allowed to form an unaffiliated association. So now with 150 of them in this group our management unit is cut in half. They'll be negotiating and I don't know whether they'll continue to be under this new system or not. But it wasn't a result of people feeling that the system was unfair. It was a result of feeling they didn't have any power over the decision as to whether they should forego a raise.

"So," Armstrong concluded, "we did in fact have what I consider to be a comparable worth study, in that we dropped classes and we also raised everybody up. We say we do have comparable worth, or internal equity, with the management group."

I was puzzled by Armstrong's statement that the city had dropped some management classes in pay, when earlier he had said that five classes were stabilized (not lowered) and the rest raised. The issue was interesting because he had defined comparable worth as requiring that high-paid classes be brought into line. He considered the management settlement to be a comparable worth settlement, but said the nonmanagement settlement was not, in part because the top classes could not be dropped.

"If you took comparable worth as strictly a philosophical exercise, an academic exercise," Sally Reed had told me, echoing Armstrong's position, "you would be bringing down the wages paid plumbers at the same time you were bringing up the wages paid your clerk. And you can't get plumbers if you don't pay the going rate. So," she concluded, "what may have great philosophical merit is, from a financial standpoint, undoable on the cost-savings side. You create a cycle. The plumber is always going to get this high wage based on demand rather than on skill and difficulty of the job."

I checked back with the Hay Report on the Management Compensation Study for the City of San Jose, and looked at the recommendations the city had followed in putting the new pay structure for management into effect. I found that Hay Associates had advised a policy of achieving internal equity in pay, based on job evaluation (Hay) points, but were firmly against doing this by moving all jobs "in line" with the "current average tendency" or, as Armstrong called it, the "trend line." They pointed out that such a policy meant that

> approximately the same number of positions are, relatively, moved up and, relatively, moved down. This approach would, in effect, penalize the relatively higher positions for the sake of establishing internal equity. Instead of this move-all-to-average approach, our recommendations move all jobs to a "highest reasonable common denominator," i.e. to a level higher than the average line but close enough to it that a large proportion of jobs are currently being paid at that level. This highest normal level was determined to be 10 percent above the average trend so *our recommendations include an increase to bring all positions to a "highest common level," approximately 10 percent above the average trend.*

The average trend, in turn, was the trend for the 66th percentile of the 14 largest jurisdictions in California. Hay pointed out that the proposed salary structure "eliminates all intradepartmental and interdepartmental pay differences immediately and creates one common salary structure and policy." It also satisfied the city's goal of giving equal weight to internal equity and external competitiveness.[3]

"The city employs individuals in diverse occupations—many of these occupational groups are in separate distinct job markets which have traditionally experienced disparate pay trends," the Hay Report said. "The greatest disparity is found between the City Attorney Department (highest salary trend) and the Library Department (lowest salary trend). Specifically, the City Attorney Department tends to pay 47 percent more (at the middle management level) to 30 percent more (at the senior management level) than the Library Department." On the other hand, the study had found that pay equity within each city department was quite good.

For several occupations with high "prevailing market rates," Hay Associates recommended that the city "adopt salary ranges for these jobs without consideration to their relationship to other city salary rates." These occupations were; attorneys, data-processing professionals, medical director, and director of convention and cultural facilities. Hay recommended setting their salaries by "close study of prevailing rates" and suggested increases for several positions. This pragmatic solution resembles that adopted by the Canadian Human Rights Commission to deal with the problem of out-of-line occupations with sellers' markets.

Hay estimated the cost of implementing their recommendations at not over 18.8 percent of payroll, in the first year. This included a 9.5 percent increase for everyone, in line with the then existing presidential wage guidelines. It included raising all classes, on the basis of their job evaluation points, to a "highest reasonable common denominator," approximately 10 percent above the 66th percentile trend line. And it included pay higher than relative job content points dictated for a few jobs with sellers' markets. The city put the new management salary structure into effect in July 1980.

The Nonmanagement Study

"When the nonmanagement study became available in December 1980, it was, in fact, absolute dynamite," Prudence Slaathaug, an AFSCME Local 101 business agent at the time of the 1980–81 negotiations, told me. "People had it Xeroxed and routed throughout the city in about five minutes, I think. And everybody, of course, looked to see what had happened to them and where they ended up in the comparability. It became something that everyone was very aware of and talked about continually. It was *the* topic of conversation. And, of course, they found the incredible inequities that have been reported all over the country."

"We believed from the beginning that it was a very high risk decision even to conduct the Hay study for nonmanagement classes," Sally Reed had told me.

"It was the manager's intent only to have a job evaluation system for management, because he never did think it ever worked for negotiations," Dave Armstrong had said.

The city's doubts and fears showed up along the way. "There were many opportunities for the city to bring the thing to a halt," Mike Ferrero explained.

I think that there was a conscious concern on the part of the city that they may have made a mistake and they were looking for places in which they could move this thing off course. One of the first opportunities, of course, was just on the makeup of who the people from the city work force would be, who would be involved in overseeing the study and then actually involved in the study.

Overseeing the study was not a big problem because we [the municipal employees] were going to have our representation on that, and that was fine. But the big thing was that, after the classification studies had been put together, there would have to be a committee of people to actually study those classifications and evaluate them—give them points. And that was going to be real critical. Because if you lose control of that then, of course, you don't have any way to validate the results of the study.

And that was political. Originally, the Hay consultants and management seemed to work out a deal on who should be on that committee. I believe that the original committee that they put together had *one* union representative on it. And then it had six or seven people from personnel, and a Hay consultant. So we would get outvoted on any major issue. We went at it real hard, at that point. We said, "This is going to turn it into a political committee. These are all personnel people. They don't understand the jobs. We should have employees on these committees so that we get a fair and accurate evaluation."

Personnel and management resisted that with everything they had. But we fought it on a political level and the council eventually said, "If we're going to do this, this has got to be fair." And so an evaluation committee was put together with one person from personnel, who would have a vote, and the rest of the voting members were employees who were chosen jointly by management and the unions involved—there were a number of other unions, but AFSCME was much the largest. So we had a lot of input on that evaluation committee.

The committee members were described by business agent Bill Callahan as senior within their classifications, with a broad knowledge of jobs outside their own classes, and respected by both management and employees. "We found that to be very important in establishing the credibility of the committee," he said. And, in fact, I heard no criticism of the non-management evaluation committee from anyone. Nor did anyone that I talked to question the evaluation results.

The union was also adamant about an important ground rule for the evaluation process—that it would be a study of internal pay equity only, with no dollar valuation of Hay points for jobs by relating them to the external market, and no written recommendations from the consultants. As Maxine Jenkins's letter to the city manager had explained, the union did not want to carry over the external market's sex discrimination in pay to the evaluation process. Furthermore, the union insisted that wages should be set by collective bargaining between union and management. The data would be available to both sides, and the study results would be a "guide but not the gospel," as Bill Callahan put it. The city agreed to these union demands.

"From talking to people on both sides," Prudence Slaathaug told me, "it appears to me that, once the committee was chosen, the council simply let those people go away and work for 18 months and rarely had either a progress report or any indication from them of what they were finding, or any discussion of the implications. So you had a decision being made, and kind of disappearing for a year and a half, while a group of ten people, who were deemed credible by both sides, were developing this explosive data."

The study covered 2,860 positions (377 classes), according to Hay Associates.[4] It excluded some 1,500 uniformed fire and police employees. AFSCME represented the majority of the workers, with about 500 represented by unions of the crafts and the operating engineers.

"In a comparable worth study it is important to look at everyone, across the board," Bill Callahan maintained. "If you exclude the craft workers, who are male, you weaken the study for the agency. This study did include all the classes, other than uniformed police and fire and management, and this was very important, I think, in validating the study and establishing credibility to both employees and management and the community, too.

"It's interesting that in the contract negotiations in 1980, before the completion of the study, we had a significant stumbling block in those negotiations," Callahan said. "The administration initially refused to give us the results of the Hay study, which we had been assured that we would get when the council commissioned the study in 1979. And secondly, they would not agree to a reopener of our contract in order to negotiate the results of that study. And so we went, for almost two weeks, away from the bargaining table, lobbying the city council and, in essence, I guess, just raising hell about it."

The city finally agreed in writing, in July 1980, to furnish to the union "a complete copy of the study," and to "meet and confer" on any proposals for salary adjustments coming out of the study. The city pointed out, however, that implementation of any agreements on salary adjustment "will be based on the city's ability to pay."[5]

"The city initially hesitated," Callahan said, "because I think that after they commissioned the study they saw that they may have started to open a can of worms. And that if the results showed, which everyone thought they would, that there was a pay gap, that the city did not want to be put into the position of having to negotiate this. They wanted to keep it quiet or shove it under a rug, or something else. It became evident to us that there was some concern on their part."

The study found the "incredible inequities" that Prudence Slaathaug described. "There is," it reported, "significant dispersion around the general pay trend—one third of all classes are paid more than 15 percent above or below the overall pay trend." The report found "strong relationships" between pay and occupation, pay and sex, and pay and type of working conditions. The highest-paid occupational classes were the male-dominated skilled trades, paid up to 38 percent above the general trend. The lowest paid group was the female-dominated recreation group, paid "up to 46 percent below the overall trend." Library and clerical classes, also female-dominated, were low paid.

The report found that classes with 50 percent or more female workers averaged 2 to 10 percent below the overall pay trend. Male classes averaged 8 to 15 percent above it.

The city paid those holding jobs with working conditions described as "medium and heavy," typical of male physical labor, "up to 20 percent above the overall trend." The summary reported that classes with the type of working conditions found in an office were paid along the trend. The clerical group, however, was getting paid about 15 percent below the trend, according to personnel administrator Dave Armstrong. In line with the conventional wisdom about office work, the committee's scale ranked office working conditions as "none," the least onerous of all the working conditions in city jobs.

None of these findings about pay differences was surprising, according to Hay Associates. "It was a foregone conclusion that such comparisons [between the pay practices of male- and female-dominated occupational groups] would show substantial differences," Hay Associates pointed out to their clients in their "Client Briefing" on the San Jose case.[6] "There is no question in any informed person's mind," the Hay Briefing continued, "that there are occupations and jobs in which equal opportunity and civil rights regulations have not eliminated disproportionate sexual representation, and that differences in pay exist between occupations that are female-dominated and those that are male-dominated. If one chooses to compare relative internal worth of jobs in an organization, a competently designed and implemented job measurement system will show that some of the female-dominated jobs have relative worth that is equal to or greater than male-dominated jobs, but the male-dominated are often paid more."[7]

"The City of San Jose as an employer, and the AFSCME local representing employees, each agreed to establish a 'leading edge' posture on the issue of comparable worth," Hay Associates told its clients. Both parties in the San Jose instance selected "the Hay Guide Chart-Profile Method of job measurement . . . as the appropriate methodology to rank jobs within the city organization without reference to the particular incumbents, external markets or how the results might be interpreted." These methods, they said, were "well accepted" by both city and union.

In terms of technology or applied professional skills, the work performed by Hay with the City of San Jose was not novel. A similar project with similar results could have been conducted by Hay consultants at any given time during the past 30 years. . . . The only basis for national publicity is that the theory of equal pay for work of comparable worth was being spotlighted in a public forum and in the collective bargaining process. Previously that theory had only been debated legislatively, fought (without final decision) in the courts, and proposed by government regulators and various special interest groups.[8]

Bargaining Comparable Worth

"The study results became available to the employees union in December 1980, in the middle of our contract," Bill Callahan told me.

The issue at that point was a single issue—pay parity. We got the study results on December 18 and we began negotiations on December 22. We felt that that was a very important move, in that, by bringing the city to the bargaining table, it established the legal requirement to negotiate—to conclude those negotiations that had begun on the twenty-second. And we did it because in November a new council was elected, not the council that commissioned the study, but a new one. This added many complications to the whole process, not the least of which was that the council went from a five-member council to an eleven-member council, so you had many more people and personalities to deal with.

As we began negotiations in December and continued on through January, we found that the city was very reluctant to do much of anything about implementing the Hay study. They were not willing to adjust the wages significantly upward for female-dominated classes, in line with the study results.

And so we went through January and February with many, many meetings and with very little movement on the part of the city. As we moved into early March and found that we were not getting much progress at the bargaining table, we decided we'd have to do a little more. So we started some political action by contacting local groups concerned with this issue—women's groups, labor groups, civil rights groups—anyone and everyone that we knew of that might give us support. We formed an advocacy committee of these groups that would help in contacting more groups and in getting more support. And we used this as an outside form of leverage, away from the union, to try to move the city council and the administration.

"Do you think this had some effect on the council?" I asked.
"I think it had a significant effect," Callahan replied.

We all live in a social atmosphere. And politicians live in a much narrower sphere, where they're influenced by one group or another—whether it's to get a sandbox in a local park, or a theater and arts center downtown. We're all swayed to one degree or another by advocacy groups. And in this case we were able to enlist the "reputable" organizations such as NOW, and the National Women's Political Caucus, the American Library Association, and the Leisure Association, an organization of professional recreation people. And we worked with the county and the state commissions on the status of women and received support for comparable worth from them.

But it was also still a problem at the bargaining table. And on March 27, 1981, the women workers in San Jose struck city hall for half a day. They walked off the job. It was a very dramatic incident in that it emphasized both to the administration and to the community that this was a very serious issue and one that needed to be addressed by the city administration in a more responsive way. It didn't disrupt city hall too much. But it made a point. It was more of a statement than an effective shutting down of city hall.

But it didn't change the administration's position to any significant degree. And because it didn't change significantly, we asked our membership what they wanted to do. They said, "If we do not have an agreement, or if we do not have significant movement on the part of the city, we will strike the city on May 5."

We went to the central labor council and got strike sanction from them and began preparations for a strike, while continuing to bargain with the city. On the evening of May 4, the state mediator that we called in was able to get together with me and the city's chief negotiator and we worked out what we called the mediator's agreement to avert a strike. In this agreement the city agreed to change its position dramatically.

One of the problems was that the city had said that they would not negotiate any wage adjustments for employees whose wages fell within 15 percent of the Hay study trend line. And we said you *have* to adjust those classes. They're 15 percent. They're *more* than that, because some male classes that have the same Hay value may be 15 percent above the trend. So it's not a question of a 15 percent inequity. It's a question of a 30 percent inequity. But the city wanted only to bring up classes more than 15 percent below the trend and they would bring them up only to 15 percent below the trend. And we found that to be wholly unacceptable. So the city agreed to look at that problem.

In the mediator's agreement, the city also agreed to bargain the issue of comparable worth. Before they had been sort of waffling on the issue and not calling it comparable worth or sex-based wage discrimination. Those were the two important parts of the agreement.

The other part of the agreement was to combine the negotiation for a general contract—sick leave, vacations, other issues—with the pay parity issue. We were somewhat reluctant to do that because it meant complicating the single issue negotiations with many, many more issues. But we finally agreed to do it when the city agreed to these other changes. So it was sort of a mutually acceptable compromise to avert the strike on May 5. We did not say that there was not going to be a strike. We simply said that we were postponing a strike at the time, pending the outcome of negotiations. To handle the combined negotiations we enlarged our bargaining committee from five members to eleven, which made it much more difficult, too. And the city also changed their chief negotiator. We began those negotiations on May 6.

When I talked with Dave Armstrong he reviewed the story of the negotiations and gave me the management's view on the issues. "Let's start with the union's opening position," he began. "Their opening position was, 'Pay us just like you did the management. You paid the management way up here.' " He pointed to the sixty-sixth wage percentile, above the pay trend line. " 'Pay us up there and move everybody up there and don't touch the jobs up above.' And they wanted to move *all* the jobs—men, women, everyone.

"The opening position for the city was, 'There's a 15 percent plus or minus cone. We'll move all the *women's* jobs up to the cone. And that's all we're going to do. Because the only thing we're interested in addressing is the women's issue. We're not interested in comparable worth because we believe that we're in a market situation with those jobs. And as far as negotiating is concerned, we want to do something for women and close the gap, but we don't want to do anything for *all* of your classes. We can't do comparable worth, a pure study, because (a) we can't drop all of these classes, and (b) we can't do it unilaterally anyway because we have a bilateral negotiating process in the city.'

"We got this plus or minus 15 percent from Hay," he explained. "And one of the things we didn't really check out was that in the management report they talked about a 10 percent plus or minus factor. And in the nonmanagement they talked about 15 percent. It was just a difference in calculation.

"So," Armstrong continued, "our second position was, to go with the 10 percent cone. That makes more sense, and we used it in the management study. Our second position was that we would move all *women's* classes below the line up to the 10 percent cone.

"The second position for the union," he went on, "was 'All right, move *everybody* to the trend line, all classes to the trend line.'

"What are we talking about, moneywise?" Armstrong asked. "The first union position—to do with nonmanagement exactly what we did with the management—we calculated would cost us somewhere between $8 and $10 million. We were hurting for money at this time. There was no way that anybody could go and give $8 to $10 million to this. The whole pay and benefit package for that year, for everybody, came to $10 million. To put that much money into this effort was just out of the question.

"It would have cost us somewhere between $3 or $4 million," he said, "to take everybody to the trend line. Our proposal, to take the *women's* classes to the 10 percent cone, would have cost $1.4 million.

"The council became very stiff on this whole issue. They said, 'Look. This is what it is. San Jose does not live in a vacuum. We want to make a step toward this whole issue, make a positive effort on it. But what we would like to do is to have the rest of the world catch up to us. And we want to do it gradually, over a number of years, so that the citizens do not have to pay an exorbitant fee to square away this discrimination which was created not only by San Jose but also by the rest of the world.'

"It was an economic kind of thing," Armstrong added. "They didn't have the money. So they basically said, '$1.4 million is all we're going to pay for this effort.' "

"What do you think caused the conflict?" I later asked Sally Reed, who was deputy city administrator at the time of the negotiations. "Was money a main issue?"

"Absolutely," she replied. Then she added, "The issue of money is a part of it. California governments all over, as a result of Proposition 13, are limited in their resources. And so that clearly was a piece of it. Another very related piece is public perception. If we pay our clerical staff 150 percent more than the amount that everyone else pays their clerical staff, that is simply not acceptable to the public. It may be, in an esoteric sense, a good idea, but that doesn't make it acceptable when it's taxpayers' dollars."

"Were there other public employers and private employers who were opposed to comparable worth and who put pressure on the city not to go along with this?" I asked.

"Absolutely," Sally Reed answered. "As I recall—it's been a while—the statewide chamber of commerce as well as local chambers of commerce, business groups, and clearly other public employers who knew they could not afford to see this precedent set, made many phone calls and sent letters to us saying, 'It's outrageous. If you move in this direction you're just going to open the floodgates.' And from the business side, 'You should run government like a business.' There was a lot of pressure."

The union, on the other hand, was unhappy on several major counts with the city's negotiating positions during the period from May 6 to July 4, the date when the old contract expired. The union wanted more movement on pay equity than the city offered. The union wanted *all* classes that were below the trend line moved, and not just the classes which were female-dominated. The union believed the city was dragging its feet on comparable worth as much as possible.

Furthermore, the union wanted a larger general cost-of-living increase than the 4.5 percent that the city offered. Inflation was running at

13.5 percent in 1980 and at 10.4 percent in 1981. The city had given the management classes a 9.5 percent general increase, the top figure allowed by the president's wage guidelines. The union believed that the city was trying to make the male nonmanagement classes pay for any pay equity increases it won for the female-dominated classes. Was this just a matter of money? Or was the city trying to encourage conflict within the union? Or both?

"At the end of May, we called another meeting of our membership," Bill Callahan related, "because we were still getting the same kind of stalling and foot-dragging at the bargaining table that we had received since December. We asked the members to set another strike date. They set July 4, 1981, the expiration date of our contract. The simple statement was 'No contract, no work.'

"On June 12," Callahan said, "the Supreme Court decided the *Gunther* case. And the *Gunther* case did provide another avenue for relief of sex-based wage discrimination, that avenue being the judicial process. When, by June 18, we felt there was still a lack of progress in our negotiations, we filed a complaint with the state Equal Employment Opportunity Commission. The complaint alleged that even though a job evaluation study had been done, and both parties accepted the results of the study, the city continued to pay employees discriminatorily based on sex.

"We were accused of bad faith negotiations in filing that complaint. But we felt that we would be remiss in our duty to our membership if we did not use every possible avenue to resolve this issue," Callahan explained. "If the issue was not resolved at the bargaining table we would have to go to litigation. And there was a time limit for filing. But we did not wish to go to litigation. We were hopeful we could bargain it out successfully.

"And we continued to bargain. But on the evening of July 3, after a day and evening of marathon negotiations, we were not able to reach agreement although we came close, we felt. So on July 4, the strike began."

The Strike

"Immediately it became evident that the strike was a major event for labor," Callahan said, "it being the first strike on the issue of sex-based wage discrimination. And it attracted national attention. It brought in the media from as far away as Canada and England. We had reporters here in person from the Boston *Globe,* and the L.A. *Times,* and the Washington *Post* as well as having innumerable telephone and radio interviews. It was such a media event that, two days after the strike started, the vice president of the chapter and I flew to New York to appear on "Good Morning America."

"It was exciting to us," he explained, "because it was really showing that this was an issue that people were concerned about. That it was really an issue that caught the imagination, and in many cases provoked the indignation, of people throughout the country, because we were talking about institutionalized, sex-based wage discrimination."

"It was a very risky strike I think, in retrospect," Mike Ferrero, president of Local 101, told me. "You know you never look at these things the same way until you get away from them. It was a risky strike," he continued, "in that probably they could have beaten us. But, for whatever the reasons, they didn't. Either there was too much national publicity to really wait us out, or we had internally enough political clout so that some of the council members couldn't afford to see us get clobbered in that kind of a strike. To this day I'm not sure what exactly were the elements of our not being beaten on the strike, but it was risky.

"You could never count on that much national publicity," he added. "When we went in, publicitywise we grabbed the high ground. And they were never able to take that away from us. So we were the 'good guys' through the entire thing. And that was very difficult for the city to cope with."

"Well, I remember the publicity myself," I commented. "And I think that it was puzzling to an outsider to read the stories about San Jose as the 'feminist capital of the world,' with a female mayor and so on, and yet to read that the city opposed this."

"The mayor used that kind of publicity a lot," Ferrero commented. "She liked calling San Jose the feminist capital of the world. She liked being seen as a real feminist herself, a champion of feminist causes. She never liked us. We never got along very well. And I think that once the confrontation began, there was a real unwillingness there to share the spotlight. And as we got down toward the end, I think that probably was one of the things that she really begrudged us. The union was getting the credit for doing this. She wasn't getting the credit.

"It never had to work out the way it did," he said. "We could have settled this thing. But essentially the strike happened because they were cheating us on the general salary increase."

"The strike was not over comparable worth?" I asked.

"It was, in the sense of how they were going to make us pay for comparable worth," Ferrero answered. "They would give us comparable worth but they were going to make us pay for it out of the general salary increases of all the other members in our units. And they couldn't understand why we didn't think that was fair.

"You don't give pay equity on one hand," he explained, "and then take it away on the other, in the general wage increase."

"It's a little hard for a union to do that, anyway, isn't it?" I asked.

"Yes," he replied. "Politically, we would have committed civil war. We were real concerned all along that that could happen," he added, "and were trying to avoid that at every step. And then the city set that scenario up for us."

"The irony was that there we were with our bargaining team, which had a number of women on it, and they were looking at an agreement on pay equity that they wanted. But they would have sold out the other members at the table if they were to buy that package, which they couldn't do. That's when the strike happened. Apparently that is a point of view that some cities have, I suppose, that that's an easy way to pay for it—'They can bite the bullet. This is an easy way to pay for it.' "

"The city was clearly testing waters, trying to see how much strength the union had, and clearly forcing the issue of men versus women on us at that time," Prudence Slaathaug told me. "And we, as a union, had to decide whether we were going to remain a unified union or, as the city would have liked it, have the women somehow isolated by a group of men who said, 'We're not going to give you dames any more money than you deserve.' So it really became an issue of identity and strength and unity among men and women, which I think is another important story in San Jose. And that's the story of men sticking to this issue."

"Why did the men stick with this issue?" I asked.

"It became for them very much a trade union issue," Slaathaug answered. "It became an issue of a living wage. And in the end we kind of got on the right track. The union began to realize that this was a family issue, that it was a much broader issue than Mary in the personnel department or Jane in the library. And that, in fact, it really touched on something a lot of men had seen their wives and mothers go through and suspected their children might have to go through.

"I remember one young man whose mother worked for the city, as he did. She had worked for 25 years and had a responsible secretarial job, he was a draftsman. He said, 'How can I not support this? I make more money than my mother. It's just incomprehensible.'

"In addition, the union was able to hold people together because the pay equity negotiations became part of a general contract negotiation, which in the beginning they were not," Slaathaug explained. "So we combined the issue of comparable worth with the usual collective bargaining issues. It became clear that the union was only going to settle on all of these together and would not allow them to be pulled out and dealt with separately.

"That, in retrospect, was an important difference," she added. "To not let this become a woman's issue, in a very isolated and rarified atmosphere, but to make it more 'business as usual.' That this was one thing that the women wanted and, you know, somebody else wants safety glasses. In that context the men began to understand that the settlement was going to be made with all of these issues in mind. If they wanted theirs, they were going to have to support another very large group of people.

"I think at that time," Slaathaug said, "the implicit guarantee that the union made to their membership, when they combined all of the issues, was that the men would not buy comparable worth out of their own salaries—that the union would not settle for something which said, 'Well, you could have had 8 percent but we're going to give *you* 6 so we can pay for this change in the salaries of *women*.' This tactic had become, in other conflicts, a very important issue, when management tried to play off one group against another."

The union asked for a four-year pay equity program, with all the low classes moving up to 15 percent below the trend line the first year, to 10 percent below trend the second year, to 5 percent the third year, and to the trend line by the fourth year. The union estimated this would cost $650,000 the first year and $3.2 million over four years. The union wanted a four-year program to ensure that the city would not discontinue pay equity in midstream. They also asked for an annual 10 percent cost of living raise.

The city offered $1.3 million over two years to correct pay inequities for female-dominated classes only. They refused to consider the low-paid male-dominated classes, like the male stock clerks. And they said they could not commit future city councils to a four-year program. They proposed a 6 percent annual general pay increase.

The union membership rejected the city's offer. And so the strike began. It went on for nine days.

"It seemed like nine *years*," Dave Armstrong said.

The national media publicity that Callahan spoke of put the city on center stage, in a difficult spot—"a very tight situation," Armstrong called it. Public and private employers opposed to pay equity policy pressed the city to resist the union's demands. On the other hand, as Callahan had told me, many diverse local, state, and national groups strongly supported the union's position and some, like AFSCME and NOW, sent representatives from their national organizations to San Jose to help the union .

But it was the city manager, Jim Alloway, who finally forced the city's hand. "He had put out an edict that he was going to fire everybody who was out on the picket line," Dave Armstrong told me. Alloway sent out termination letters. "That hurt us badly," Armstrong said, "because some of our best people were out there on the line. And we had to come up with some kind of a compromise with the union."

So the city and union went back to the bargaining table. Initially the city's negotiator and the city manager agreed to the four-year contract term that the union had wanted. But the city council turned it down. This reversal of the city's negotiator incensed the union members, and some 70 of them stormed into a closed city council session to demand good faith negotiation. Then they went back to the bargaining table and finally came up with a two-year contract agreed to by both sides. The union also asked for, and received, a written agreement that the city would bargain on further pay equity adjustments when the contract expired.

The contract took the union about half way toward its four-year pay equity goal, although the equity adjustments were distributed somewhat differently from those initially proposed by the union. In the 1981 agreement, all classes with 50 percent or more women workers, which were more than 10 percent below the pay trend line, received pay equity adjustments ranging from a minimum of 5 percent to a maximum of 15 percent. The city agreed to spend $700,000 each year for these adjustments, making a two-year total of $1.4 million. According to Bill Callahan the pay equity adjustments affected about 78 classifications. These classes were either female-dominated, with 70 percent or more women workers, or mixed, with 50 percent or more women workers. The 78 classes accounted for about 75 percent of the workers represented by the union. The city also agreed to a 7.5 percent general increase in wages in the first contract year and an 8 percent general increase in the second year.

Aftereffects: Hope Prevails

"The strike was short, but very intense," Bill Callahan said. "There was so much going on, so much media attention. Every person who was on the picket line was subjected to an interview by someone or other, or had a camera in their face. It became very much of an event for the people on strike. It was not something where people were isolated, out on the picket line, and forgotten. It was very much of an event in San Jose.

"We feel that the strikers were the best employees in the city," he added. "These were the people who had been there 10, 15, or 20 years and were the most qualified employees within their positions.

"And we really feel that the strike dramatically changed the lives of those people who went out on strike," Bill Callahan said. "It was a turning point in their lives, something that they will never forget. It was the highlight of their lives, in many cases. When the strike was over, these people walked back to their jobs in city hall and in the library with their heads held high. They even received applause from the management for their strength and steadfastness in holding to an issue that they felt was an issue of theirs."

Prudence Slaathaug told me that when the city manager sent out termination letters, it enraged the strikers so much that it strengthened the union's hand. "The employees ended up burning their termination letters in front of the city hall," she said, "which is extremely radical behavior for a 55-year-old legal secretary. It really angered them and pushed them well beyond what their experience had been.

"Right after the settlement," Slaathaug said, "there was a mayor's race in San Jose, and the candidate the union was supporting did a poll on issues. It turned out that 70 percent of the people responded favorably to the issue of comparable worth. And this is in a right-to-work area," she pointed out. "This is a fairly antiunion and conservative town. And there had just been a strike. Still the public sentiment was very high on the side of women getting a fair wage."

"The strike almost broke the union in the city," Armstrong told me, bringing out what he saw as a negative aspect of the strike for AFSCME Local 101. "I thought that for the union it was an absolute disaster," he continued. "The union is at least half men. And you see, there was absolutely nothing in this for men."

"What effect do you think the strike had on the union?" I asked Sally Reed, looking for another city management opinion on the strike's effects.

"The union leadership, both nationally and locally, I think benefited from the whole issue," she replied. "It certainly raised their visibility. It gave them an identity. Within the union itself, I think it was probably— and this is *purely* my own personal opinion, I haven't had anyone tell me—it was probably at least as harmful as it was helpful. It's a divisive issue in a union that is not predominantly female."

None of the union people I talked to agreed with management's assessment that the strike hurt the local union. They pointed out that the union's membership had increased by about 20 percent, from 500 to 600 members, since the strike. They explained that many men were in the "mixed" 50 percent male–50 percent female classes and so benefited from the equity adjustments. They said that the union men saw pay equity as an economic issue of two pay checks rather than one and a half pay checks in the family. And they said that the men supported the strike because the city wouldn't give the union a decent general wage increase. The fact that the union continued its support of comparable worth pay demands in the 1983 bargaining, even though the bargaining team's members were largely from male-dominated classes, supports their view.

"What we received out of it was a total benefit, as far as an organization goes," Callahan told me. "The strike cost about $15,000, which was fully borne by the national union. I think the press that the local union and the national union and the movement in general got you couldn't buy for $15 million. You really couldn't buy the coverage the issue got in the radio, newspapers, and TV. So we benefited from that. The union is still fully committed, both locally and nationally, to the issue of resolving sex-based wage discrimination. And we're seeing many other unions that we had thought would not support this issue, coming out strong on it.

"The only thing I might say, as far as Dave Armstrong's remark about the strike is concerned," Callahan added, "is that I don't know whether we could do it again in San Jose. The circumstances were such that it was ideal at that point in time, from all sides, the city administration, everyone. But now I'm really not sure. There's the problem now of the lack of prosperity in the economy. Strikes are not occurring because of the fear of losing job security. But as far as the strike in 1981 is concerned, it was a total success for the organization and for those people participating."

Both city management and union representatives agreed that the 1981 pay equity settlement improved clerical wages in the private sector in Silicon Valley, and that it had made it easier for the city to hire help, so the ripple effect that other employers feared and women workers hoped for did occur.

In August 1983 the city and AFSCME Local 101 negotiated a new, one-year contract. In it, they continued with the third year of the four-year pay equity program. According to Mike Ferrero, the new agreement takes all classes with 50 percent or more women workers to within 7½ percent of the trend line, adjusted for the 15½ percent general increase since 1981. The policy affected classes within the 10 percent cone for the first time, in all about 15 more classes than in 1981. The city employees also received a general increase of 5 percent.

Mike Ferrero reported that a major unresolved issue of 1983's negotiations was the agency shop. (The agency shop is a union security provision, often sought by public employee unions, which requires nonunion members to pay a fee for the union's bargaining services.) "But other than that," he said, "we were pretty pleased with the settlement."

"We didn't go back to the point that we worked very hard on last time and that we still feel very strongly about," Joan Goddard added, "which is that we are leaving some of the men in the low male classes behind. We were working, this year, on continuing the third year of the proposal, which had been agreed to with the city before. We are starting now to work on updating our pay equity data. And we're working on the political angle by including interested city council members in the union considerations of what we should do next and how best to approach the issue. There are only two council members who we're sure are adamant against it, and maybe two or three who are willing to forget about it very easily. But the mayor and vice mayor and several other council members are interested."

"The San Jose strike helped the women's movement immeasurably," Callahan told me, summing up his view of its effects. "The one thing that came out of the strike," he continued, "was the recognition by other women workers that the device men have used for years to better their condition is collective bargaining. And that unions are not dominated by thugs and goons but are professional organizations with professional staffs using all the modern techniques to negotiate—research departments, legal departments, and the media.

"As Eleanor Holmes Norton said, 'Comparable worth is the working woman's issue of the eighties.' Well," he concluded, "it started out a little slow, but with San Jose the spark was lit and it really became a major issue and has remained so."

Notes

1. Hay Associates, "Client Briefing," No. 102, August 6, 1981.

2. Hay Associates, "Management Compensation Study," Personnel Department, City of San Jose, 1980.

3. Ibid. Italics theirs.

4. Hay Associates, "Client Briefing."

5. Agreement between the city of San Jose and MEF, Local 101, AFSCME, AFL-CIO, July 3, 1980.

6. Hay Associates, "Client Briefing," p. 2.

7. Ibid.

8. Ibid.

6

PAY EQUITY IN THE FACTORY:
IUE v. *Westinghouse*
Electric Corporation

"Blatant sex discrimination exists today in virtually every industrial plant in the United States. I believe that the most effective way to combat discriminatory conditions is to file charges and lawsuits under Title VII, the Equal Pay Act, the federal executive order governing government contractors, and state and local equal opportunity laws," stated Winn Newman in 1975 at a conference on occupational segregation at Wellesley College. At the time he was general counsel for the International Union of Electrical Workers (IUE).[1]

"It is time—eleven years after the effective date of the Equal Pay Act and ten years after the effective date of Title VII," he continued, to stop discussing how "to educate people as to how badly women are treated" and to start doing something about the treatment. "The best kind of education," he asserted, "is the kind that results from success [in] making those who break the law give restitution. . . . The best way to do this," he repeated, "is to enforce the law by filing charges and lawsuits."[2]

Winn Newman followed his own advice. Filing charges of sex-based wage discrimination against electrical equipment manufacturers is exactly what he had been doing since early 1970, a few months after he became the IUE general counsel. Like water wearing down a stone, the union, under his legal guidance, began to win gains for women workers in settlements of charges and suits and in collective bargaining negotiations. In 1980, after ten persistent years, the IUE won a landmark victory in the third circuit court of appeals in the case of *IUE* v. *Westinghouse Electric Corporation*.

The district court in Trenton, New Jersey, had ruled against IUE on the grounds that the Bennett Amendment to Title VII of the Civil Rights Act restricted sex-based pay discrimination claims to cases where women were doing substantially the same work as men. And the women in the

Westinghouse lamp factory in Trenton did not claim they were doing "equal" work.

The circuit court, however, reversed the lower court, holding that: (1) [the] Bennett Amendment to the Civil Rights Act

> does not mean that the prohibition against sex-based discrimination in wages in the Civil Rights Act is limited to situations where employees are performing the same or substantially the same work, in the manner that the Equal Pay Act is limited, and (2) [the] claimed policy of employer in deliberately setting wage rates lower for those job classifications which were predominately filled by females than for job classifications which were predominately filled by males would, if proven, be a violation of the Civil Rights Act of 1964 even though the jobs predominately held by women were not the same as the jobs predominately held by men.[3]

Both IUE and Westinghouse asked the Supreme Court to review the case. In 1981, about a week after announcing its decision in the *Gunther* case, the Supreme Court refused review, thereby letting the appeals court decision stand. This effectively reaffirmed the Supreme Court's opinion in the *Gunther* case that Title VII of the Civil Rights Act covered sex-based wage discrimination in the same way that the title covered claims of pay discrimination based on race, color, religion, or national origin. In other words, women workers were not limited by the Bennett Amendment to situations where they were doing the same work as male workers.

"Once you knocked out Bennett then you simply had a statute that banned discrimination in compensation, that's all," Winn Newman told me when I interviewed him about *IUE* v. *Westinghouse Electric Corporation* and *AFSCME* v. *the State of Washington,* another precedent-setting sex-based wage discrimination case that he had recently argued in a Washington state district court and won. He later lost the appeal of the Washington state case, however, in September 1985.

"And you don't have to worry about whether it's labeled comparable worth or anything else?" I asked.

"I don't," he answered. "The statute doesn't say anything about comparable worth. I wouldn't try to prove anything about comparable worth. I don't know what comparable worth is any more. But I know what discrimination in compensation is.

"The statute bans discrimination in compensation. And once you knocked out Bennett, race- and sex-based wage discrimination are the same thing.

"I think Westinghouse is going to show up as a major case. It is a far more significant case than *Washington State,*" he asserted.

"Why?" I asked.

"Well," Newman answered, "because it was early and now *Washington State* can lean on *Westinghouse.* In the days of *Westinghouse* we didn't have *Gunther* as precedent. *Westinghouse* is the first case."

The Plaintiffs: Filing Suit

The plaintiffs in the history-making *Westinghouse* case were five women workers in the Westinghouse lamp plant in Trenton, New Jersey, suing "on behalf of themselves and the class they represent"; their IUE Local 449; and the parent organization, the International Union of Electrical, Radio and Machine Workers, AFL-CIO-CLC. The Trenton plant was around 60 years old then. From the late 1930s to 1950 it was one of the largest lamp plants in the country, and, indeed, in the world. It had peaked in production between the end of World War II and the beginning of the 1950s.[4]

At the time of the suit there were 213 women and 76 men working in the Trenton factory, almost three times as many women as men. According to Westinghouse general manager Jack Kusler, this preponderance of women workers was typical of the 13 Westinghouse lamp plants.[5] Moreover, more than a million women work in the electrical equipment industry as a whole, making up about 40 percent of its labor force. "No other durable goods manufacturing industry in the United States has any comparable number of women workers," Winn Newman told a conference on "Positive Action for Women at Work" held in London, England, in 1981. The IUE represents about 300,000 of the industry's workers, Newman reported. About 40 percent of its members are women.

The Trenton case started out as part of a national charge the IUE filed with the EEOC against Westinghouse in 1973. "The union alleged discrimination against women and minorities in hiring, initial assignment, wage rates, promotion, transfer, training, upgrading, and seniority. The original charge covered 40 Westinghouse locations."[6]

In 1974 the IUE filed suit against Westinghouse in Pittsburgh, in the western district of Pennsylvania, where Westinghouse has its headquarters. This suit claimed wage discrimination against female employees in four Westinghouse plants—Trenton, New Jersey; Fairmont, West Virginia; Bloomfield, New Jersey; and Buffalo, New York. The Trenton, Fairmont, and Bloomfield plants made lamps. The Buffalo plant made electric motors. This suit was later parceled out for trial in the different areas where the plants were located.

Of these four suits, the Trenton case was the one that finally went to the Supreme Court. In West Virginia, district court judge Haden dismissed the IUE Fairmont claim of wage bias on the grounds that "the only sex-based wage discrimination claims cognizable under Title VII were

those where women were paid differently from men for equal work. . . .
The Court . . . held that Congress intended to incorporate the 'equal work'
standard into Title VII."[7]

The union appealed the West Virginia district court's decision. But
while the appeal was pending, the union and the company and the
EEOC, an intervenor in the Fairmont case, agreed on a settlement involving 270 employees. In the settlement Westinghouse "agreed to raise the
rates for 16 traditionally female job classifications a total of 25 labor
grades, and to pay ½ of the accrued back pay ($45,000) to employees who
had worked in the female jobs during the past five years. Approximately
100 women are employed in these jobs and eight men. *The cost divided
among the 1,882 employees in the entire plant was .6 cents per hour.*"[8]

Soon after the IUE filed its suits the company made "voluntary" adjustments in grading and pay of some female jobs in the Bloomfield and
Buffalo plants. Westinghouse "upgraded thirteen female job classifications at the Bloomfield plant from three to seven labor grades each (between 15 and 72 cents per hour in future pay and approximately
$1,000,000 in back pay)."[9] They were forced to recognize, Newman says,
that "these female jobs were underrated in comparison to the worth of
male jobs *which were different in content.*"[10] In Buffalo, "90–95 percent of
the predominantly female jobs were upgraded from one to two labor
grades."[11]

In both cases, the union locals found the "voluntary adjustments" inadequate and continued to press their lawsuits for more wage discrimination relief. The company and union reached a settlement for the Bloomfield plant after the court decision and settlement in the Trenton case. According to Carole Wilson, associate general counsel of the IUE, "the
Bloomfield plant was much larger than the Trenton plant and the settlement there was much larger—$200,000 in back pay with much more up-
grading."[12] IUE and Westinghouse are still negotiating a settlement at
Buffalo, the fourth location in the original lawsuit.

The Complaint: "No Rate Below the Rate of Common Labor"

What were the plaintiffs in these suits complaining about? What was
their evidence of wage discrimination?

Their complaint was simple—in the electrical equipment factories
where the women worked, "gender, rather than skill, determined the
wages to be paid for women's jobs."[13] The evidence was overwhelming.
"All but a small fraction of the women's jobs are rated substantially below
male common labor despite the fact that many, if not most of these jobs,
clearly involve more skill, mental aptitude, and responsibility than the
male common labor jobs."

This statement accurately describes the situation in 1975 at the Westinghouse plant in Trenton, New Jersey. But it was made in 1945 by Lloyd K. Garrison, chairman of the World War II Labor Board, in his decision on wage inequities at Westinghouse and General Electric plants.[14] The union found that this discriminatory pay policy dated back to at least the late 1930s, "when the company maintained a work force completely segregated by sex. There were 'male' and 'female' jobs, but no jobs open to both men and women."[15]

In arguing its case the union supplied evidence of sex-based wage discrimination from that period—the Westinghouse "Industrial Relations Manual" put out in 1939 to guide plant officials in structuring wages in each plant. Following the manual's wage-setting process, the company first did a job evaluation study, rating each job "on the basis of skill, effort, responsibility, and working conditions."[16] Then plant officials put each job into a labor grade, based on the job's assigned points. "The Manual emphasized that the jobs were to be rated and assigned to labor grades without regard to whether they were filled by men or by women."[17]

So far there seems to be nothing to complain about. But then the manual went on to instruct "plant officials to compensate women's jobs at a lower rate than men's jobs which had received the same point ratings and were assigned to the same labor grade."[18] In its 1945 investigation of the electrical industry, the War Labor Board found that Westinghouse reduced the wage rate by 18 to 20 percent for jobs done by women. General Electric was even tougher, paying women one third less than it would have paid men for the same job evaluation ratings.[19] In effect, the companies had separate wage scales and "key sheets" for women's and men's jobs.

This discriminatory wage policy coupled with the company's practice of segregating women's jobs and of not allowing women to work in any job above grade five resulted in the incongruous situation where "the highest skilled women's job, a '5W,' paid less than the lowest [unskilled] male entry-level job, a '1-M.' "[20]

How did Westinghouse explain paying women employees less than men for jobs with equal point ratings? The manual says the policy is justified "because of the more transient character of the service of the [women], the relative shortness of their activity in industry, the differences in environment required, the extra services that must be provided, overtime limitations, and the general sociological factors not requiring discussion herein."[21]

The War Labor Board, nevertheless, "stated *as a rule of thumb* that any female job rate below the rate paid male common laborers was probably discriminatory."[22] In its 1945 Westinghouse-GE decision the board ordered a four-cent increase for women workers, thereby acknowledging discrimination, but not fully compensating for it. But according to counsel for Westinghouse, the board "excepted from even the four-cent increase the Westinghouse lamp plants, such as Trenton, because 'intra-plant comparisons of men's and women's rates would be of doubtful validity' therein since the proportion of women to men was so great."[23]

The Suit: Union Charges, Company Defense

In its 1975 suit the IUE claimed that Westinghouse still practiced sex-based wage discrimination in much the same way that it had since the late 1930s by setting "wage rates lower for those job classifications which were predominantly filled by females than the wage rates for those job classifications which were predominantly filled by males." This, the union claimed, violated Title VII of the Civil Rights Act.[24]

The company had made one change in its wage-setting practices in 1965. Title VII had made it illegal to have labor grades and wage rates designated as "female" and "male." Consequently management set up a single "key sheet" or wage scale in which, as Judge Higginbotham explained, "the grades had no explicit sexual designation. The plaintiffs contend that the new wage scale, which is still in use [in 1980], embodies the deliberately discriminatory policy of the prior plan."[25] What the company did was to add four labor grades, making a total of thirteen grades instead of nine. Then it put most of the women in the lowest four labor grades.

As the judge said, "Westinghouse . . . generally accorded female jobs labor grades in the new scale below those of male jobs even though these jobs had been at corresponding labor grades before the merger."[26] As a result of the pay down-grading the most skilled women's jobs were being paid less than the lowest-level unskilled men's work.

After the 1965 change to a single key sheet, men who had formerly been in men's labor grades one to five, with the same number of points as women's grades one to five (but with higher wages), went into labor grades five to nine. The result was that in 1975 only one male was in labor grades one to four while 85 percent of the women were in these grades. Moreover, the top labor grade for all but one of the women was labor grade six. The men still got higher wages, because they were in higher grades. The union's argument boiled down to the charge that they were in higher grades because they were men and not because of the job evaluation rating of their jobs.

In the appeals court the company's attorneys argued that "Westinghouse and the IUE and Local 449 reviewed all the jobs in the Trenton Plant and agreed in writing in 1968–1970 that all jobs were classified in proper relationship to each other. The IUE and Local 449, by means of this suit," the attorneys complained, "now want to renege and ignore those agreements (after having gotten the benefit of them) and draw the Court into a massive review, going back to the 1930s, of the entire Trenton wage structure which has 108 separate job titles."[27]

Clearly, in 1975, the union leaders and lawyers did not agree with the proposition that all jobs were properly classified. The union did say in its brief before the court that "there have been some changes in job content over the years, and some rate adjustments," but it charged that nevertheless "the changes have not eradicated the wage inequities established by the [1930] system."[28]

The Trenton plant made incandescent lamps, "what we call bread and butter lamps," Jack Kusler told me, "the kind you use in your home— 60 watts and 100 watts that you just screw in the socket." To get a first-hand picture of what the jobs in the Trenton plant were like, I talked to Marge Brophy, one of the five women appellants in the Trenton *IUE* v. *Westinghouse* case. She had come to work in the plant after high school and stayed for 37 years till the plant closed in 1982. She was chief steward of Local 449 for 16 years, negotiating workers' grievances with the management. Marge Brophy was one of the women who "bumped up" to maintenance work after the settlement of the court case in 1981, when management agreed to allow women to bump up to these men's jobs.

Before that she was doing utility work. This was "a labor grade six, the highest paid women's work in the plant," she told me. "A utility girl," she explained, "was a person who could do any job in the place. She moved from one job to another, when other workers were out."

Darrell Snider, who had worked at the plant for nearly 36 years, started as a supply server taking flares to the women workers on the lamp assembly line. "A flare is a little piece of glass that is shaped to form the base of the lamp," he explained. "We made those there."

Later the union elected him chief steward. Then he became part of management as a foreman, and finally a lead supervisor of production.

"What does that entail doing?" I asked him.

"That just about entails everything," he replied. "From being in charge of total production to the supervision of other supervisors and so forth."

"How are the lamps made?" I asked him. "The women did the assembly of the lamps?"

"Right," he answered. "They took all the parts and put them through the equipment. There were four women in each group. They worked on a kind of assembly line, which consisted of mounting machines, sealex, basing, and final inspection. The mount machine operator fed flares, coils, exhaust tubing, and wires into the machine. She had to put the mount in the machine and the bulb on a turret which takes it around, etches it, and drops it down over the mount. Then it went around to the sealer and was sealed. The air inside was exhausted and it was filled to 600 millimeters with argon gas. Then the bulb was tipped off and sent through a cooling tower to the baser, who straightened out the wires and put a base on it. She put it into a basing machine where fires sealed the cement to the lamp, the wires were cut off, it was soldered, and then it went through a flasher. Then the final operator got a hold of it, inspected it, repaired it if it needed a touch up on the solder or something. Then she put it into a wrapper and packed it into a case where it went on to a conveyor."

"And all the people who were doing this sort of work were women?" I asked again.

"Yes, until—they did try some men on it but it didn't work out," he said. "They didn't have the dexterity and the speed. And then after they got on—I guess a woman is used to being tied to a certain position and can keep doing repetitive work. The men didn't have too much success at it."

"Would you classify this as unskilled, semiskilled, or skilled work?" I asked.

"After they got on the job I would call it more or less skilled," he said. "You soon picked out the ones that couldn't get skilled."

"The workers weren't skilled when they were hired," he added, "but they had a progressive training period. Actually, the training period was always about twice the labor grade. If you went in as a labor grade three then by the first six weeks you were there you would be on probationary. Then you would be on six weeks of qualifying before you made standard. Making standard is top pay."

"A baser was a grade four," he said. "And the rest of the group was a grade three. A baser had to have a little extra 'umph,' " he explained, "to be able to put the base on."

"Would you say that the women's work on assembly line jobs was more skilled than that of the men who were janitors?" I asked Marge Brophy.

"Oh, definitely," she said. "And more of a responsibility, too. All of those jobs were more skilled. Even more so than a supply man. A supply man was a grade five, and the girls were threes, and the baser, four. The company didn't call it skilled," she continued. "I would say that for the sealer it would take a month to learn the job. And for the baser it would take six months to a year to be really efficient."

"What were the working conditions like on the line?" I asked. "Were they tiring? Was it hard on your eyes?"

"Oh, yes. It was hard on your back and your eyes. To put out nine or ten thousand lamps a day you were just moving constantly."

"Did you have rest periods?"

"Yes. We had 15 minutes in the morning and 15 minutes in the afternoon."

In its brief for the appeals court review, the union asserted that "the low rates for all female jobs—including the few classified above Labor

Grade Three—are not justified by the nature and content of the jobs, but are solely the result of sex discrimination."[29] To justify its assertion, the brief referred to some of the interrogatories in which the plaintiffs' answers gave comparisons of women's and men's jobs. Judge Van Dusen, in a note to his dissent to the third circuit decision, quoted from one of these interrogatories at length. The judge was using this evidence to make the case that the work of the men and women was clearly not "equal." But the comparison he cited bears out the union's point as well, as the union counsel intended.

The answer to the interrogatory compares the job of mount machine operator with that of janitor.

A Mount Machine Operator must work at a fast pace feeding [materials] into her machine. This demands great skill and dexterity. . . . The operator must be able to work from a schedule sheet, must notify other personnel of type changes and the anticipated time of changeovers, must keep production records, must analyze and record shrinkage, and must take note of irregularities in the machine's operation and in the materials she receives. The operator must clear jams and remove defective parts with tweezers, relight fires, and do other maintenance functions.

The description lists more duties involved in sending the bulbs to the next line position and in cleaning up the area.

Much of this work is heavy; for example, the lifting of heavy boxes of flares and tubes, and the moving of even heavier cullet boxes and bulb hampers. The work is constant and involves tension and pressure, since the operator must keep up with the machine and the plant's production depends on the operator's ability to keep the machine fed and running, and to identify problems in the operation of the machine as well as defects in the materials which go into the machine and the mounts which come out of it.

In contrast, the Janitor job involves virtually no skill. Moreover, the janitors can work at a leisurely pace, and often have no duties to perform for substantial periods of time. And of course, the performance of the janitors does not have a direct effect on production, unlike the Mount Machine job. Furthermore, for the most part the janitor's work is very light. Janitors have seldom been required to sweep the factory areas (except the warehouse janitor), because this work is done by the operators in the areas. The cleaning done by the janitors is of a light nature, requiring little exertion. . . . And equipment such as powered sweepers and automatic hand tracks minimize the effort required in the few areas where the work might otherwise be heavy.[30]

The company's counsel responded to the union's charge of deliberate sex segregation of jobs in the Trenton plant by arguing in its brief that few women moved into higher paid men's jobs even though

> the jobs in the plant have been open to both sexes and paid on a revised single key sheet since 1965. . . . Furthermore, it is clear that it has been a voluntary decision by the women in the Trenton Plant to occupy the jobs which they hold and which largely consist of light assembly or production work or inspection work, frequently performed while they are seated. Despite special efforts and programs, Westinghouse has not been able to get many women to bid out of these jobs which they prefer into the jobs largely performed by males that generally involve more physical effort or craft skills.[31]

As evidence the brief cited the lack of female response to a "special program" for women and minorities "created" in November 1975. In this "special effort" the company asked all active women and minority employees as well as those on the inactive list whether

> they desired any job which they had not yet been able to obtain. . . . In essence the Company advised the women that they would receive *special consideration* for placement upon that job (unless it was one in which a significant number of women were already working) at the time of the next immediate vacancy on that job and that *special training* would be considered to qualify them for the job, if they currently lacked qualifications.

The brief pointed out that *"only four (4) women requested jobs upon which women were not already working in a significant number."* It concluded that "to the extent that there are clusters [of women in certain jobs], it is because women want those jobs."[32]

"We couldn't bump until the local negotiated a signed local supplement," Marge Brophy told me. "And for 67 years we never had one. The company would say it would do something about women moving up, but never in writing."

IUE counsel, Carole Wilson explained to me that a supplement is a local agreement that supplements any situations that aren't covered by the national agreement between IUE and Westinghouse. She said that typically the bumping procedure had to be negotiated between the local union and its plant management.

"It was company policy that women couldn't bid on men's jobs," Marge Brophy said. "It would *never* let us bump up. We'd been pushing that in negotiations for years, you know, so that women would have the opportunity to go into these higher jobs. After the judge ordered the company to work out a signed supplement we could bump all the way up to a grade ten. That was in 1981, toward the end. In 1982 we closed up."

"Even before the supplement you could get some male jobs within a department, if there were jobs vacant," she continued, qualifying her previous "never." "And while it was all in the court being settled some women started moving into these areas. But all of this revolved around the court case, because years ago you just couldn't get into those jobs—warehouse jobs, supplies, maintenance were all men's jobs in those days."

Marge Brophy explained that "in those days" the foremen routinely discouraged women from trying to move into men's jobs. "They told us we wouldn't know how to use the tools. Or that the jobs were too hard for us. And they didn't encourage us to try for the men's jobs when they hired us."

After the Civil Rights Act spurred the company to get rid of the sex designation of jobs as "men's" and "women's" in 1965, Marge Brophy bid for a labor grade five job. It had formerly been a "men's" job and the foreman discouraged her from taking it. I asked her what the job was.

"That was a getter mixer job," she said.

"A which?" I asked.

"A getter mixer job, that's mixing coils. You know the coils that go in the light bulbs? I signed a posting for an upgrade on that job. And they discouraged me and took me to the elevator and said, 'Look, you couldn't even work this elevator, which you would have to do in this job.'

"So, knowing no women went on that job, I just was discouraged and I didn't attempt it. But then when I became Chief Steward, I was going around the whole plant. And I was going up and down in the elevator constantly."

After the union and management negotiated the written supplement that allowed women to bump up, however, Marge Brophy did bump up into a "man's job," this time doing maintenance at grade nine. The company said they were going to cut out the grade six "utility" job she had been doing.

"We had put in the grievance [on bumping] and worked out the supplement so I thought, well, this would be a good chance to make the move," she said.

"Were you apprehensive about taking what was known as a man's job?" I asked.

"Yes, I was apprehensive. I thought, oh, I'll never make this. I don't know anything about tools. But I knew the company would have to put the utility girls back in because they needed them. And I thought, well, I'll take it. But so what. I'll be on it a week or maybe a month and I'll go back to utility.

"Well, about a month later they said they'd made a bad mistake and they did put utility back on. You always have 'last off, first back,' so they came to me and said 'do you want last off, first back to utility?' And me being on this maintenance job, I said, 'No way.' I just really loved it. And it was a lot easier than I'd thought it would be. I made standard before the usual time."

"Was it more skilled than the other job you had?"

"Oh, definitely. It was where the finished products came down. The cases had to be sealed and bundled. There was a glue machine that the little boxes came through. It had all kinds of parts on it. And then there was a printing machine that printed the sleeves. And I'd have to take the machines apart and clean them out and keep them in good running shape.

"I had training," she added. "I had machine shop men training me, and my foreman, and a girl who was working there before me. I really got the cooperation of everybody. I loved it," she repeated.

I asked both Carole Wilson and Winn Newman about the claims made by Walter DeForest, counsel for Westinghouse, in his brief—that the company had allowed women to be promoted on the same basis as men since 1965, that in 1975 the company initiated an upward mobility training program for women, but only four women had requested "men's jobs."

"I know that," Carole Wilson responded. "That's the argument that we often meet—that the equal employment law only requires equal employment opportunity as opposed to actuality. And as we point out in the testimony we gave before the EEOC, we have situations like the Trenton case where 85 percent of the unit was female. And so in a hundred years you couldn't possibly have them promote out into the higher-paying jobs. Especially," she stressed, "in times when the work forces are reducing rather than increasing. So that was our answer to that."

"The union opposed that training program," Winn Newman said.

"Why?" I asked.

"Because they were giving women training for jobs that required no training," he answered. "It was such a flagrant case of fitting into the argument, 'I'd hire a woman if I could only find a qualified one.' These were entry level jobs that men were hired off the street for and they made a big show, *after* the charges were filed, and *after* the lawsuits were started, of fighting the lawsuits by introducing the program. It was a purely defensive action," he went on. "There was no intent to do anything for women *at all* until after the lawsuits were filed."

"In 1973," he said, "which were the first negotiations after I got there, we proposed all kinds of things—like moving everybody up to the common labor rate, because the jobs that were below the common labor rate were the female jobs. We proposed a study of wage rates. We proposed posting and bidding, which we did get some semblance of. We proposed that all disputes over wage rates be submitted to arbitration, with the arbitrator having all the authority of the federal courts so that the arbitrator would not be bound by the contract but would be bound to adjust pay based upon the relative worth of the jobs without regard to past practice.

"That program proposed by Westinghouse was put in purely as a defense to the whole issue," Winn Newman repeated, "so that they could say 'women are in these jobs because they want to be in them.' The fact is that when they hired people Westinghouse *made* the assignment and Westinghouse *assigned* women to women's jobs and men to men's jobs. People who apply for entry level jobs don't go around saying 'I want to be an assembler.' They just come into a plant and say 'I want a job.'

"Paper standards are not very meaningful," Newman continued, "when you have a history of a door that's closed, and the plant has an established practice of not having jobs for women, and you're not prepared to do anything to encourage women and to do something about the harassment that occurs when the first women move into the men's jobs, and when you have supervisors who discourage women orally and who find them not qualified to do the work.

"Besides," he added, "if you really want to integrate the plant, you eliminate wage discrimination and then you will find men moving into women's jobs."

The Suit: In the Courts

On October 28, 1975, the IUE suit alleging "a pervasive scheme of sex-based discrimination at Westinghouse's Trenton, New Jersey, plant, all in violation of 703(a) of Title VII" of the Civil Rights Act, came before the United States District Court for the District of New Jersey.[33] The complaint alleged "discriminatory practices in compensation, job assignments, transfers and promotions, tenure, job classifications and other terms and conditions of employment growing out of an official company policy dating back to 1938."[34]

The court granted Westinghouse's motion for partial summary judgment on the parts of the complaint alleging sex-based discrimination in the payment of wages. According to Chief Judge Barlow's opinion, the question at issue was

> whether a sex-based wage discrimination claim may be maintained under Title VII in the absence of allegations that male and female employees are paid disparate wages for the performance of equal or substantially equal work. More specifically, the question is whether the Bennett Amendment to 703(h) of Title VII . . . limits sex-based wage discrimi-

nation claims under Title VII to conduct which would also be actionable under the Equal Pay Act of 1963. . . . The answer to the question is purely a matter of statutory construction."[35]

Because the issue was one of statutory construction the court deemed it proper to issue an order prior to decision on the factual issues involved in the IUE allegations, so that it could be appealed.

During the discovery phase of the trial the union witnesses said that they were not going to try to prove that the women were doing equal or substantially the same work as men for unequal pay. As a result of this "admission" that the union could not prove the work to be equal, Judge Barlow stated that "this Court believes that plaintiffs' allegations of sex-based wage discrimination . . . are insufficient in law and that defendant's motion should, therefore, be granted."[36]

The court's decision, like the Westinghouse counsel's brief, hinged on its interpretation of the Bennett Amendment to the Civil Rights Act. It held that the amendment limited claims of sex discrimination in pay to equal pay for equal work claims. The court based this decision on its examination of the legislative history of Title VII, on EEOC interpretation of the law, and on the relevant case law.

Congress had added the prohibition of sex discrimination to Title VII almost as an afterthought. It had adopted the Bennett Amendment late in the process of working on the act and with little explanation or discussion. As Judge Higginbotham of the appeals court later said in his *IUE* v. *Westinghouse* decision, "The legislative materials on the Bennett Amendment are remarkable only for their equivocacy and turbidity."[37] Consequently there has been room for much legal and judicial difference of opinion on the meaning and effect of the amendment. In addition, the EEOC's interpretation of this legislation appeared to change over time, adding further confusion to the legal deliberations. And both sides relied on the case law to reach different conclusions.

The union opposed the Westinghouse motion, arguing that "Congress did not intend to incorporate the entire 'equal work' formula of the Equal Pay Act into Title VII, but only the four affirmative defenses."[38] In other words, the union contended that the Bennett Amendment simply said that employers accused of sex-based wage discrimination could use the four defenses provided to them in the Equal Pay Act. As Judge Barlow wrote,

Plaintiffs strenuously argue that Congress could not have intended to allow purposeful sex-based wage discrimination, on the pretext of keeping the courts out of the business place, when Congress exhibited little concern for judicial interference in the business place when wage discrimination was based on race, color, religion, or national origin rather than sex.[39]

Judge Barlow commented on the union's hypothetical case, which they said could occur under the court's interpretation of the law. They described a situation where "an employer could isolate a job category which was traditionally all female, arbitrarily cut the wages of that job class in half for the sole reason that its holders were female, and yet not run afoul of the broad remedial provisions of Title VII."[40] Judge Barlow observed that "such discrimination could not be maintained" because Title VII "would still prohibit sex discrimination in hiring, firing, promotion, transfer, classification, and terms and conditions of employment, and any attempt to perpetuate the effects of such purposefully discriminatory yet allegedly lawful activities would run afoul of these prohibitions." He concluded, "We therefore do not believe that our decision will have the dire consequences predicted by the plaintiffs."[41] In other words, according to the judge, when sex discrimination in compensation occurred in unequal work situations outside the reach of the Equal Pay Act, women workers, unlike other protected groups, would have no legal protection against such discrimination but they still could, and indeed would, move to other higher paying jobs. If they had difficulty moving they would charge sex discrimination in hiring, transfer, or promotion and get redress in that way.

As expected, the IUE appealed the district court order to the third circuit court of appeals. Circuit Judge A. Leon Higginbotham wrote the court's majority opinion, holding that the Bennett Amendment "merely incorporates into Title VII . . . the four exceptions outlined in the Equal Pay Act, and does not mean that the prohibition against sex-based discrimination in wages in the Civil Rights Act is limited to situations where employees are performing the same or substantially similar work. . . ." The court further held that

> the claimed policy of employer in deliberately setting wage rates lower for those job classifications which were predominately filled by females than for job classifications which were predominately filled by males would, if proven, be a violation of the Civil Rights Act of 1964 even though the jobs predominately held by women were not the same as the jobs predominately held by men.

Therefore the circuit court reversed the district court and sent the case back to the court for trial on the unsettled claims. Circuit Judge Van Dusen dissented from the majority opinion for reasons similar to those given by the district court for its decision.

Judge Higginbotham began his opinion with the comment that "the instant case pushes us to the edge of subtle concepts of statutory construction." He therefore believed it essential to define the issues clearly. The charge, he said, was "that Westinghouse allegedly used a system which set the wage rates lower for any classification if the group covered within that category was predominantly female." He then pointed out that

> under the applicable law it is clear that Westinghouse could not create job classifications whereby different wages were paid to one group solely because of considerations of religion, race or national origin. The statutory issue here is whether Congress intended to permit Westinghouse to willfully discriminate against women in a way in which it could not discriminate against blacks or whites, Jews or Gentiles, Protestants or Catholics, Italians or Irish, or any other group protected by the Act. Because we hold that this alleged intentional discrimination in formulating classifications of jobs violates Title VII, we will reverse.[42]

In arriving at this decision, the court of appeals examined the legislative history, the administrative interpretations, and the case law relating to the civil rights legislation, just as the district court had done. Noting that "the legislative history . . . is not totally free of ambiguity," the circuit court found that its research pushed it "slowly but firmly" to its conclusions about the meaning of the Bennett Amendment.[43] It disagreed with the district court's assessment of the EEOC's interpretation of the legislation. And it found that the "case law, for the most part, adds little to our inquiry." The opinion did cite the *Gunther* decision of the tenth circuit court with approval, noting that "that court's interpretation of the Bennett Amendment's legislative history is consistent with our own."[44]

Both the IUE and Westinghouse asked the United States Supreme Court to review the circuit court decision, by filing petitions for a writ of certiorari. In his petition to the Supreme Court, Walter DeForest, counsel for Westinghouse, pointed out that it was an "unusual step" for the IUE, "which had prevailed in this case in the Third Circuit," to seek review.[45]

"It was most unusual," Winn Newman said, when I asked him about DeForest's comment. "But then," he added, "no one has ever accused me of being a conformist. I filed that because, although we had won, I thought it was the best case to go up to the Supreme Court."

"We were trying to get a joint agreement with Westinghouse to file for cert, which would have helped to get it. But Westinghouse stalled around and we lost the timing. Christmas and New Year's fouled up the

Court's schedule. And *Gunther* went ahead. We had wanted to get joined in with *Gunther*. It would have been a much better case for the Court to review. We won *Gunther* anyway, but it was a 5–4 vote," he explained.

"We knew that the *Gunther* petition for cert was pending and we thought that the facts in *IUE* v. *Westinghouse* were much stronger and that it would make a better case for the Supreme Court to consider," Carole Wilson told me, when I put the same question to her. "As it turned out the *Gunther* decision very much paralleled the Westinghouse facts— the failure of employers to follow their own objective job evaluations in the payment of women's wages. But when *Gunther* was on appeal it did not seem to us to be that type of case. And we thought that ours, with the smoking gun—the Industrial Relations Manual quote that women weren't getting paid as much as men in part because of general sociologi- cal reasons not necessary to go into herein—was the stronger case to get the court's attention and a good decision. But, in hindsight, it worked out fine. And, of course, the Court was very much aware of our case because we, along with the AFL-CIO, filed a friend of the court brief in *Gunther*."

After the Supreme Court refused to review the case it went back to the district court for trial. But instead of going to trial, IUE and Westing- house arrived at an out-of-court settlement. Westinghouse agreed to up- grade jobs for some 85 women workers at the Trenton plant. It also agreed to a back-pay fund of $75,000 for around 600 women employed at the plant from 1972 to the settlement date.

"Were you satisfied with the settlement?" I asked Carole Wilson.

"Yes, we were pleased," she said. "There was upgrading of jobs so they all earned at the higher rate in addition to getting back pay. We knew the company was in financial trouble when we were negotiating the set- tlement. We thought it was better for the women to get the jobs upgraded and earn the money then, rather than go through a lengthy trial. Had we gone to trial, by the time we got any order it would have all been back pay because the jobs wouldn't have existed then to go back to."

Epilogue

The union and Westinghouse agreed on the settlement in January 1982. Early that year the company also announced that it planned to close the old, multistory Trenton plant by the year's end. In December the plant closed. And in 1983 Westinghouse sold the lamp division—all its lamp plants—to North American Philips, part of a Dutch company.

Was there any connection between the closing of the Trenton plant and the settlement of the IUE suit? Both union and management people to whom I talked agreed that there was not.

"If we thought they closed it down to retaliate because of the settle- ment we would have filed suit," Carole Wilson, IUE counsel, said. "No," she continued, "it was due to business reasons. We were satisfied of that."

"It was an old plant. It was a multistory plant. It had to depend on elevators to move material," Jack Kusler, retired general manager of the lamp division, explained. "And you just couldn't put the latest automated equipment in there. It didn't lend itself to that. That's why it eventually had to shut down."

Output in the Trenton plant peaked right after World War II, he told me. By the end of the 1940s Westinghouse was already moving the production of incandescent "bread and butter" lamps out of Trenton to its modern plant in Little Rock, Arkansas.

"Trenton began to be more specialized in later years," he said, "because it didn't have the high-speed modern equipment, being an old multistory plant. It became a specialized plant. It built high-wattage lamps and very special usage lamps that took quite a bit of hand labor. It wasn't quite as automated. That's why it shut down."

"What happened to the workers when the plant shut down?" I asked Marge Brophy.

"Anyone over 50 got a pension when the plant closed," she said. "That was in the contract. The people under 50 really got hurt. One woman was 48 and had been with Westinghouse for 28 years. But she didn't get a pension. While others who had been there fewer years but were over 50 got pensions. This woman fought. And she got a job in the Bloomfield plant. Some workers went to work for GE in Trenton," she added.

Marge Brophy herself got a pension and retired. But after six months at home she couldn't stand it any longer, so she took another job making electronic components in a plant nearby in Pennsylvania. She seems happy to be back at work. "I've worked ever since I left high school," she said.

The plant she works in is owned by a Swiss company. It is nonunion. The workers get $3.55 to $4.00 an hour—"the same pay as all the places that do this," she explained. She was making $9.33 an hour when she left Westinghouse.

"The management says they can't pay any more or they would go out of business," she said. "My friends ask, 'Marge, why don't you organize a union?' " She didn't answer this question. But it is clear that she is acting in her former role of shop steward, handling grievances for the workers and advising the management on how to deal with problem employees.

"I could have taken a transfer," Darrell Snider said, explaining why he chose to retire a year or two early. "But I just couldn't see it for another year or two, moving—I've been to El Paso, Texas. No way.

"A lot of the Trenton plant workers got different jobs," he added. "Several of them went to a small Hungarian lamp plant in New

Brunswick. Some of the maintenance people went into supervision and transferred down to the southern plants. Some went to Texas, some to Owensboro, Kentucky. These are now Philips plants."

"Why do you think Westinghouse sold the lamp division to North American Philips?" I asked Jack Kusler.

"Because the lamp business takes an awful lot of capital investment," he replied. "You can't buy lamp equipment from any vendor. It's very specialized. Our lamp division designed and built most of its own equipment. It was very capital intensive. To be competitive with Sylvania and GE, and with Philips coming in, you had to invest in equipment. And it took a lot of research and development in your new HID [mercury vapor] lamps and fluorescent lamps—trying to fit fluorescent lamps into little incandescent sockets. We were putting $20 million in the business for one year, the last year I was there. And the corporation just didn't want to go along with that any more. They felt they could get a better return on investment in something else."

"Was foreign competition a factor?" I asked.

"Yes," he said. "To us as well as to GE and Sylvania. Tungsram was one of the big factors; it was a Hungarian operation. We got into a dumping suit with them, and we lost it. They were dumping lamps here cheaper than we could make them.

"And the Japanese, in the decorative type of lamps—the little bent tip lamps that you put in the fancy chandeliers. We couldn't compete with Japan, or Korea, or Taiwan, even. Some of our people visited Hong Kong and said they were paying ridiculous wages to those people. We just couldn't compete in that market. And it was the same way with automotive lamps, the little light bulbs you put in your car. They were coming from Korea and Taiwan.

"Then of course with photoflash it wasn't foreign competition so much as cutthroat business here in the States. And then new flash technology coming along and fast film—that just about put photoflash out of the picture."

"How is North American Philips doing with its plants?" I queried.

"They are investing heavily and I think they are going to be successful," Jack Kusler answered. "They already had a small operation here in Lynn, Massachusetts, and in Hightstown, New Jersey. And they were familiar with some of the American markets. They make lamps all over the world. And they sell a lot of equipment to these small countries. They are very good in lamp equipment design."

In a cover story titled "Operation Turnaround: How Westinghouse's New CEO Plans to Fire Up an Old-Line Company," the December 5, 1983, issue of *Business Week* describes the deteriorating financial and management situation of the company in the early 1970s. "Poor management had let some core businesses deteriorate," the article says, "while the company embarked on a wild acquisition spree costing hundreds of millions of dollars." When, in 1975, "Westinghouse was sued by a group of utilities for reneging on contracts to deliver 80 million lb. of uranium at fixed prices that were then far below prevailing market prices,' one director said, 'We could have gone down the tubes.' "[46]

In its effort to improve profits, the company got rid of some of its old-line businesses, like the lamp division. This was done in part, according to *Business Week,* to hold down labor costs. The company "has sharply reduced the number of unionized workers by unloading product lines— such as appliances and light bulbs—that depended on union workers," the article asserts. "New businesses have been started in smaller plants, often in the South, that are less likely to organize—and easier to manage—than the old giant plants in the Northeast. Overall, less than 50 percent of Westinghouse's eligible workforce is unionized, down from more than two-thirds in the mid-1950s."[47]

"For more than 20 years," a *Wall Street Journal* article on March 17, 1983, reports in the same vein, "electrical workers and their unions have watched helplessly as Westinghouse Electric Corporation pursued what the unions call a 'Southern strategy,' closing old plants in the North and moving production to states where laws and attitudes make union organizing difficult." The *Journal* article describes the workers' opposition to the company's alleged plan to close a motor controls plant in Chicago.

"Westinghouse company officials are, in my opinion, very antiunion, although publicly they say differently," Vincent Vingle of the IUE told me when I asked him about these two articles. "In 1979, I believe it was, the day that we went into negotiations for the 1979 three-year contract," he said, "there was a story on the front page of the Pittsburgh *Post Gazette* quoting one of the company officials as saying that they would do everything legally possible to keep the unions out of their plants. They don't like unions."

I tried to get interviews with some of the present Westinghouse management so that I could ask them about their employment and pay policies both in the past and the present. But Stuart Saltman, their chief counsel, human resources/law, wrote me that that would not be possible inasmuch as Westinghouse has a policy of not discussing issues under litigation. Many of the issues in the Trenton case are still being litigated in the IUE case at Westinghouse's Buffalo plant.

The IUE has suffered substantial membership losses, Carole Wilson told me. "We're down about 25 percent since 1979. And we're at our lowest in history," she said. "We seem to have stabilized at about 180,000 members."

Vincent Vingle attributes this to the decline in the basic industries— auto and steel. The decline in employment there affects the demand for housing, he explained, and for the electrical products that go with it. He also pointed out that the diversification of the electrical equipment companies into other businesses reduced the number of production jobs.

But despite its reduced membership the IUE, with 40 percent of its membership female and with its strong concern about the economic issues affecting women, is still one of the most important organizations representing blue-collar working women. And the *IUE* v. *Westinghouse* case is, as Winn Newman pointed out, a major case—a milestone—in the legal effort to get rid of sex-based wage discrimination.

"We won that case, which was really a great thing," Marge Brophy told me when I asked her what she thought about the future of pay equity. "You would understand it if you were directly involved. And I think now there'll be more and more unions and women going for these things they never had. Like the Willmar Eight."[48]

Notes

1. Winn Newman, "Policy Issues," *Signs: Journal of Women in Culture and Society* 1 (1976): 265–77.
2. Ibid., p. 266.
3. *IUE* v. *Westinghouse Electric Corporation*, 631 Federal Reporter, 2d Series, p. 1094.
4. Interview with Darrell Snider, retired supervisor in the Trenton plant, January 5, 1984, and with Jack Kusler, retired general manager, Westinghouse lamp plants, March 7, 1984.
5. Kusler interview.
6. Winn Newman and Jeanne M. Vonhof, " 'Separate but Equal'—Job Segregation and Pay Equity in the Wake of *Gunther*," *University of Illinois Law Review* 2 (1981): 295, note 118.
7. Brief of Defendant-Appellee, Westinghouse Electric Corporation, U.S. Court of Appeals for the Third Circuit, p. 41. Hereafter cited as Westinghouse brief.
8. Winn Newman, "Statements before EEOC Hearing on Job Segregation and Wage Discrimination under Title VII and Equal Pay Act," *Daily Labor Report*, Bureau of National Affairs, Washington, D.C., April 28, 1980, pp. E-3, E-4.
9. Ibid., p. E-3.
10. Ibid. Italics added.
11. Ibid.
12. Interview, December 12, 1983.
13. Newman and Vonhof, "Separate but Equal," note 113.
14. Ibid. Lloyd Garrison was the former dean of the University of Wisconsin Law School.
15. Ibid., p. 292.
16. Ibid., p. 293.
17. Ibid.
18. Ibid.
19. Winn Newman, "Policy Issues," p. 267.

20. Newman and Vonhof, "Separate but Equal," note 109.

21. Ibid., citing the Westinghouse Industrial Relations Manual, p. 158.

22. Winn Newman, "Statements before EEOC Hearing," p. E-3.

23. Westinghouse brief, p. 5.

24. Judge A. Leon Higginbotham, Jr., Opinion of the Court, *IUE* v. *Westinghouse Corporation,* p. 1096.

25. Ibid., p. 1097.

26. Ibid.

27. Westinghouse brief, p. 6 and n. 14.

28. Brief for Appellants at 10–11, cited by Judge Higginbotham, Opinion of the Court, p. 1098.

29. Ibid. at 69a, cited by Judge Van Dusen in his dissent, *IUE* v. *Westinghouse,* p. 1109, note 5.

30. *IUE* v. *Westinghouse,* p. 1109, note 5.

31. Westinghouse brief, pp. 6, 8.

32. Ibid., p. 8.

33. Chief Judge Barlow, Opinion, *IUE* v. *Westinghouse Electric Corporation,* 19 FEP Cases, p. 451.

34. Ibid.

35. Ibid., p. 452.

36. Ibid.

37. Higginbotham, Opinion of the Court, p. 1096.

38. Barlow, Opinion, p. 453.

39. Ibid.

40. Ibid., p. 457.

41. Ibid.

42. Higginbotham, Opinion, pp. 1096–97.

43. Ibid., p. 1096.

44. Ibid., p. 1107.

45. Walter P. DeForest, III, Counsel for Petitioner, Westinghouse Electric Corporation, Petitioner, v. International Union of Electrical, Radio and Machine Workers, AFL-CIO-CLC, et al., Respondents, Petition for Writ of Certiorari to the United States Court of Appeals for the Third Circuit, October Term, 1980, p. i.

46. "Operation Turnaround," *Business Week,* December 5, 1983, pp. 124–33.

47. Ibid., p. 127.

48. The Willmar Eight were eight female bank tellers in Willmar, Minnesota who went on strike for union recognition and stayed on the picket lines through a bitterly cold Minnesota winter. A film, "The Willmar 8," and a television movie were made about them. The bank received much bad publicity and the next effort of Willmar bank tellers to organize, in 1982, was successful.

7

DEFEAT IN DENVER:
Economic Chaos Averted?

"This case is a case certainly of substantial importance to the plaintiffs," District Court Judge Fred Winner said as he began his oral opinion on *Lemons* v. *the City and County of Denver.* "It is a case of substantial importance to the tax payers of the City and County of Denver, it is a case of substantial importance to the entire community, it is a case which is pregnant with the possibility of disrupting the entire economic system of the United States of America." After observing that he was not going to "open the Pandora's Box in this case of restructuring the entire economy of the U.S. of A.," the judge found against Mary Lemons and the nurses employed by the city and county of Denver.[1]

Nurses are not usually considered radicals or revolutionaries. What did the Denver nurses do that Judge Winner found so threatening?

What they did was to present nursing as a disturbingly clear example of sex-based wage discrimination. Nursing is an occupation that is 98 percent female. It requires substantial training and skill and carries heavy responsibilities for the welfare and, indeed, the lives of patients. The working conditions are hard, often unpleasant and hazardous. The hours include night work, weekend work, and holiday work. The work schedules are frequently unpredictable. In spite of its requirements and working conditions, nursing is an occupation that is historically low paid.

Moreover, low wages in the profession cannot be explained by the law of supply and demand, although Judge Winner mistakenly tried to do this. An oversupply of nurses was not the reason for low wages in Denver or elsewhere in the country in the 1970s, nor is it an explanation now. On the contrary, the federal government has long been seriously concerned with the issue of how to ensure an *adequate* supply of registered nurses to meet the country's health care requirements. During the past two decades it has implemented programs to encourage the education of registered nurses and to increase the supply in the geographical and occupational areas where they are needed. Despite these efforts, the American Hospital Association in the early 1980s estimated "the hospital nurse vacancy" at between 65,000 and 70,000 nationwide.

According to Eunice Cole, president of the American Nurses' Association, this shortage is "a shortage of nurses which has been reported for decades. . . . If the market forces were working to establish wage rates," she said, "obviously this shortage would have led to higher wages for nurses. This has not happened. Nurses' salaries have not increased faster than other occupations and have not outpaced the cost of living."[2]

"In the nursing case," Dr. Helen Remick of the University of Washington asserted, "there is more than an adequate number of personnel with proper certification to fill all vacancies, but there is an acute shortage of those willing to accept present wages and working conditions."[3]

In its fourth *Report to the President and Congress* in May 1984, the Department of Health and Human Services forecast that requirements for registered nurses in all their various types of employment will "outstrip supply" by the 1990s. The department finds this a particularly serious problem in the areas of critical care, administration, and nursing education.[4]

"The wage and salary concerns of all women," Eunice Cole testified,

> are embodied in the wage and salary concerns of registered nurses. No other profession provides a stronger picture of a working woman. No other profession is so closely identified with working women. No other female occupation has provided such a glaring example of the failure of market forces to determine wage rates. Nowhere is it more obvious that the occupation is undervalued because it is work performed by women. . . . In fact, to a large extent registered nurses have become a symbol of the persistent inequities against women who work."[5]

Nursing is a centuries-old service, originally unpaid—"voluntary or missionary work," Cole described it. Florence Nightingale, "widely regarded as the secular saint of nursing," is the model for the volunteer, female, nurturing nurse.[6] Henry Wadsworth Longfellow eulogized Nightingale's nineteenth-century work in his poem about "the lady with the lamp" passing "through the glimmering gloom," whose shadow "the speechless sufferer turns to kiss." The powerful "Nightingale mystique" of dedicated altruism still pervades attitudes toward nursing.[7]

"Nurses have traditionally been taught not to be concerned with salaries," Ada Jacox, a director of the American Nurses' Association, testified at the 1980 EEOC Hearings on Job Segregation and Wage Discrimination. "We have come out of a strong, religious, voluntary tradition in which it was anticipated that we would get our rewards in heaven. We are concerned," she emphasized, "and as Denver nurses are illustrating, we are becoming more aggressive in taking actions to reverse the situation in which what we do is undervalued because we are women."[8]

"Hospital workers are not called the New Nightingales because they have abandoned the traditional altruism of nursing," New York University professor Patricia Cayo Sexton said in her study of hospital workers and unions. "On the contrary, they have extended it, learned to care in newer and better ways, and recognized that saving others does not require one's own suicide."[9]

"We have chosen to utilize the forum of the judicial system to ask our questions," the Denver nurses wrote, "but there are many avenues. On the surface we ask, 'Should sex determine our salary?' More fundamentally we ask, 'What is nursing?' And, 'What is the worth (value) of nursing care?' "[10]

How the Lemons Case Began

"How did the suit get started?" I asked the five Denver nurses who had come to talk with me about *Lemons* v. *the City and County of Denver.* All of the nurses—Sharon Shumway, Ann Jumper, Marilyn Shahan, Charlene Lark, and Ruth Ryan—were active workers on the case from its beginning. The first three were listed as plaintiffs in the class action suit along with Mary Lemons—from whom the suit gets its name—and Margaret Lewis, Lois Cady, Dolora Cotter, Jean Mitchell, and Judith Ives.

"There are two nursing groups in the Denver Department of Health and Hospitals," Ann Jumper replied, "the hospital nursing service and the visiting nurse service. Mary Lemons was the director of nursing at Denver General—the hospital nursing service director. And Margaret Lewis was the public health service director—the director of the visting nurse service. As I recall, around January 1973 the two nursing directors got both groups together to talk about salaries. They said they couldn't tackle the salary issue alone and asked if any of us would be interested in meeting with the attorney for the Colorado Nurses' Association to talk about what seemed to be a disparity in the proposed salary increases."

"Career Service—the Denver personnel agency," Sharon Shumway explained, "published enough information for us to know that the first-level administrative series, which did not include the nurses, was paid higher than the nurses. I think that was one thing that really caught our attention."

"And we had been through a lot of things," Ann Jumper said. "There was a lot of push to get nursing salaries up."

"The history of the suit goes back to the time when we marched on city hall and attended the city council meeting," Marilyn (Shady) Shahan said when the nurses met in 1980 to record some of the history of the case.[11]

"October 1966, according to my notes," Ann Jumper said. "It was at the 1966 ANA (American Nurses' Association) convention where they passed a resolution that starting salary be $6,500. In October 1966, the Denver Career Service recommendations for nursing salaries created inequities at all levels. They wanted to give us each a $50 increase and we wanted a percentage increase. All this resulted in an appeal to the city council by DGH and VNS nursing staffs, resulting in the reversal of the Career Service recommendation."

"I think we should recall some of that meeting," Shady said.

"Who said you should go . . . and what was the purpose of the meeting?" Ruth Ryan asked.

"It seems it was the director of services [Margaret Lewis]," Shady said, "and we decided we should all go in uniform, so the room was full of white and navy blue. Over 200 of us present. Both nursing services had prepared speeches from every level of nursing. . . . Every class was represented. This was quite an accomplishment."

"I remember Arnold [Arnold McDermott, head of the Career Service Authority] being very angry," Ann Jumper said. "The city council was very understanding and overwhelmed. We got an immediate reversal before we left that night at midnight."

"Then we went along, complacent[ly]," Shady added. "The first meeting I went to was in January 1973 . . . at CNA [Colorado Nurses' Association], with their lawyer. . . . We were going to do a preliminary exploration of salary discrimination based on sex. . . . Wasn't 1973 the year they [ANA] did the national survey for directors?" she asked. "When we got back [from the ANA convention], in January 1974, that's when we really got started to roll with it."

And so the original impetus in the case came from the Denver city and county nursing administrators aroused by what seemed to them clear discrepancies between their salaries and those of males in positions requiring similar backgrounds and involving similar types of responsibility. The growing activism of nurses and other working women, nationwide, also supported their concern. As they dug into the facts, however, they saw that all the nurses, from the licensed practical nurse on up, were subject to the same kind of wage discrimination. The issue of pay equity for their profession became a matter of principle for them.

Eight of the nurses met again with the CNA lawyer Fred Miles and, for the first time, with his associate, Craig Barnes. They discussed the results of the nurses' preliminary investigation and efforts.

"Fred did not think that we had a case or understand that we did," Sharon Shumway said. "We knew we needed someone who could."

"Craig picked up on it right away," Shady said. Barnes, who had just finished arguing the Denver school desegregation case in the Supreme Court, became the nurses' chief lawyer.

The nurses knew they wanted to pursue the issue, but how were they going to pay for it? After talking with Barnes they estimated it would cost them $10,000 and take six months to a year. They would save money by doing the work of getting the information needed to make their case, analyzing it, and presenting it in tables and charts themselves.

"Ten years later we're still raising money," the nurses told me. The final cost was over $100,000—one nurse estimated it at $170,000. And it was more than seven years before the case was through the courts.

"They spent more time working on the case, for volunteer people, than any case I ever tried," Craig Barnes said. "They spent hours and hours—I suppose some 10,000 hours—preparing materials. I've never seen clients work like that," he said. "They were invested in it with their whole philosophy, it wasn't just money."

They raised their first money by asking the supervisory group of nurses for two monthly contributions of 5 percent of their pay. They also had fund-raisers.

"Our first fund-raiser was a flea market and it raised $174.52," Charlene Lark said. "We were just so proud that we made that much money. And disillusioned that it took that much work to make that much money."

They incorporated as a nonprofit organization, N.U.R.S.E., Inc. Between 1974 and 1979 they raised $17,000 from a variety of activities—plays, a wine and cheese party, selling cookbooks and calendars, a fashion show, a raffle. The American Nurses' Association gave them $30,000. They passed the hat at ANA conventions. By December 1979 they had raised close to $86,000 but had incurred expenses of $133,000, leaving them with a $39,000 deficit to pay off.

"We didn't realize the extent of our analysis," Ann Jumper told me, explaining the hours of work they put in. "We started out fairly small. But each time we would analyze something it would indicate the need to broaden the analysis to look at different kinds of comparisons, more data. And it just kept growing like Topsy. The city has 800 job classifications."

"And that meant we needed a description—a job specification—for each one of those," Charlene Lark explained. "It took us years, and lots of people."

"What kind of comparisons were you making?" I asked.

"We finally settled on the criteria of education, experience, supervisory responsibility, and occupational category—which was a designation assigned by the city to all of their jobs," Shady answered. "They had about seven or eight categories—supervisory, professional, technical. . . . And then male or female incumbency in any given job classification."

"How did you go about comparing yourselves?" I asked. "They don't give points to jobs."

"We got all the job descriptions and requirements," Shady answered. "They classify them according to the things I just listed, so we could compare them. We could compare the licensed practical nurse with the people who were similarly situated. And the graduate nurse I, and the person with the master's degree and first-level supervisory responsibility to the nurse who had that."

"Did you do that for all the job classifications?" I asked.

"We looked at 800 job classifications, [compared] against the nurse," Shady answered. "So that for the director of nursing service you'd have— I don't remember exactly—but it's 15 or 20 positions in the city system where a master's degree was required and you had administrative responsibility for a whole department with x number of employees. So there might be 20 other positions that she might be compared against. The graduate nurse I was compared against maybe 70. We have the information available."

"We used several approaches," Ann Jumper said. "We compared them against all occupational categories, whether they were technical or professional. And then we compared them against the professional—the nurse was listed as professional."

"Craig was always willing to go with what we had, but often felt it would be nice to know such and such," Shady said. "Then there would be another six-week project."

"And the other thing we had to do," Ann Jumper said, "was to make all the charts, and do the lettering, and put in color. And have them Xeroxed in color, which was very costly at the time."

"The nurses actually took all of the 800 jobs in the city and spread them out—diagrammed them—over thousands of hours of time," Craig Barnes said. "It was a very extensive job and the Career Service Board had never done it themselves."

When the nurses started doing the job comparisons Barnes called in George Bardwell, a professor of statistics at the University of Denver, to work with them on the correct statistical tools and methods to use. Then after doing this analysis they decided they needed a job evaluation study to reinforce their work.

"So I got a call and went down," Dick Beatty, professor of management and organization, College of Business Administration and Graduate School of Business, University of Colorado at Boulder, told me. "And spent the next two years of my life working on this case. Two graduate students and I went in and designed a factor comparison job evaluation system based on job content to assess the value of those jobs as you would do for any kind of compensation study. I do a lot of compensation work," he said, "and I teach for the American Compensation Association."

"Did the nurses try to reach some settlement of their grievances before suing?" I asked Craig Barnes.

"There was a long history of discussion about it, yes," he said. "They had talked to the Career Service Board on a number of occasions about the apparent discrepancies. They noticed that other jobs of similar professional prerequirement qualifications paid substantially more, or were classified in a different way. They were classified in the general administrative and professional series. And the nurses, seeing themselves as professionals, wondered why they weren't classified in the professional series, and asked the question early on, even before they saw me. They were told that they were not going to be moved into the professional series. They tried to work that out with the Career Service Board and ran into a stone wall."

"We did a couple of things," Shady told me. "We talked with the hospital administration and they were *very* supportive, at that time. And we met with the Career Service Authority and shared all of our concerns with them and told them we were going to need some data. We went to a public hearing on the salaries, too, and stated our case there. And nothing happened."

In February 1975 the nurses filed a complaint with the EEOC. Before filing they met with Arnold McDermott, head of the Career Service Authority, and Clyde Hocking, who ran the classification system, and Herb Abshire, another personnel officer who replaced McDermott when he retired.

"We met with them and told them we were going to file with EEOC and they were so shocked," Shady said, at the nurses' history taping session. "I'll never forget Arnold's words, something to the effect, 'You're going to sue us?' Like we have always thought of the Career Service and the city as one big happy family. He was really taken aback."

"They couldn't see any point [to it] at all," Sharon Shumway added. "[They didn't have] any understanding of what we were talking about. They paid fairly, that's what they kept going back to. 'We pay what the community pays.' . . . They were nervous and we were pleased."

"Later on, after we filed the suit," Craig Barnes said, "there was always the question of whether or not we would seek some kind of a compromise settlement for a 7, 8, or 10 percent increase in salaries, which seemed quite within reach. By that point, after working on it for a year and a half or two years, the nurses were deeply wedded to the principle of it.

"I remember a meeting," Barnes said, "where we sat around my conference room and I said, 'You know we could go for a salary result right now and the chances are we would get it. You have to make a decision whether or not you want to go for a salary result or try and cut some new ground. Your chances are much less if you do that.' Uniformly, absolutely universally, unanimously, the decision was not to go for the short-term salary result but try to cut the high ground. That was a very conscious decision they made."

"We didn't want to be bought out again, and there was a principle involved," Sharon explained.

"We thought about the staff, too, and what they thought," Ann said. "In 1966 we got an immediate response [from the city council] and we knew we could get a similar type of thing, but it would probably not be a lasting change. What we wanted was a change in the system."

The Nurses' Case

Many of the comparable worth cases that have been brought to court to date have based their defense on the principles of "disparate impact" or "disparate treatment." What do these two terms mean? In a 1981 decision, *Heagney* v. *University of Washington,* the ninth circuit court explained that "In a disparate impact case, a plaintiff must show some facially neutral employment practice has a substantially disproportionate impact upon a group protected by Title VII." These "outwardly neutral employment practices" may, for example, be requirements, such as height and weight specifications, that are not, in fact, related to the job and operate to exclude a protected group such as women. Another example is employment tests that exclude "those of certain cultural backgrounds," as the court put it, but are not validly related to the job.

The theory of disparate impact does not require a finding of intent to discriminate. The ninth circuit court explained:

> Once plaintiffs have shown the existence and impact of such a practice, which constitutes a prima facie case, the employer will be held liable unless the practice can be justified by "business necessity."
>
> A "treatment case" involves a situation where an employer treats an individual protected by Title VII differently simply because of the person's minority status, religion, or sex. In a treatment case, unlike an impact case, it is necessary to show an employer's intent to discriminate, but intent can be inferred from circumstantial evidence.

A plaintiff can make a prima facie case of disparate treatment by introducing credible evidence that the defendant "had an intent to discriminate." To avoid being liable, an employer must then "articulate legitimate, nondiscriminatory reasons for disparate treatment." If the employer does this, the plaintiff can try to show that these reasons "were a pretext to hide bias."[12]

"What were the nurses' chief arguments in their suit?" I asked Craig Barnes. "Intent to discriminate? Disparate impact? Was it a comparable worth case?"

"It was a Title VII disparate impact case," he replied. "The pivotal point was that the procedures by which the Career Service Board arrived at salary decisions were so infected with bias that there was no way that they could come up with a nondiscriminatory result. And so the process resulted in disparate impact across the board against women.

"The way in which the salary classifications, the salary comparisons, were made was—is—in itself a comparable worth system and it's a subjective one. So a second major element of our approach was that it's not a choice between comparable worth evaluation and something else. Comparable worth evaluation was going on across the board. It was only a question of whether or not it would be fair."

The city uses what is called a "key class" system to organize its pay structure. In 1977 there were some 8,000 employees in 800 different job classes organized around 30 key classes. The city determines the prevailing wage for each key class annually by surveying Denver area wages. These are the only job classes tied directly to the market. The other 770 jobs in the city are grouped into job clusters around one of the 30 key jobs. Each of these job families consists of a hierarchy of jobs linked to the pay of its key class. So the critical question for job holders is what key class their job is linked to and where their job is in the pay structure of that job family. The classifiers for the Career Service Board make these decisions. In setting up these family trees of jobs the classifiers use what personnel people call "whole job analysis."

"We have, as I recall, some 16 different elements of the job that we look at," Maxine Kurtz, personnel officer at the Career Service Authority, told me. "And then we look at anything else that comes up.

"Some of those considerations are (1) supervision received, (2) supervision given, (3) impact of error, (4) independence of judgment, (5) interpersonal relations, i.e., how does this kind of nurse relate to patients, to co-workers, to supervisors, to the public. But it is *not* a checklist of 16 elements," she stressed. "There was a great deal of to-do [in the court case] about the fact that we didn't use a checklist. We didn't consider everything for every job. [But] we look at all facets of the work and compare them on everything that's relevant.

"And a crucial point," she added, "is we do *not* go across occupational lines. We do not compare nurses to tree trimmers. We do not use internal relationships outside of the job families. What we have is a marketplace-based plan.

"The second thing that is crucial about this," she said, "is that this is based entirely on the kind and level of duties and responsibilities. We don't care who the incumbent is. And furthermore we don't care how well or poorly the job is being done.

"By using the 'whole job' we can look at any unusual circumstances that may be around a given job," she explained. "We're not straitlaced into the four categories that statistical systems use—(1) knowledge and skills, (2) responsibility, (3) accountability, and (4) working conditions." I suggested that "problem solving" belonged in this list of factors used in point factor job evaluation systems like Hay's, with Kurtz's (2) and (3) being considered together.

"Is 'whole job analysis' a system that's commonly used?" I asked.

"It's one of the very common systems among government agencies," she said.

"The women's movement and AFSCME and some of the consultants—notably Hay, and to a lesser extent Willis—have been pushing the statistical systems. Now that's what happened with *Gunther* [*County of Washington, Oregon et al.* v. *Gunther et al.*]," she said. "Whatever the statistical system was that the state of Oregon used, it showed that matrons' jobs were worth 95 percent of what [male] guards' jobs were worth. I'm not sure what they thought they were going to do with this system once they put it in," she added.

"They initiated this on their own," I said. "They weren't asked to do it."

"That's right," she said. "Well, in fact, any of those cases that have been lost have revolved around a point system initiated by the jurisdiction in question. Jurisdictions have been hanging themselves with these point systems.

"Then they [the county of Washington] went into the marketplace and did a prevailing wage study and found that they could hire matrons for 70 percent of what it cost them to hire male guards," she said. "So they did.

"The Supreme Court said, 'We're not passing on the value of jobs. You set them up. You were the ones who said that the matron's job was worth 95 percent of what a male guard's job was worth. But you decided, on a different basis, that you were only going to pay them 70 percent of what you pay the guards. Now that comprises intentional discrimination under Title VII.'

"That is exactly what the state of Washington did, as well," she said. "The state, in four studies and two statutes passed by the general assembly, announced that they were discriminating and proceeded to prove it, using this Willis point system. Now anybody who goes in for one of these point systems is setting themselves up to be knocked over on the comparable worth argument," she said. "And the fatal first step is to do a statistical point study. Once you embark on that you've gone past the point of no return.

"And it's 'in,' " she said, "because it's pseudoscientific. And I mean it's pseudoscientific. Probably not even as objective as our system. But it does have numbers to crunch."

The nurses charged that although the city's key class pay system was facially neutral—apparently nondiscriminatory—the Career Service Board administered it in a discriminatory way. The board, they said, "used different classification criteria for males than females, and . . . the controlling criteria for females is sex." They argued that the system picks up "historic sex discrimination" against nurses by using community wage scales and "that the result of all these practices is massive wage and salary disadvantage for nurses compared to male job classes."[13]

The nurses asked the court "to have the nursing 'key' class which reflects historically depressed wage scales discontinued, and to be paid on an existing scale that the City maintains for professionals and administrators known as the 'General Administrative Series.' " The Career Board exempts many administrative and professional jobs from the key class system by putting them into the general administrative series (GAS). According to the plaintiffs' complaint, filed in the U.S. District Court of Colorado, the GAS classification includes "a majority of all Bachelors-trained personnel in city employment and a majority of all professionals." But these are the bachelor's-trained males and "professional" males. The majority of bachelor's-trained females and "professional" females are not in the GAS classes.

The Career Service ties the salary of the GAS classes to a composite of administrative and professional salaries in both Denver and the nation as a whole. The nurses' complaint states that

> this wider composite survey, including many classes and incorporating the benefits of higher professional salaries nationally, effectively eliminates, or reduces substantially, the skewing effects of discrimination which may depress wages within any one profession, as in the case of nurses who have suffered historic wage discrimination. While a majority of male professionals enjoy the benefits of the composite survey, defendants arbitrarily exclude nurses such as [the] plaintiffs.[14]

Despite being classified by the city as "professionals," the Denver nurses of all grades, from the graduate nurse I to the top administrators of nursing in the city hospital and visiting nurse systems, are classified in the key class system with their wages tied to the community wage for the entry level nurse, the graduate nurse I. The nurses provided voluminous testimony that the market wages of nurses are historically low, following a centuries old tradition that predated Florence Nightingale. Furthermore, they told me that the 16 Denver private hospitals set local nursing wages, to which the city and county wages are tied, by acting together at meetings of the Colorado Hospital Association.

"They would get together and set the salary for the nurse in the community, private and public," the nurses explained. "And you would find that any nurse's salary in the city would be within their range. Their meetings had been open, but they closed them to us, so we couldn't prove it. But the hospitals would raise their salaries January 1. And we could do our own survey of those hospitals and determine what our increase was going to be."

"Hospitals may be monopsonistic employers," Dr. Lois Friss, professor in the School of Public Administration, University of Southern California, writes. "There is little or no competitive bidding for the local supply of nurses, and the larger metropolitan associations have well-developed wage stabilization programs."[15]

In testimony at hearings before the California State Department of Industrial Relations, Dr. Friss gave an example of monopsony in the nursing labor market by describing the wage-related activities of the Hospital Council of Southern California. The Hospital Council, she said, is an organization of about 200 hospitals in six counties. The council's personnel practices committee annually reviews benchmark—key class—jobs and rewrites descriptions as needed. It hires a consulting firm to do an annual survey of wages and to make wage projections for the coming year.

"The Council publishes and distributes this report to member hospitals who closely follow these projections," Friss testified.

> The effect of this is to eliminate intra-regional rate differentials. David Thomsen, . . . an authority in the field of bias-free job evaluations, describes this benchmark ranking or market pricing job evaluation as a method of price fixing which allows the freedom to discriminate against selected groups. [He says] it is the perfect plan for those who wish to pay only what they must, the bare minimum, agreed upon via surveys while trapping employees in economic conditions from which there is no escape.[16]

The main thrust of the nurses' argument was that the city's pay system was organized on the basis of sex. They argued that the organizing principle for classifying women's jobs was to put them with other women's jobs no matter what the requirements for education, training, or management responsibility might be. This, they said, was not the classification principle for men's jobs.

"There are 30 key class clusters," the plaintiffs' brief stated.

Twenty-six of these are sex segregated (75 percent–100 percent all one sex). The overwhelming majority of the City's employees are found in these clusters. . . . The City's jobs are also sex segregated. In 1974 the chance that a male would be sex segregated in his work was 89 percent. . . . The chance that a female would work in a sex segregated environment was 83 percent. In 1977, the chances were 79 percent and 83 percent respectively for males and females.

Thus the way the City administers this system, women work with women and women's job classes are clustered with other women's job classes for purposes of establishing pay relationships. There is no tradition or "market" to follow that causes the Family Health Counselor I to be in the same cluster with the Director of Nursing Services. That is a discretionary, entirely free, choice of the City's classifiers.[17]

The nurses found in their research on the system that the organizing principle for male-dominated classes was education, that is, that most male clusters have similar educational prerequisites. But they found that five of the key class job clusters were exceptions to this rule. They had no educational homogeneity whatsoever. In 1974, four of these five exceptions were female classes. In 1977, three were female. And the nurses' class was one of these exceptions. Only 9 percent of the job classes clustered around the key class graduate nurse I required the same education as the key class, although 84 percent of the other job clusters showed uniformity in educational requirements. The education required in the nurses' cluster ranged from high school to a master's degree.

The city's pay policies tied the wage of the key class graduate nurse I, to the prevailing nursing wage in the Denver market. This was a low wage because of historic discrimination against nurses. Then the city personnel people grouped a variety of female jobs into the nursing cluster. Jobs with substantial educational and training requirements and administrative responsibility were tied to this low entry level wage instead of being related to jobs with equivalent requirements, as male jobs typically were.

Maxine Kurtz said that a "crucial point" in the Denver system was "that we do *not* go across occupational lines." The plaintiffs' brief points out, however, that in the job cluster tied to the key class graduate nurse I for pay purposes "were such other predominately female classes as the Dental Hygienist, the Child Educational Consultant, the Family Health Counselor I, the Program Aide III, the Social Services Director, and the social worker. Obviously," the brief states, "these jobs do not all relate to nursing or even to health care. On their face they do not all work in hospitals. They do not . . . share the same educational level."[18]

The brief finds "the clue to this grouping" in the fact that these jobs are female. It points out that male-dominated classes in the health field such as "the Health Center Administrative Officer, the Executive Hospital Housekeeper, the Laboratory Technicians I and II, the Health and Hospitals Controller, and all the physicians, dentists, public health veterinarians and the environmental health director"[19] are not included in the graduate nurse I grouping, but are linked to higher-paying male classes.

In 1975 the city made an effort to get rid of sexist titles for jobs, such as office girl and laundry washman. But when asked by the plaintiffs' counsel what procedures the Career Service Authority currently followed to screen out sex stereotyping of jobs, the city's chief job classifier, Clyde Hocking, said, "None of the procedures that we go through has anything to do with stereotyping. . . . In classification, in fact, as long as I have been in classification, I have never known of sex stereotyping."

"What study or analysis have you made to determine that it doesn't exist, other than your ipse dixit?" Judge Winner asked Hocking. "What do we have to go on?"

"I haven't made any study of this, Your Honor," Clyde Hocking replied. "The fact that it has never been considered by myself or my staff is all that I have to go on."

The plaintiffs' counsel spent a good deal of time questioning Hocking about the city's classification methods, both in pretrial interrogatories and during the trial. According to Hocking's testimony, the city uses the "whole job" classification system in a subjective, judgmental way. The classifications are made in informal meetings of the classifiers. No written criteria are used. The classifiers make a "professional judgment." Different criteria are used for classifying different jobs.

> Sometimes the criterion is functional similarity of jobs, as for example, with two jobs related to food. Supervisory authority is another criterion. Educational level another. One whole collection of jobs was conceived of as a college graduate series. Another rationale . . . was that both jobs were housed in the same physical facility, such as in a hospital.
>
> Under this system, the latitude for imagination and creative classification is limited by no regular, identifiable criteria of any kind. The Laundry Washman is not classified with the Laundry Manager, but instead is classified with the Hospital Attendant I. The Hospital Supply Tech I is also related to the Hospital Attendant I, but the Hospital Supply Tech III is related to the Licensed Practical Nurse, and the Hospital Supply Tech IV is classified in a third group, the Dietician. . . . the Accountant III is not classified with the Accountant I and II because, although they are functionally similar, there are other "criteria."[20]

Counsel Barnes asked Hocking how he resolved differences of opinion among the classifiers on classifying a job. He replied that he adopted the classification with which he was "most comfortable."

". . . At any given time or [for] any given relationship an outside observer would be completely unable to tell, would he not, which of those several criteria might be possible for any single one of these relationships?" Barnes asked Hocking, during the trial.

"That's right," Hocking answered.

"And there is no reference point or no document or no guideline, no weighting which would tell us, nor any record which would tell us exactly what criteria was used, is that correct?" Barnes continued.

"That's correct," Hocking said.

Barnes, citing a tenth circuit decision, argued that the principle is firmly established "that subjectivity combined with discriminatory effect constitutes unlawful discrimination." And in this case the nurses had proven, he said, "the combination of discriminatory impact and vague and subjective standards."

Furthermore, the nurses provided statistical evidence of the discriminatory results—the disparate impact—of the city's classification procedures. Professor George Bardwell worked on the statistical analysis. Professor Richard Beatty, an expert in the field of compensation studies, did a job evaluation study of the 800 city positions.

The statistical and job worth studies showed that salaries tracked maleness. "Starting salary is significantly correlated to the percent of males in the job class; that is, starting salary increases as the percent of males in a job class increases," the plaintiffs asserted. "At every corresponding level of job worth, 100 percent male classes are paid significantly higher starting salaries than 100 percent female classes." The studies showed that for nursing classes

the average starting salary . . . is less than the average starting salary for all 100 percent male classes, although average job worth for nurses is greater than the average job worth of 100 percent male classes in four of five traditional job worth factors. In addition, average educational and licensure requirements are greater for nurses. . . . Nurses within the same general range of job worth as 100 percent male classes had a salary deficiency ranging from 43.9 percent to 79.6 percent.[21]

The plaintiffs' brief cited the experience of individual nurses, such as that of Mary Lemons, the director of nursing services, from whom the case took its name. Plaintiff Lemons, their brief said, is "an administrator who does not deliver direct patient care and who is a supervisor of over 400 persons, is Masters-trained and has comparable administrative responsibilities to the Hospital Administration Officer, who is also Masters-trained." Professor Beatty's compensation team rated the director's job, "using customary standards of job worth analysis," at 855 points. They rated the job of hospital administration officer at 805 points. This job, held by a male, pays a starting salary $144 a month higher than that of the director of nursing services. The female director's job is not classified with the hospital administrator's job, or other administrative jobs with similar requirements, but is grouped with the female key class graduate nurse I.

Similarly, the job held by plaintiff Ann Jumper, public health nurse IV, classified by the city as a "professional, Level 2 Supervisor job," requiring a master's degree, was not grouped for pay purposes with other professional, master's degree, level 2 supervisor's jobs. It was put into the graduate nurse I key class. As a result, a male level 2 supervisor, like the city planner IV, drew $109 a month more in starting salary, although the job's worth was rated at 545 points compared to the public health nurse's 710 points.

The plaintiffs' evidence showed the same sort of inequity for classes throughout the graduate nurse I key class cluster. The best-known comparison, which became identified with the case, was between the monthly entry level salary for graduate nurse I, $929, and the starting salary for city tree trimmers, $1,040. Other frequently cited male starting salaries for city workers were $994 for a parking meter repairman, $1,017 for a tire serviceman, $1,088 for a painter, and $1,245 for a sign painter.[22]

The nurses also complained that nurses, and several other female classes, suffered from a compressed salary range. The key class graduate nurse I had, in practice, a nine-step salary range, while most male jobs had an eleven-step range. The graduate nurse I salaries began at step 3 for the entry-level hiring rate, rather than at step 1, and ran to step 11. The Career Services Board had to vote each year to use this step 3 "Board-Approved Hiring Rate [BAHR]." Although the practice continued over a period of time, the board did not change step 3 to step 1. This BAHR policy effectively cut out the top two salary grades for graduate nurse I, which affected all the jobs tied to the key class. The nurses saw this as discriminatory.

The plaintiffs'-appellants' Table of Contents for their tenth circuit appeals court brief summarizes the nurses' case:

A. There was Overwhelming Evidence that the City Organizes its Pay System on the Basis of Sex

B. There was Overwhelming Evidence that the City Uses Vague and Subjective Standards which Disadvantage Nurses Compared to Males

C. There was Uncontradicted Evidence that the City Picks up and Affirmatively Reproduces Patterns of Historic Discrimination

D. There was Evidence that Nurses are Denied Promotional Opportunities Allowed Male Classes.

The City's Defense

In its defense against the nurses' claims the city argued before the appeals court that the nurses had failed to prove a prima facie case of discrimination under either Title VII or the Fourteenth Amendment to the Constitution. The defendants also argued that the nurses had failed to prove any Title VII violation under the Griggs theory of disparate impact. They supported the first claim by contending that the Bennett Amendment to the Civil Rights Act of 1964 limited sex-based wage discrimination claims to Equal Pay Act claims, that is, to equal pay for equal work cases.

"Counsel for the nurses [in the district court trial] stipulated that the nurses were not making any claims under the Equal Pay Act for any pay differences based on jobs substantially equal to nursing classifications," the defendants said. The argument that women not working in jobs "substantially similar" to men's were not protected against sex-based wage discrimination by Title VII had been made successfully prior to *Lemons,* most notably in a 1977 eighth circuit court of appeals case, *Christensen* v. *State of Iowa.* It continued to be a stock argument of employers until it was thrown out in the 1981 post-*Lemons* Supreme Court decision *Gunther* v. *the County of Washington* and the almost simultaneous Supreme Court refusal of review in *IUE* v. *Westinghouse Corporation.*

The city further argued that the nurses had "clearly failed to prove any intentional discriminatory treatment of nurses by the City." But the nurses had not claimed that the city intentionally discriminated.

"It was not a 'let's go out and discriminate against the women' case," Craig Barnes told me. "There is a great deal of discrimination in it but it is all unappreciated by those who are doing it. The fact that 85 percent of the women are lumped with women was unknown to them. They just thought all women were alike. If you've got a women's group then throw another women's group in, and that seems right. Even women did it. All the classifiers are not men. It's just the way we think."

The city also denied that its job classification and pay system had a disparate impact on the nurses or resulted in disparate treatment of them. The city's brief said that the system was begun in 1954 when a city charter amendment was adopted requiring the city council to enact a classification and pay plan based on the duties of the jobs.

"Pay rates," the amendment said, "shall be equal to prevailing rates and shall provide like pay for like work." The amendment set up the Career Service Authority to run the plan. The plan's purpose, like that of other governmental units' pay plans, was to get rid of the spoils system—a once common political patronage practice of letting the party in power control the hiring and pay for government jobs.

The city said that the use of annual community wage surveys to determine prevailing market rates for jobs was an objective way of tying city workers' wages to the market as required by the charter. The city also said that paying market wages was necessary to meet competition, although it was not clear to the nurses how that argument justified paying them low wages.

"In the key class system only the key classes had their pay rate determined directly from the community pay surveys," the city's brief stressed. "The majority of the classes are not key classes and are assigned a pay rate on the basis of their direct or indirect relationship to one or more of the key classes. . . . Non-key classes must be related to key classes in order that their pay may be determined consistent with the Charter Amendment requiring *like pay for like work.*" (Italics added.)

But the nurses saw the way in which the city related nonkey classes to key classes as crucial and found it discriminatory in effect, if not in intent. This occurred, they said, primarily because the evidence indicated that the city used sex as a standard for organizing women's job classes. Furthermore, they argued, the city used subjective standards for setting up classes, standards that varied from class to class in an unpredictable way.

The city, however, viewed their use of the "whole job or position classification" system to be objective, nondiscriminatory, and thoroughly professional. The system was set up and operated, they said, "in absolute good faith." They said that the sex of job holders was not a consideration in organizing key class job clusters.

Maxine Kurtz explained to me that the city used detailed job specifications that, on a complex job, might run to three single-spaced pages of job description. Considering the "whole job," she said, enabled the classifier to look at the interrelationship of these factors for each job and then to link the jobs in a structure. Some factors, like number of people supervised or skill or education required, might be more important in one job than in another. But in relating jobs the classifier would be concerned with the overall combination of the different factors considered. The outcome of this method would, she felt, be more informed than that of the point factor systems.

Certainly, as Barnes pointed out, it was harder to understand and challenge because the criteria and their weighting were not obvious and they changed for each case. Kurtz implied that this flexibility was an advantage of the system. Barnes suggested that it was a way of justifying doing "whatever you felt most comfortable with." Professor Beatty termed the classification decisions "ambiguous and inconsistent." When I mentioned Kurtz's view that using a "statistical" job evaluation system that assigned points to each job was an invitation for suits, he commented that yes, ambiguity was a way of hiding the evidence.

"But they'll get hung with it," Beatty said. "It takes longer to find them out. And you have to do more work as a plaintiff. But eventually they will."

"Now the notions that were raised by the nurses that you compare jobs on the basis of education and experience required," Kurtz told me, "that is not the basis of our comparisons. Education and experience are considerations derived from duties and responsibilities, not determinants of the value of a job. Our experience," she continued, "was to discover that using education and experience to set minimum qualifications was credentialism carried to the ultimate. . . . We have alternate ways for people to get into the system. But if you start comparing jobs on the basis of education you'd wipe out all this affirmative action which has been so successful." Neither she nor the city's brief, however, addressed the nurses' contention that education appeared to be an organizing principle for predominantly male jobs.

To back up their view of the rightness of their methods, the city called in an expert witness, Carl Lutz, who testified that the whole job classification system was widely used. He said that the city's pay program "followed the standards of the profession." And, he testified, the Career Service's pay survey is a "highly respected survey." Finally, he noted that Arnold McDermott, who set up the system, received an award from the International Personnel Management Association for developing the Denver system.

The Courts Decide

"As far as we knew," Craig Barnes told me, "and we had someone do a computer review, Judge Winner had never decided a case in favor of plaintiffs in a civil rights case in all the years he'd been on the bench. So we knew that we were in for a lot of trouble as soon as we got Judge Winner.

"The judge said it was the best tried case he'd ever seen, on our side," Barnes said. "He repeated that remark voluntarily to a number of people. So we tried a good case. But the women actually ran into the bias in the system that they were trying to combat. At one point in the trial he quoted the Declaration of Independence to us—'All men are created equal.' The preference for men, that's what it says—as if to say that this was not a problem he could solve or really wanted to solve."

"Dr. Barbara Bergmann, professor of economics at the University of Maryland, testified for us at the trial," one of the nurses told me. "Judge Winner asked her, 'Do you want me to call you Mrs.?' And throughout the trial the judge and the defendants' lawyers referred to the male experts as 'Dr.' and to Dr. Bergmann as 'Mrs.' "

"At one point," Ann Jumper said, "Dr. Bergmann started to respond to a question with more than a yes or no, and the judge leaned over his bench and screamed at her, 'Hey, lady. Just answer the question.' It was embarrassing."

"Then he told this anecdote about how he always addresses our congressional representative, Patricia Schroeder, as Mrs. James Schroeder," Sharon Shumway said. "He gave that example in court."

"There were so many sexist remarks in that trial," Ruth Ryan said.

"You have to picture this kind of impressive court room and Judge Winner with his back to the room, running an adding machine back there during the proceedings," Marilyn Shahan explained, "sitting facing the wall, away from the attorneys, away from the witnesses, away from the audience."

"What was he adding up?" I asked.

"Who knows?" Marilyn answered. "Maybe his grocery bills."

"Salaries of basketball players and ice skaters," Ann Jumper said. "He gave examples of those."

"He was kind to us the first day," Sharon said. "He seemed interested. And then it appeared he had already decided."

"It was all downhill after his 'Hey, lady' remark," Charlene Lark added. "That remark depressed everybody."

"There was probably more discrimination in the courts than in the work setting," Sharon said.

"I think we were all appalled," Ruth Ryan commented. "We thought that the court was the last answer. Well, it was only the beginning."

"He's a very eccentric, shoot-from-the-hip judge," Craig Barnes said, "given to flamboyant statements and often vitriolic in his attacks on lawyers from the bench. And he's a mercurial judge. When, early on in the case he was going our way, he was 100 percent our way. Nothing the city could do was satisfactory. He threatened to throw the city's Hay Associates witness in jail. It was incredible.

"Then, halfway through the trial," Barnes said, "one of our witnesses began to lay out the comparable worth analysis. As soon as he saw the full implication of that—that a federal judge might be involved in comparable worth, and that he might have to be that judge—he did an instantaneous flip-flop. And from that moment on there was nothing we could do. And though he never failed to treat me with respect, for which I was grateful," Barnes added, "he went after my associate and just tore him apart in front of a packed courtroom. It was most distressing for everybody there."

"Could you tell me why he didn't give a written opinion?" I asked Craig Barnes. "It was an oral opinion which was transcribed from the court reporter's notes, wasn't it? Is that usual?"

"It is not usual," Barnes answered. "Although for this judge it is not unusual. It is not surprising that, at the end of the trial, he would say,

'OK, I'm ready to rule.' But the nurses were very disappointed after the hours and hours of time they had spent in preparation. It was an affirmation to them that the discrimination against which they fought wasn't limited to the Career Service Board or the hospital, but that they had run into it again at the bench."

"It's been a very interesting case," Judge Winner said at the beginning of his oral opinion.

> It's been a very well prepared case, it's been a very well presented case. Counsel seem more than happy to wind up their part of the case here today. . . . I can decide the case today, too. If they can argue it, I can decide it. . . .
>
> The entire theory of the plaintiffs' case is that the defendant does not discriminate among its own employees, but rather that there is occupational discrimination which has come down through the centuries and that Congress intended that the Courts should take over the restructuring of the economy of the United States of America. Plaintiffs say, and I don't quarrel with this . . . that their skills are such that in a truly egalitarian society, they would receive more money.

He then said that he had looked up "egalitarianism" and found it defined as "a belief that all *men* are equal in intrinsic worth . . ."

"I mention that simply to emphasize what we are confronted with here today is history," he said. ". . . a history which I have no hesitancy at all in finding has discriminated unfairly and improperly against women. But," he said, stressing a point that he made throughout his opinion, "Congress did not, in my judgment decide that we were going to roll aside all history and that the Federal Courts should take over the job of leveling out centuries of discrimination."

> The plaintiffs here say they want their pay to be compared with other occupations. Of course they do. If that were done, it would give them more pay. But I can find nothing in the law that requires that. It would be nice for the plaintiffs. It would be completely disruptive of our way of life, and we've got enough disruptions now. . . .
>
> I think that they have established that, by and large, male-dominated occupations probably pay more for comparable work than is paid in the occupations dominated by females. . . . [But I] cannot conceive of how a system would work where a group of employees' pay was to be determined by comparison with the other jobs available in that employer's economic structure.[23]

This was a point made by the employers' association, the Equal Employment Advisory Council, in their friend of the court brief in the *Lemons* case. Employers' groups and other opponents of pay equity commonly stress the impossibility of making pay comparisons between jobs.

"Both the judge and the employer association were unaware, or chose to ignore, the purposes of position classification in governments," Professor Lois Friss explained. The purposes are twofold, she said; first, to see that variations in pay to different employees are proportionate to the differences in responsibility, difficulty, and skill and training requirements of the work done, and second, "that individual positions will be so grouped and identified by classes and grades that the resulting position classification system can be used in all phases of personnel administration. Indeed," she concluded, "*public personnel systems are designed to compare apples and oranges, and the methodology exists to do so.*"[24]

Judge Winner argued that Congress did not interpret either the Fourteenth Amendment or Title VII as requiring such comparisons. He agreed with the courts that had ruled that the Bennett Amendment to Title VII limited claims of sex-based wage discrimination to Equal Pay Act claims of unequal pay for equal work.

"I expressly find that the plaintiffs failed to prove any pay differential based on sex for the performance of substantially equal work," Judge Winner said. He recognized that they had not tried to make a claim of discrimination under the Equal Pay Act. But he saw no grounds for any other type of claim under Title VII or the Fourteenth Amendment. He found no prima facie violation of Title VII when women and men receive different pay for different work of comparable value to the employer.

Frequently in his *Lemons* opinion Judge Winner indulged in an extravagant distortion of Title VII plaintiffs' pay equity claims, a distortion common to pay equity opponents, which assumes that the discrimination claims are economywide and not limited to an employer and his or her employees, as the law clearly says. "I am unable to believe that the Congress of the United States has mandated that the job of every person in the United States be evaluated skill-wise, productive-wise and otherwise to the job of every other person," he said, "and that we have a completely new pay scale set up by some group of experts or pseudo experts."

The judge found that the city had not excluded any males from nursing because of their sex. And he found that the city had not excluded females from any other occupation on the grounds of sex.

He found that the city's classification system "was set up in good faith" and that structuring it as the plaintiffs "seek to structure it would be unrealistic." He thought that the city had shown its good faith effort by paying prevailing wages as the city charter required. "This country got where it got—I don't know whether that's good or bad—but it got here by meeting competition," he said.

"Congress cannot, and never has been able," Judge Winner asserted, "to repeal the law of supply and demand. And the situation, unfortunate that it may be," he said, either ignoring or ignorant of the prevailing shortage of nurses, "is that the supply of nurses is very large as compared to the demand, and it puts the nurses in a somewhat disadvantageous negotiating position. But," he said, "the discrimination, as I see it, is not a discrimination in the nursing profession against females.

"Plaintiffs' very statistical evidence," he claimed, standing the sex segregation argument on its head, "demonstrates that if there is discrimination within the nursing profession, it is in favor of females because females outnumber males by a tremendous percentage."

"I have said," he held, "and I repeat, historically there has been discrimination against females. I condemn it. It's wrong. But Congress has not seen fit to bring it all down to date. . . . The Courts aren't qualified to do it, the Courts ought to stay out of it. And if history is that bad, the plaintiffs should direct their appeals to the Legislature, the Congress. . . .

"I don't think plaintiffs have proven any grounds for relief in this case," he concluded, "and accordingly, the Clerk shall prepare a judgment denying plaintiffs relief."

The nurses appealed Judge Winner's district court decision to the tenth circuit court of appeals. The three circuit court justices affirmed the district court decision largely on the grounds "that the plaintiffs are seeking relief far beyond that contemplated by Congress or the Constitution." They described the suit as "based on the proposition that nurses are underpaid in city positions, and in the community, in comparison with other and different jobs which they assert are of equal worth to the employer."[25]

They held that the Bennett Amendment limited Title VII claims of sex-based wage discrimination to Equal Pay Act claims of unequal pay for equal work. They saw a similarity between this case and *Christensen* v. *State of Iowa*. In *Christensen* women clerical employees at the University of Northern Iowa compared their pay with that of male employees working in the university's physical plant. Hay Associates had graded the jobs, using a point factor system. Despite the fact that the clerical employees and the plant workers had similar point ratings, the university paid the men more because they were paid more in the local labor market.

The eighth circuit court ruled that the purpose of Title VII was to provide equal employment *opportunities*. They said that they found "nothing in the text and history of Title VII suggesting that Congress intended to abrogate the law of supply and demand. . . . We do not interpret Title VII as requiring an employer to ignore the market in setting wage rates for genuinely different work classifications."[26]

The tenth circuit court found that the city's classification and pay system provided equal pay for equal work. It found that the city provided equal opportunities for women workers. "The parity the plaintiffs seek," the judges concluded, "is not a remedy which the courts can now provide."[27]

The nurses and their counsel, Craig Barnes, decided to petition the Supreme Court for review of the circuit court *Lemons* decision. They reported strenuous opposition to this move from well-intentioned pay equity supporters, among them the American Nurses Association and EEOC Chair Eleanor Holmes Norton.

"They thought it was too tough a case for us to win as a comparable worth case," Craig Barnes said. "They thought that you've got to go into court with a very select strategy and pick your cases carefully. *Gunther* was a simpler case. It didn't require this massive leap that analysis of the evaluation of a whole city system did.

"I argued to Eleanor Holmes Norton that actually this was *not* a comparable worth case," Barnes said. "That it was a disparate impact case. That the Bennett Amendment problem was serious. And that we needed to make our maximum effort. I don't know if I was right about that but as it turned out it didn't matter."

"Everybody pressured us not to go," the nurses told me, "including a phone call from Eleanor Holmes Norton where all of us got on the line. But you know, we felt that so many nurses had helped to support this. And we really were on a shoestring. And we had been at it so long. Not to take the last step, even though it was very doubtful anything would happen—it would have been awful."

In his petition for review to the Supreme Court, Craig Barnes argued once again that this was a *Griggs* v. *Duke Power* disparate impact case. It was, he said, a classification case brought under section 703(a)(2) of Title VII of the Civil Rights Act. The city of Denver's classification practices appear facially neutral, the first test, according to Barnes, of "a *Griggs*-type disparate impact case." These practices tend "to expand and ramify a discriminatory history," the second characteristic of a *Griggs*-type case. In *Griggs,* Barnes pointed out, it was a question of applicant testing procedures that perpetuated a history of race discrimination and low wages. In *Lemons,* he argued, "there is a history of sex discrimination and low wages which is perpetuated by the subjective classification system of the Career Service Authority."

Both the district court and the tenth circuit had erred in holding that the nurses' claim was an Equal Pay Act claim, he said, inasmuch as "nothing in the Equal Pay Act addresses discrimination in classification which is the grievance of the nurses in the present case. . . . The Bennett Amendment is not relevant to the claims of this case. . . ." The nurses made the comparisons between the worth of comparable jobs to show the discriminatory *effects* of the city's sex-segregated classification and pay structure. But their claim was against the sex-stereotyping, segregation, and classification procedures.

The nurses' petition for certiorari went to the Supreme Court in 1980. The Court turned it down, leaving the decisions of the appeals and district courts standing. This was a year before the Supreme Court's landmark decision in *Gunther* v. *County of Washington* that held, by a five-to-four vote, that Title VII sex-based wage discrimination claims were not restricted to Equal Pay Act claims by the Bennett Amendment.

What could be learned by comparable worth advocates from the *Lemons* case? The nurses had worked hard on it for over eight years. Were they too early? Were they unlucky in the judge lottery? Was it the wrong case for the sex-based wage discrimination issue? Could they have presented it in some better, more convincing way?

It may well have been a little of all of these. The law on disparate impact in sex-based wage discrimination claims is still developing, seven years later. In retrospect, no matter how good the case, it was probably too much to expect to win then, before those judges, on that issue alone, without any showing of intent to discriminate.

As the next chapters relate, District Court Judge Tanner, in his 1983 *AFSCME* v. *State of Washington* decision, was the first judge to recognize disparate impact as grounds for finding sex-based wage discrimination. The disparate impact arose from the state's use of prevailing wages for its benchmark or key classes—wages that perpetuated historic discrimination against women workers. This is an argument the nurses made in *Lemons*.

Judge Tanner, however, also found intent to discriminate. Before *Washington State* it seemed to be necessary to prove intent. Depending on the courts' rulings in *Washington State* on appeal, this may continue to be true.

In any event, as Winn Newman, lawyer for the plaintiffs in *Washington State* has pointed out, judges need some support for their decisions. Even the most adventurous will not get too far ahead of the temper of their times. Both Judge Winner and the appeals court judges were described as conservative and unlikely to break new judicial ground.

"It was a huge case," Craig Barnes said. "I felt, looking back at it, that we had so much material in front of Judge Winner, and then so much material in front of the court of appeals that somehow they were overwhelmed. Tactically maybe we should have tried to slim the case down. Judge Winner said it was the best tried case he'd ever seen. But he didn't decide in our favor.

"The appeals court was a bit of an enigma," he said. "They had this 15 inches of trial record in front of them. They did not appear to go into it at all. And in our argument we sensed a kind of lack of interest. If they were lesser men you would say it was laziness—'this is a huge case and the easiest thing we can do with it is to just deny it.' "

"It was a class action suit," Sharon Shumway explained. "Some people said we would have done better if we had sued as eight individuals and not on behalf of the whole class, that because it was a class action they wouldn't decide the case for us because it had such far-reaching implications."

"What is the argument against class action?" I asked.

"Well, maybe that the judge wouldn't have felt like he was opening Pandora's box," Sharon answered. "And that as individuals he could see how the director, for example, had been discriminated against, or the staff person."

"Dick Beatty said he urged you just to have the nurses in administrative positions make the case rather than the whole group," I said. "He thought that would have made a much stronger case."

"It's interesting," Ann Jumper said. "It wasn't the union point of view of the beginning-level person taking on management. It was the management nurses taking on the rest of the system."

"On behalf of the staff nurses, too," Sharon added. "And the licensed practical nurses, and 'women who worked for the city and county.' "

"How many nurses were represented?" I asked.

"About 500 or 600 at Denver General Hospital and 300 at the visiting nurse service," Shady said.

"How many of them were staff nurses?" I asked.

"I would guess about two thirds of them, easily," Shady answered. "The rest were supervisory—administrative—head nurse or above."

"Were there any aftereffects of the suit on the nurses?" I asked. "On the city? Any effect on nurses' salaries? On union organization?"

"I think there were some things that happened to the eight individuals," the nurses said. "There were some administrative nurses—people in the lawsuit—who found that they couldn't function in their current job with the pressures and could not find another job in the same area. Mary Lemons, who had been the director of nursing for 14 years here, went to Lubbock, Texas. Margaret Lewis, the director of the visiting nurse service, retired. Dolora Cotter left Denver and went to work in Grand Junction. Lois Cady left—she would have to say why. Shady experienced a demotion which was supposedly tied to budget issues, not just once but twice. The pressures were terrific afterward," they agreed.

"Another thing that happened at our agency," one of the nurses said, "was that the Career Service description for the director of nursing was changed. Always before it had required a master's degree. And suddenly it didn't. We heard that the Career Services thought that the degree nurses were part of the problem here. That if they hadn't had so many educated nurses they wouldn't have had the trouble. We were worried that we might not have a nurse as director, because of the way the job description was rewritten. It could have been anybody, even a business major."

"As for salaries," Sharon said, "the beginning level salary is now equivalent to the general administrative series salaries. I think that we *do* make more than tree trimmers now. So salaries *have* improved overall though they didn't reclassify us."

"There was a threatened strike in some of the private Denver hospitals, right after our suit ended," Sharon said. "Some of the same community nurses at the staff level who had been very supportive of us were involved."

"I don't think they wanted to let the issue die," Charlene commented.

"Management-level nurses couldn't be involved in the unionization activities and the strike," Shady added.

"The year after the trial the voluntary hospitals in the area increased the pay of nurses mid-year and again at the end of the year," Maxine Kurtz told me. "That year the nurses had a 17 percent increase. A shortage of nurses developed here. And there was a private sector job action against the voluntary hospitals.

"The suit didn't affect the city," Kurtz asserted. "When we won the case we won the case. That was the end of that. It was natural economic forces that caused the increase in pay of the nurses, not the effect of the lawsuit. We weren't ordered to do anything different than we'd been doing right along. And we didn't. It's fatal to be intimidated by lawsuits," she added. "Because that just invites more and more lawsuits. If you've got no reason to change, don't change."

Department of Labor statistics for major metropolitan areas show that the average annual earnings of full-time general duty nurses increased 13.8 percent in the Denver/Boulder area between 1978 and 1981. Only Kansas City—home of the American Nurses' Association—had as high an increase. The Denver/Boulder average annual salaries went from $13,603 to $20,030. This raised Denver/Boulder from sixteenth place out of the 23 metropolitan areas in 1978 to seventh place in 1981.

"I think it's an issue that's going to be with us for a while," Maxine Kurtz said, when I asked her opinion on the future of pay equity. "AFSCME said it was going to push all over the country with lawsuits and legislative efforts, which it is doing. And the consultants will be their allies on it. I agree with the analyst who said that he thinks that the Supreme Court has gone as far as it's going to in finding intentional discrimination.

"So if the jurisdictions are obliging enough to go out and *prove* they are discriminating, the courts won't argue with their conclusion. And I expect the naïveté to continue for a while longer," she said. "At the end of which time this fad of quantitative job analysis will run its course and probably not be instituted again.

"I'm not sure how much is going to be left by the time we get through with it," she said. "But in any event, I think anybody who's undertaking one of these quantitative systems has set themselves up for a *Washington State* or *Gunther*-type lawsuit. And I think those of us that have the more sophisticated systems are going to be all right."

"Craig Barnes would never have gotten a favorable ruling from Judge Winner, no matter what," Dick Beatty said, when I asked him for his views on pay equity's future. "That was a foregone conclusion. The only hope was to get stuff in the record for the appeal. But the appeal didn't go well either. There was probably too much in the record.

"I think they tried to do too much with this case," he said. "Half a loaf is better than none. You're not going to have swooping change with these things. Incremental change is the best women's strategy. And the cases are still hard.

"The nurses have the best argument," he continued. "There are more identifiable, comparable things about their job. Clearly you can make arguments about how risky it is to be a nurse. And how much you have to know to be a nurse. Given the data from the city, for example, it's pretty hard to justify paying a zookeeper, or an oiler, or many of those other jobs which have severely lower skill requirements, more than a nurse. I feel even more strongly that the nursing managers are critically underpaid."

"What do you think the outlook for the future is for nurses here and elsewhere?" I asked the nurses.

"I wish we had waited about five years before we started the suit and then we might have won," Sharon Shumway said. "We were ahead of our time."

"We would win it today," Ann Jumper said. "And we would have a computer today and we wouldn't do that by hand again. And we would know what a mean and a median and a mode were. And we would know it would cost more money."

"We would win today," Ruth Ryan agreed. "We would be more politically savvy. We wouldn't trust the courts. We would do more politicking on the side. That's an error we made all along. We didn't go down and politick enough people."

"Which people?" I asked. "You mean city hall?"

"City hall. Representatives. The council," Ruth said.

"The nurses back then were not that politically astute," Charlene agreed.

"I think we thought, too," Ruth said, "that the public loves a nurse so much—you're always there, soothing the brow—that it just couldn't go against you."

"Some of us wondered how we could have drawn this judge, of all the federal judges, that had such a close relationship with the city and a terrible civil rights record," Sharon said. "We thought the courts were fair and found out they were not."

Notes

1. *Mary Lemons et al.* v. *the City and County of Denver et al.,* U.S. District Court, District of Colorado, No. 76-W-1156, April 17, 1978, as corrected April 28, 1978, FEP Cases, pp. 906–914.

2. Testimony of Eunice Cole, *Joint Hearings,* Committee on Post Office and Civil Service, House of Representatives, 97th Cong. 2d Sess., 1982, Part I, pp. 273–74.

3. Helen Remick, "The Comparable Worth Controversy," *IPMA Public Personnel Management Journal* 10 (December 1981): 7.

4. U.S. Dept. of Health and Human Services, *Report to the President and Congress on the Status of Health Personnel in the United States, Nursing* (May 1984): C-3.

5. Eunice Cole, *Joint Hearings,* Part I, pp. 273, 280.

6. Patricia Cayo Sexton, *The New Nightingales* (New York: Enquiry Press, 1982).

7. Ibid., p. 23.

8. U.S. Equal Employment Opportunity Commission, *Hearings on Job Segregation and Wage Discrimination* (April 28–30, 1980): p. 519.

9. Sexton, *The New Nightingales,* p. 23.

10. N.U.R.S.E. Inc., *A Case for Cooking,* Preface. This is a cookbook published by the nurses to raise money for their suit.

11. Transcript of tape from first session, 1980.

12. Plaintiffs' Proposed Findings of Fact and Conclusions of Law, *AFSCME et al.* v. *State of Washington et al.,* October 14, 1983, pp. 52–53. For a discussion of the case see Chapters 8 and 9.

13. Plaintiffs'-Appellants' Brief, *Mary Lemons et al.* v. *the City and County of Denver et al.,* U.S. Court of Appeals, Tenth Circuit, No. 78-1499, April 21, 1980, p. 3.

14. Plaintiffs' Complaint, *Mary Lemons et al.* v. *the City and County of Denver et al.,* U.S. District Court, no. 76-1156, December 3, 1976, pp. 14–15.

15. Lois O'Brien Friss, "Work Force Policy Perspectives: Registered Nurses," *Journal of Health Politics, Policy and Law* 5 (1981): 699.

16. Lois Friss, Pay Inequity Hearings, State Department of Industrial Relations, February 25–27, 1981, p. 2.

17. Plaintiffs'-Appellants' Brief, pp. 38–39.

18. Plaintiffs'-Appellants' Brief, p. 40.

19. Ibid.

20. Ibid., p. 44.

21. Plaintiffs' complaint, p. 17.

22. Friss, "Work Force Policy Perspectives," p. 702.

23. *Mary Lemons et al.* v. *the City and County of Denver et al.,* U.S. District Court, District of Colorado, no. 76-W-1156, April 17, 1978, as corrected April 28, 1978, 17 FEP cases, pp. 906–14.

24. Friss, "Work Force Policy Perspectives," p. 704. Italics added.

25. *Mary Lemons et al.* v. *the City and County of Denver et al.*, U.S. Court of Appeals, Tenth Circuit, No. 78-1499, April 21, 1980.

26. *Christensen* v. *State of Iowa*, 563 F.2d 353, Eighth Circuit, 1977, at 356.

27. *Mary Lemons et al.* v. *the City and County of Denver et al.*, U.S. Court of Appeals, Tenth Circuit, No. 78-1499, April 21, 1980.

8

THE WIN IN WASHINGTON STATE:
"A Huge Victory for Women?"

"I feel very good about the outcome for this case on appeal," Peggy Holmes, a plaintiff in *AFSCME* v. *State of Washington,* told me. "I feel we can't help but win. If you were in the courtroom, and listened to the arguments, it just seemed so obvious that we would win.

"But more than that," she added, "I think we *have* won, whether we make it past this stage or not. I think it's a huge victory for women. It's given women a lot of hope that they didn't have before. And that's really important. It will make it easier for women to stand up and fight for what they need. Women out there are saying, 'Sure, it would be great to get the back pay and everything. But if they'd just start recognizing us for what we're worth *now, from now on,* that would be quite a victory.' "

Judge Tanner's district court decision ordering Washington State to correct sex-based wage discrimination immediately and levying back pay for aggrieved workers brought other employers and the Reagan administration to full attention. The *Wall Street Journal* reported that the Justice Department "is seriously considering challenging" the federal judge's order. "Despite the issue's political sensitivity," the paper wrote, "William Bradford Reynolds, assistant attorney general for civil rights, called the decision one of tremendous importance that could set a dangerous precedent." Reynolds explained that the department could file a friend of the court brief in the case or it could try to become an intervenor and get the right to appeal the case itself. "If this issue is properly understood," he told the *Journal,* "I think we'll have the full support of a large majority of the public."[1]

How It All Began

"Why Washington State?" I asked Helen Remick, director of the University of Washington's Office of Affirmative Action for Women. "Why was Washington the first state ever to do a pay equity study, starting with top-level management in 1973 and then for all the state's classified employees in 1974?"

"I've asked that question, too," she answered. "It's interesting. The management study was apparently done because the top managers in state government, who were exempt from the civil service system, felt their salaries were too low. And so in order to raise their salaries they wanted a job study done, not so much for internal alignment but they wanted to compare their jobs with the outside. So they negotiated with the governor and he hired Willis and Associates, a Seattle firm, to do the study of top management.

"That study," she continued, "while it did indeed make some changes in internal alignment, was used to point out how low the salaries were in state government in Washington. Which was true.

"The study was implemented by the legislature in 1976," she said. "And it did result in substantial salary increases. That Willis study, using point factor job evaluation methods and outside market comparisons, is still in place. It then spread to several other state agencies where larger parts of the state agency use it. And then Willis was hired as well to do several state colleges and several community colleges, again covering people exempt from civil service.

"In 1973–74 a management study was done on this University of Washington campus, though by a different firm, Hay Associates, from Chicago. That's still in place. Now on this campus," she explained, "the study was done in response to criticism that we had a big overall salary gap between men and women and between minorities and non-minorities. And the institution responded by saying, 'Well, we don't have a salary system, but we'll implement one and it will show you that there's no problem.'

"This was done," she said, "not calling it comparable worth but just calling it a salary study. The study showed that 39 percent of the women were making less than the minimum of the range that would be recommended for them. Some 20 percent of the minorities—and that includes men and women—and 19 percent of the males were also underpaid. So it resulted in substantial salary increases to many women workers. It's been in place since 1974. It was not called comparable worth until it occurred to me one day when I was working that, by God, this is the same thing!

"So in 1973 there were several forces at work," Helen Remick continued. "There was a state women's commission, and they were very instrumental in this area. And I can tell you who says he was the father of all this—Larry Goodman of the Washington Federation of State Employees. Larry says he started it."

By the time I talked to Larry Goodman I had learned a good deal more about the Washington State personnel systems. Dorothy Gerard, a top administrator for the Department of Higher Education Personnel (HEP), explained to me that there are two completely separate personnel systems in Washington State. The oldest is the Department of Personnel (DOP), which was set up in 1960 by the state's first civil service law in order to get away from the political patronage system. It covers about 35,000 "classified" employees. It does not include the state's higher education employees nor those of some smaller agencies like the state liquor board.

In 1969 the legislature set up a second civil service system for higher education, which covers some 15,000 classified employees of the institutions of higher education. Another 15,000 higher education employees— faculty and administrators—are exempt from civil service. They deal with the boards of trustees of their respective institutions.

In Washington, state employees cannot bargain collectively on compensation if a state board controls the terms of their employment. To get some uniformity in pay scales across different state agencies, the state employees' union supported the legislative requirement that the salary-setting system reflect not less than prevailing market rates. But when this setup went into effect for higher education personnel in the early 1970s, women employees and women's organizations, like the Washington State Women's Council, complained to the union that prevailing rates discriminated against many women workers.

"What are we going to do about this?" the women's council asked the Washington Federation of State Employees.

"Well, we'll go to the governor," replied Norm Schut, the director of the Washington Federation of State Employees, AFSCME-AFL-CIO. First, he talked with the governor's staff about what he termed "the very serious business of discrimination based on sex in the setting of salaries by the state's two personnel boards."[2] On their advice, he then wrote to Governor Evans detailing the union's concerns.

> The point of issue is not that the Personnel Boards have ignored wages paid for comparable work in the private sector, but rather that the Boards have perpetuated the discrimination against women in salary setting that permeates through the private sector and other governmental units.
>
> Our two state civil service laws require the Boards to survey wages paid for comparable work in private industry and in other governmental units and then come up with a salary schedule for state employees that reflects not less than, and I repeat not less than, prevailing rates on the outside. The not less than prevailing rate provision of the law, in our view, simply requires that that be a minimum or a floor.

He said that the state had made "considerable progress" in improving women workers' access to jobs. "The major issue, however," he declared, "is still unresolved, namely blatant discrimination in the salary setting process against women who work." He attributed the problem not solely to state actions but also to "an historical situation."

> I strongly feel, however, that the state has a unique opportunity to turn this thing around and set policy, at least as it affects state employment, which will eliminate and prohibit the discrimination in salary setting which adversely affects the incumbents of those positions substantially occupied by women.
> Because of the forthright stand you have consistently taken against all forms of discrimination, I am asking that you take the leadership in immediately dealing with this problem by requesting both the Higher Education Personnel Board and the State Personnel Board to address themselves to this issue and to act on proposals that will rectify this situation . . . as soon as possible.[3]

A few days later, Washington's Republican governor, Dan Evans, wrote to the heads of the two personnel boards asking them to "immediately and jointly initiate a thorough study of the Higher Education and State Personnel pay plans to identify those job classifications predominately and traditionally held by women where salaries fall below job classifications typically filled by men having a comparable level of skill requirements and job responsibilities."

"It is the position of this administration that the state take the lead, by enforcement and example, in eliminating all forms of discrimination," he wrote. "If the state's salary schedules reflect a bias in wages paid to women compared to those of men, then we must move to reverse this inequity." The governor asked that the study be done quickly so that he could present it to the legislature in early 1974.

The two directors of personnel, Douglas E. Sayan, HEP Board, and Leonard A. Nord, DOP, sent the governor a report on the requested study in January 1974. They pointed out that because of time pressure and the lack of precedent for this type of analysis, their study was "of an introductory nature."

"Although the findings are limited to and by the scope of the instant study, we are confident," they asserted, "that a further, more technically valid study would support the conclusions contained herein." They indicated their interest in "a more thorough analysis of wage and salary setting in state employment."[4]

How did they do their study and what did it show? Both agencies studied entry- or lower-level job classes that were two-thirds or more male or female. The Department of Personnel selected classes "which are heavily populated, and/or directly related to a series of classes representing a relatively high proportion of the workforce. Further, while the classes are not directly comparable in duties or nature of work, they do have measurable job elements which allow for comparisons that can be illustrated."[5] The Higher Education Personnel Board selected 22 job classes, 11 predominately female and 11 predominately male. "The job series represented by these classes includes about 6,000 employees," the report said, "nearly one-half of the higher education system employees."[6]

Both agencies used a point factor rating system—the same system used by Norman Willis in evaluating the state's top management jobs, with the addition of one factor, working conditions. They rated the jobs on five factors—working conditions, complexity of work, physical effort, responsibility, and education and/or experience. They selected job class raters from their respective agencies "who represented a wide range of job evaluation experience, knowledge and skills."

The study graphs the relationship between the points allotted to each job category and the salaries of those jobs, for the male jobs and the female jobs studied in each agency. The analysts fitted a regression line to these points for the predominately male jobs and another line for the predominately female jobs. "The difference between these regression lines," the Department of Personnel reported, "shows that predominately male classes are paid a little over $100 per month more than predominately female classes for jobs of comparable value as rated by the method used."

The Higher Education Personnel Board study found that "at a point value of 10.0, salaries for classes held by men tend to average $50 per month higher than salaries for classes held by women (9.06 percent higher). At a point value of 18.0, predominately male class salaries tend to average $78 per month higher than predominately female class salaries (9.29 percent higher)."

The joint report of the two agencies concluded that:

1. There are clear indications of pay differences between classes predominately held by men and those predominately held by women within the state systems.
2. Such differences are not due solely to job "worth."
3. Further study is necessary to accurately determine the amount of salary difference and all classes to which a "correction" would apply.
4. It has been determined that any full "correction" or adjustment cannot be confined to the entrance level.

The report estimated that the cost of full implementation of rectifying sex-based pay inequities could range between $27 million and $34 million for the rest of the two-year legislative salary-setting period.

"In our discussions with the governor and others about the issue," Larry Goodman, director of Personnel Board activities for the Washington Federation of State Employees, told me, "we said we weren't talking about equal pay for equal work. We were talking about equal pay for comparable worth. We coined the term 'comparable worth.' " The 1973 study that came out of these discussions was the first comparable worth study in the country—the first investigation of discrimination in pay by an employer between male and female jobs with similar job worth, as measured by the jobs' requirements for knowledge, skill, responsibility, and working conditions.

"What was interesting," Goodman said, "was that we really weren't doing anything revolutionary from the standpoint of internal pay alignments.

> The governor, because he was having a difficult time recruiting and keeping his very highest level of management—directors of agencies, major division heads—had previously brought in a consultant who used a nationally accepted system of evaluating jobs in four components, converting these point factors to dollars and then making an analysis of the relationship of the values of these jobs. Now, ironically, these jobs were almost exclusively white, almost exclusively male, and very high paying.
>
> What we suggested to him was that the same system that he had adopted to set wage scales for these top management jobs could also be used to analyze the relative value of other state employees—a nurse vs. a secretary vs. a truck driver, and so on. And so, because we had some confidence in this consultant, Willis, and because the system was acceptable inasmuch as Willis had worked for large industries like Boeing, Weyerhauser, the Bell system, he brought Willis in after the initial report of the personnel departments and had Willis do the first study, actually labeled a comparable worth study. In fact, it's called Comparable Worth Study on the title page. This was in 1974. That's when they started accepting our terminology.

This 1974 "landmark study," as Governor Evans called it, was done by the two state personnel departments under the direction of Norman D. Willis and Associates. "The purpose of the study," according to the Willis report, "was to examine and identify salary differences that may pertain to job classes predominantly filled by men compared to job classes predominantly filled by women, based on job worth."

The study committee selected for evaluation 121 classes traditionally occupied by men or by women. Of these, 62 were female dominated, that is, 70 percent or more occupied by women, and 59 were male dominated, 70 percent or more occupied by men. An evaluation team determined the job worth of these classes, using the Willis point factor system of job evaluation. The consultants graphically determined female and male "salary practice" regression lines by relating the monthly salary for each job, on the Y axis, to the job's total job points, on the X axis. They compared these male and female salary practice lines for each personnel department separately and for both departments together.

"At all evaluation point levels, and considering both systems, women's salaries tend to be less than men's salaries," the Willis report said. The study found that, taking both systems together, women's pay ranged from 80 percent of men's pay for jobs evaluated at 100 points to 74 percent of men's pay for jobs evaluated at 450 points.

Carroll Boone, member of the advisory committee to the 1974 Washington State Comparable Worth Study and legal researcher for the plaintiffs in the Washington State case, wrote of the study:

> At a press conference on December 14 Governor Evans announced: "We have just concluded a study on comparable worth which could prove to be a landmark study not only for state government but for industry, other governments in the state of Washington and perhaps even a landmark study insofar as the United States is concerned. . . . We found . . . an average [salary] of about twenty percent less for women than for males doing equivalent jobs. . . . If . . . the case made here is valid in other areas and throughout the country . . . steps ought to be taken to rectify the imbalance which does exist."[7]

The governor's charge to the 1974 Willis study group asked them to provide "alternative suggestions to correct disparities that may be disclosed." This the Willis report did, laying out three "Alternative Courses of Action" to help correct the "significant differences, relative to job worth, [that] do exist within the two state salary systems."

"But," said Larry Goodman, "for two years our union saw nothing happen. Our executive board said, 'OK, they've done the study. It was their own study. They've verified the discrimination. But they're not doing anything about it.'

"Discrimination is our term," Goodman explained. "Willis never used the word. He used the term 'disparity that can only be attributable to sex.' Still does, as a matter of fact.

"So," Goodman went on, "I wrote a letter again to the two boards and to Dan Evans, saying, 'We're going into a legislative session. Nothing except studies and verification have taken place. We think the study ought to be expanded and include, this time, a plan for implementing comparable worth.'

"To his credit, Dan Evans did that," Goodman said. The state hired Willis to direct the update study and to help develop a plan for implementing it. The study broadened the original analysis by evaluating an additional 85 benchmark classes used by the two personnel systems in their salary setting systems. These classes included female-dominated male-dominated, and integrated job classifications, ignoring sex differences. The two departments said that they selected these classes "to cover the major occupational areas of the Compensation Plans thereby enabling the 'indexing' or salary alignment system to operate.

"Dan Evans put over $7 million in his budget for a very small, phased-in, first step, partial implementation," Larry Goodman said. But Evans was a lame duck governor. When the budget went to the 1977 legislature, Dixy Lee Ray was governor, and one of her first acts was to remove the $7 million for implementing comparable worth from her budget request. In doing this she claimed that ranking the worth of different jobs was a statistically unsound procedure.

"A group of us women went to talk to Ms. Ray when she was running for office," Peggy Holmes, at that time a secretary at Central Washington University and state secretary of the Washington Federation of State Employees, told me. "We went to talk to her and tell her how we felt about comparable worth. And she got on the bandwagon with us and said, 'Oh yes.' She knew because she was a woman and a professor at the University of Washington. She had come up through the ranks, herself, and had had trouble with pay. She understood exactly what we were talking about. She talked a real good line. And so a bunch of us women went out and worked for her to become governor. My big mistake. Immediately upon getting into office she called comparable worth 'apples and oranges and a can of worms'—her famous quote."

"Why did she turn around like that?" I asked Peggy Holmes.

"I don't know. She was very cantankerous as a governor. And she had her own interests she spent the money on. But in her campaign comparable worth was in her platform. And when she was running for office a second time she started putting out press releases that she was all for comparable worth. So the Federation let the press know it wasn't true. She got defeated by Spellman the second time."

"The real irony," Larry Goodman said, "is that in that same 1977 budget she had put in several million dollars to upgrade the pay of her new top management team that she brought in. And she used as the rationale the very same system and the very same statistical methods that were used in comparable worth—the point evaluation system. She used the point factors to justify these large salary increases. Yet she couldn't understand it for middle and low income people."

In his decision on the Washington State case, Judge Tanner emphasized that Governor Ray "took the appropriation out of the budget even though there was a surplus in the 1976-77 state budget that could have been used to pay plaintiffs their evaluated worth." He also pointed out that the State Personnel Board had adopted a resolution stating that ". . . the Board supports the correction of disparities identified by the [1976] study and that salaries will be based on prevailing rates except where such criteria do not adequately compensate the employee based on the concept of comparable worth."

In 1977 the legislature directed the two personnel departments to conduct a comparable worth salary survey biennially, along with their usual biennial survey of market rates for benchmark salary classes. The legislature asked for

a supplementary salary survey which indicates those cases where . . . prevailing rates do not provide similar salaries for positions that require or impose similar responsibilities, judgment, knowledge, skills, and working conditions. This supplementary salary schedule shall contain proposed salary adjustments necessary to eliminate any such dissimilarities in compensation.

Therefore, the legislature has had the information it neeeds to correct the wage inequities found by the personnel departments in the state's pay system. In the 1980 comparable worth survey, the departments evaluated an additional 78 job classes. In 1982 no new classes were added. But in 1984 the departments have been doing a much more extensive pay equity survey, partly in response to the state legislation on implementation and particularly to Judge Tanner's court order requiring this.

"We attempted," Larry Goodman told me, "in virtually every legislative session in this ten-year period, to get either the governor's office or the legislature itself to move toward a recognition of their own studies and a commitment to their law. But we didn't get it. Therefore, in 1981, after many years of frustration we, in conjunction with our international union, AFSCME, brought charges against the state.

"The first step," he explained, "was to file charges with the EEOC. They did absolutely nothing. When their time period ran out we had access to the federal courts. And we sued."

The legislature's response to the suit, after a year of pulling and hauling, was to pass an amendment to the Civil Service Act providing for the implementation of comparable worth by 1993.

"Two pieces of that are ironic," Larry Goodman said. "The first is that they never appropriated any money for the first biennium of the ten years. So that was suspicious. The other thing is that the legislation is such that under our constitution it really is not a commitment because one legislature cannot bind the expenditures of another legislature. The ten-year plan is a promise of this legislature with the hope that subsequent elected bodies might go along with it.

"However," he added, "in the operating budget during the waning days of the session, they appropriated $1.5 million. . . . So those people who are 20 percent or more below the average salary practice line will get an increase in their salary of $100 for the year, or $8.33 a month.

"Well, we didn't oppose that legislation," he said. "But it wasn't ours. And we pointed out to our own members that if this is an indication of their ten-year plan, they'd have to adjust it. Because at that rate, not even counting inflation—presuming a static economy—it would take 104 years instead of ten to implement comparable worth. So we were not exactly convinced that either piece of legislation indicated a good faith effort to correct discrimination."

"The peanut increase is what I call it," Carroll Boone said.

Wage-Setting in Washington State

"How does comparable worth fit with the prevailing rate system?" I asked Bob Boysen, manager of standards and surveys for the Department of Personnel. "You have two systems mandated by the legislature going on at the same time."

"The big issue today," he answered, "is how to reconcile the two. That's one of the things we are giving some study to."

"You find the prevailing market rates for your benchmark jobs," Larry Goodman said, when I asked him the same question. "Then you do a job evaluation on the jobs you surveyed. And come up with what amounts to the Willis method of comparable worth, and then analyze them to see if, for instance, that secretary market rate reflects the evaluated worth of the job.

"Comparable worth, or job evaluation, in our opinion," he said, "is not a substitute pay plan. We have taken the position that comparable worth, as a means of eliminating sex discrimination, is a rifle and not a shotgun. Prevailing market rate is the foundation and comparable worth is the way of correcting those areas of prevailing rates that are found to be discriminatory."

"We do a biennial market salary survey, both in and out of state, of about 100 benchmark classes," Bob Boysen explained. "And they become the drivers for the entire compensation plan." In other words, the pay for 100 out of a total of some 3,000 job classifications, or only 3 percent of the total classes, is directly related to the market.

"The remainder of the classes are set by what we call indexing," Boysen said, "which is a system of internal relationships. So every class is indexed, or aligned to one of the benchmarks. So as the benchmarks move, they pull along their own group of classes."

"How do you determine the indexing?" I asked. "That would be the key to the whole thing, wouldn't it?"

"Well, yes," Boysen answered. "We have a kind of computerized system of relationships. For example, here is secretary 1 shorthand, class 0160, benchmark #4 in the out-of-state survey. Secretary 2, the highest-level classified secretary, is lined-in four ranges higher than secretary 1. One range is 2½ percent, so four ranges is 10 percent. Clerk stenographer 2 is lined-in four ranges below secretary 1. All you have to do is plug in the salary for the benchmark and then the computer sets the rates for everything else.

"But how do you decide that this job is going to be four ranges higher?" I asked. "Somebody has to decide that."

"That's been kind of hammered out over a period of time," Boysen said. "That's been a judgment call. But it's kind of a rule of thumb that we have either four or six ranges difference in classes in a series."

"Not only do we have classes in the same series indexed," he added, "but we might have other classes, like the legal secretaries aligned to that secretary 1 benchmark. So that requires another judgment, where should the legal secretary be aligned to the general secretary? That's been a matter of controversy over the years. I suspect that comparable worth will have some impact," Boysen said. "Those relationships, those traditional class relationships, will all be up for grabs as we get more and more into making comparisons based on point factors."

"Do you have a committee that determines that a particular secretary class would be four ranges below or above the benchmark?" I asked.

"Well, yes," Boysen said. "Our department makes recommendations on points of debate but agencies and employee organizations can make a presentation against them, before the Personnel Board. And then the board would make a decision."

"Traditionally, the classification system that is used in this state is called the whole job match type of classification methodology," Dorothy Gerard, administrator of salary structure for the Higher Education Personnel Board told me. "You look at individual position descriptions completed in written form by employees and then simply sort them into like piles. Then you take the pile of position descriptions and write a specification sheet which encompasses the *typical* task performed by that group of people. And then comparisons are made as to overlap, redundancy, or inadequate class specifications to cover the work being performed. Those job specifications are adopted by the two personnel boards. Each board has its own, entirely separate system and set of job specifications.

"It's a real sort of antiquated way to do classification," she added. "But it works. And that's how it's been done in the state. In fact, we're in the process now of revising our mainline clerical series. There are about 20 job classes and we're collecting a sample of position descriptions of about 40 percent of the 4,000 positions. And then we'll sort and make some determinations about whether or not we have too many or too few job classes to cover all of those positions."

"Is there a routine system for updating job classifications or specifications?" I asked.

"There is not," Dorothy Gerard answered. "We've never reviewed all of the job specs since we converted to the common class plan in January 1974. We reviewed the library technical specifications a couple of years ago. I think it took two years and that was only 500 people. And, as I mentioned earlier, we're reviewing the 20-odd clerical classes now."

Jennifer Belcher, chair of the legislature's Joint Select Committee for Comparable Worth Implementation, agreed that the lack of a system for updating job descriptions was a problem. "Most of our job descriptions were written when the [DOP] system was instituted twenty or twenty-five years ago," she said. "The requirement for getting a job description updated is either you decide you're working out of class, or your employer decides you're working out of class. You can request the department to look at it and upgrade it" she explained. "But unless you, as an individual, do that the whole class could sit there for the next ten years and not be updated."

"That is really a problem in the clerical field where you have so many technological changes," I commented.

"Incredible changes," Belcher agreed. "The last ten years have just been phenomenal in the clerical field. But we haven't had any automatic updating of those positions."

"One of the things that's coming out of Jennifer Belcher's study committee," Helen Remick said, "is that the [comparable worth] evaluations are being done from existing job descriptions which are over ten years old. And what that means, especially with clericals, is that they clearly do not reflect changing technology. So we're potentially understating aspects of the work."

Furthermore, the plaintiff's trial brief pointed out that there are no written guidelines for determining how the classes are indexed. And that the state has not studied the indexing to see if it is sex-biased. Willis asked Bob Boysen, of the Department of Personnel, if he should examine the indexing when he was making his 1974 study. He was told no.

"You do a survey to get the pay rates for the 100 or so benchmark jobs?" I asked Dorothy Gerard.

"Yes," she said. "That's what's going on in this room right now. We do it every other year. We survey 2,500 to 3,000 other public and private employers in the state of Washington, and some out of state. DOP and HEP boards do it jointly. There are 60 people in the field right now collecting salary information from those employers. In November of each even year the boards pass on our findings. And they give these to the legislature to use in determining their budget for the next biennium. These findings are advisory only.

"Larry Goodman probably told you that the legislature has balanced its budget on the backs of the state employees, didn't he?" she asked. "That's one of his favorite lines.

"It's a real game of running to keep up with the prevailing rate," she went on. "There's never enough money. So, in fact, this time around, on January 1, 1985, employees will receive 50 percent of the increase recommended in the 1982 findings. We'll have the results of the 1984 survey before the 1982 survey is implemented. It sounds, in reading and on paper, like a very technical, rational way to set salaries," she commented. "But it ends up being, once again, a real political game."

"How do the comparable worth studies fit in with the general system of evaluating and ranking jobs?" I asked.

"Well, both personnel departments use the Willis methodology of evaluation," she replied. "After 1974 we evaluated just benchmarks. But the 1983 legislation said we should conduct additional studies as necessary. So we began evaluating additional job classes in the occupational groups which were due to receive the $100 per year adjustment beginning this July 1.

"And then the court order directed the special master to have us evaluate the 70 percent female-dominated classes," she said. "So we have, in each jurisdiction, established standing evaluation committees. Our department has to submit 32 evaluations every two weeks to the special master. And the DOP has to submit 64."

"Before this year we had only evaluated 10 percent of our total job classes," Bob Boysen told me. "I think we're almost up to 25 percent now, so we've made a big stride this year."

"In the past," Gerard explained, "we've evaluated the benchmark class, which is traditionally the journey level of whatever occupation is involved. We determined the comparable worth range for that benchmark job. And then," she said, "we've applied the current indexing to determine the comparable worth range for the rest of the jobs in the occupational group."

Dorothy Gerard pointed out that when the legislature decided to make $100 a month comparable worth payments to jobs tied to benchmark classes that were 20 percent or more below the average pay practice line, some higher level jobs in these classes that are actually above the line may also receive payments. The legislature has, however, set up the Comparable Worth Implementation Committee to study the changes needed in the state's pay system in order to implement comparable worth effectively.

"What is the relationship between the comparable worth mandate and the prevailing rate mandate?" I asked again. "I haven't mastered that one yet."

"Well, none of us have," she answered. "We really have contradictory compensation law right now. My guess is," she said, "and this is just Dorothy Gerard's guess, that over time and within the next couple of legislative sessions, that law will be rewritten to somehow deal with how one looks at prevailing rate at the same time one is implementing comparable worth. And that is part of what the implementation study will consider.

"Given the lawsuit and all that," she said, "my guess is we couldn't return to a purely prevailing rate methodology. But the case is under appeal," she added, "and who knows how it will turn out?"

Notes

1. Jeanne Saddler, "U.S. May Challenge Equal Pay Decision Made in Case Against Washington State," *Wall Street Journal,* January 23, 1984, p. 16.

2. Letter from Norm Schut, executive director, Washington Federation of State Employees, AFL-CIO, to Governor Daniel J. Evans, November 20, 1973.

3. Ibid.

4. Letter of Douglas E. Sayan and Leonard Nord to Governor Daniel J. Evans, accompanying their salary study report, January 8, 1974.

5. Higher Education Personnel Board and State Department of Personnel, "Salary Study Report to Governor," p. 1.

6. Ibid., p. 5.

7. Carroll Boone, "The Washington State Comparable Worth Trial," *Comparable Worth Project Newsletter* (Fall 1983/Winter 1984): 6.

9

THE TRIALS:
What Happened and What Happens Next?

"After careful review of the record herein," District Court Justice Jack Tanner wrote in his decision in the case of *American Federation of State, County, and Municipal Employees et al.* v. *State of Washington et al.,* "this Court cannot reach any conclusion other than the State of Washington has, and is continuing to maintain a compensation system which discriminates on the basis of sex. The State of Washington has failed to rectify an acknowledged discriminatory disparity in compensation. The State has and is continuing to treat some employees less favorably than others because of their sex, and this treatment is intentional.[1]

Judge Tanner found discrimination based on the theory of disparate treatment—"intentional, unfavorable treatment of employees in predominately female classifications."[2] He cited a number of types of evidence that, he said, "when considered as a whole show discriminatory intent."

He also found discrimination based on the theory of disparate impact. "The wage system in the State of Washington has a disparate impact on predominately female job classifications," he wrote.[3] He gave two pieces of evidence; first, the 20 percent female-male salary disparity found by the state's comparable worth studies, and second, the "significant inverse correlation between the percentage of women in a classification and the salary for that position."

How the Plaintiffs Made Their Case

"*Washington State* is now the first holding to find that sex-based wage discrimination is established on the basis of disparate impact," Winn Newman, lawyer for the plaintiffs, pointed out to me. "Not the first to say it *may* be established," he emphasized. "But the first to say that it *is* established. There was an earlier case that said it *may* be established but didn't find it was."

"What does that mean, in terms of what you have to demonstrate?" I asked.

"Well," he said, "I think what that means is that even absent the voluminous evidence of segregation practice that we put in, and absent the admissions by the state that its wages were discriminatory, the mere fact that you have jobs that were predominantly female, were paid less than men's, and were shown to be worth more would be enough to make the case, absent any evidence that the employer had anything to do with the segregation—as we did establish also. If that holds," he concluded, "then there's no question that every employer that hires women is guilty of sex-based wage discrimination. I don't know of any employer that hires women and men and pays women other than a disparate wage rate."

"So every employer will be subject to possible suit?" I asked.

"Well," he said, "I also think you can establish *intent* against virtually every employer. This is an easier case."

"How does this relate to Ruth Blumrosen's argument that minorities and women can use evidence of job segregation to make a prima facie case of wage discrimination?" I asked.[4]

"Well," he answered, "she made *my* argument. I made mine in 1975 and she made hers in 1979. In my 1975 article I raised the question of whether, like testing, where you establish that women are segregated and are getting paid less than men, that shifts the burden to the employer to establish why. As with testing, where a disproportionate number of blacks don't pass the test, does the burden shift to the employer to establish why?

"As far as I'm concerned," Newman continued, "*Washington State* added no law to *Gunther* except for the disparate impact. *Gunther* said that intentional discrimination is illegal. It said that disparate treatment is illegal.

"I don't understand," he added, "I never have understood, why people are afraid to file cases. There's a dearth of cases. Nobody's filing them. And it's crazy, absolutely crazy.

"You prove intent before you prove any other case," he explained. "And you don't need a smoking gun to prove intent. You don't need to have the employer say, 'Hey, woman, the reason I'm paying you less is because you're a woman,' in order to win a case. All kinds of cases involving intentional discrimination are proven every day on the basis of statistics. Statistics prove intent.

"Our judge in *Washington State* saw nothing different about this case," he added. "This is a straight Title VII case. The problem is that everybody's all wrapped up over the words 'comparable worth.' There's not a word about comparable worth in our lawsuit. The state kept talking about comparable worth and I kept saying, 'I don't know what they're talking about. They're talking about some other lawsuit, not ours.'"

"What you're talking about, then, is discrimination in compensation based on sex?" I asked.

"That's what the statute says," he answered. "It bans discrimination in compensation. It doesn't say anything about comparable worth. I wouldn't try to prove anything about comparable worth. I don't know what comparable worth is, anymore. But I know what discrimination in compensation is.

"What I'm saying," he explained, "is that once you knocked out the Bennett Amendment, then you simply have a statute that bans discrimination in compensation. That's all."

"And you don't have to worry about whether it's labeled comparable worth or anything else?" I asked.

"I don't," Newman said.

"But then you get to the problem the 1980 EEOC hearings were about," I said. "The problem of how you demonstrate sex-based wage discrimination when women are in different jobs than men. Don't you have to get involved in job evaluation?"

"Economists are all screwed up on the legal question as to how you demonstrate intent," he said. "And the moment you try to make it different from any other piece of Title VII, you're screwing it up.

"How do you prove it?" he went on. "Well, I think you use the methods we used in *Washington State.* At least I tried the methods I thought make sense. And that was to make *Brown* v. *Board of Education* the lead case. That's the landmark school segregation case," he explained. "Very simply, our theory was that separation of the sexes in the workplace denotes the inferiority of women and results in inferior wages and working conditions. And then we set about to show the employer involvement in segregation. The fact that women didn't just get there by happenstance. The employer put them there. We went back to the 1950s—as far back as I could really get evidence. I would have gone back to 1880 if I could have."

"The State of Washington maintains a sex segregated workforce," the brief, titled Plaintiffs' Proposed Findings of Fact and Conclusions of Law, asserted. "The State has and continues to recruit and assign employees on the basis of sex."

The plaintiffs' lawyers used the state's practices in placing "Help Wanted" advertisements as the key evidence buttressing this finding of deliberate sex segregation. "For example," their brief stated, "on April 23, 1972, the state ran advertisements for at least three vacancies in the *Seattle Post-Intelligencer.* Two of the vacancies—Programmer and Accountant—were advertised in the 'Help Wanted—Men' column and one—Staff

Nurses—was advertised in the 'Help Wanted—Women' column even though there was a 'Help Wanted' column without any gender identification. A disclaimer by the newspaper on the very same page states that:

> 'The advertisements presented in this column are those where the advertiser states that sex is a bona fide occupational qualification reasonably necessary to the particular business or employment.'

The brief points out that the state did not offer evidence that sex was, in fact, a bona fide occupational qualification for these jobs. And it did not deny responsibility for placing these ads. Furthermore, the brief states that "as recently as June 3, 1973, after the extension of the Civil Rights Act to public employers," the state continued to run advertisements in segregated "Help Wanted" columns. It cites as typical an ad for " 'qualified women' to work as Medical Stenographers," and another stating "the University of Washington is seeking *men* interested in the field of artificial kidney technology."

In addition to the advertisements, the plaintiffs' brief lists many of the state's job descriptions that "explicitly limit the classifications to one sex or indicate a preferred sex for a job."

"And where they didn't designate women or men," Newman told me, "when they were talking about a clerical job they used pronouns like 'she' or 'her.' And when they were talking about a chemist they used pronouns like 'he' and 'him.' " The brief lists more than three pages of other classification specifications which use this type of what it terms "sexist language."

The plaintiffs' brief details evidence illustrating "a variety of techniques for segregating employees on the basis of sex, ranging from explicit segregation to the creation of new positions to the manipulation of the indexing system." It gives the example of barbers and beauticians, an example based on testimony of the Department of Personnel and the union. "Although the duties of the beautician are more complex, the entry level pay for beauticians is less than that of the barbers," the brief states. "Barber and beautician are both indexed to the same benchmark, so the difference in pay results directly from the employer's actions, rather than the salary survey. The state's explanation that barbers were indexed higher because of greater supervisory responsibility is *not* supported by the classification specifications."

Another example is the job of safety inspector. When women complained that they were excluded from this job, the state created a new job title, "culinary inspector," for inspectors of workplaces employing women. It hired women as culinary inspectors and paid them less than male safety inspectors. In 1978 the state merged the two jobs.

A third example is the job of fisheries license supervisor. This job, the brief states,

> was traditionally paid less than Game License Supervisor, a position with substantially similar job duties. In 1979, a representative of the Department of Fisheries admitted at an SPB hearing that the salary for the Fisheries License Supervisor had been lower because it was traditionally held by a woman. The Board raised the salary of the Fisheries License Supervisor to that of the Game License Supervisor.

When questioned, the state admitted that certain jobs were traditionally segregated by sex. Some examples given were orderlies (male), nurses aides (female), custodians (male), and housekeepers (female). The union pointed out that "women were not allowed to take the examination for various jobs, such as disability claims adjudicator."

The plaintiffs' brief detailed numerous job classifications that "require similar duties [but] are segregated and the predominantly female classifications are paid less even though the required qualifications are equal to or greater than the male comparisons." The brief cites evidence that there is segregation even within predominantly female job families, with the percentage of women in a job class decreasing as the salary range increases. For example, approximately 80 percent of the class accountant 1, at a salary range of 30, is female. But only 53 percent of the class accountant 4, at salary range 44, is female. In the licensed practical nurse 1 class, with a salary range of 20, 87.5 percent of the class is female. But in the class licensed practical nurse 5, with a salary range of 34, the percentage of females dropped to 64.3 percent.

The plaintiffs' brief shows that the consequence of the state's past and present "segregative practices" is a high degree of sex segregation. Of all the job classes under the jurisdiction of the Department of Personnel 83 percent were sex segregated, that is, made up 70 percent or more of one sex or the other. Of these segregated job classes, three quarters were predominantly male and one quarter predominantly female. The female job classes, though few in number, were typically much larger than the more numerous male classes. According to the brief, "10,912 employees in DOP alone were in jobs that were 70 percent or more female."

"We have very specifically defined job classes and benchmarks for male jobs," Jennifer Belcher, chair of the legislature's Joint Select Committee for Comparable Worth Implementation, told me. "And we go out into the private sector and try to find something that really matches. But we have few benchmarks and a lot of classes lumped together for the female-dominated jobs. And the benchmark jobs in the private sector, like the entry-level clerk typist, are low paid. And so," she concluded, "not only these benchmark positions in the state employment become low paid, but all of the thousands of jobs that are tied to them become low paid. Part of that has resulted because we never really value the kinds of skills it takes to be an advanced secretary or look at the planning and organizing skills that some of these clerical functions take."

The plaintiffs' brief pointed out that "a similar pattern of segregation is evident at the University of Washington, which employs over one-half of the employees under the jurisdiction of HEPB." It cited testimony by Dr. Helen Remick, director of affirmative action at the university, that in 1976 three quarters of the job classifications at the university were 85 percent to 100 percent segregated by sex.

Thus Newman and his colleagues established the existence of substantial sex segregation of jobs for state workers and demonstrated the "employer involvement in segregation"—"that women didn't just get there by happenstance." They then went on to detail the 1974 and succeeding biennial wage studies that analyzed salary differences between predominantly male and predominantly female job classes. As we have seen, the 1974 Willis study found "an average of about twenty percent less for women than for males doing equivalent jobs," a disparity that increased to about 25 percent by the early 1980s. Their brief also pointed out that the 1974 and subsequent studies showed "a consistent, statistically significant inverse correlation between the percentage of women in a classification and the wage rate." In other words, the studies showed that the more female the class was, the lower the wage rate relative to male rates for equivalently valued jobs. The brief concluded that "intent to discriminate on the basis of sex" can be inferred from all of this evidence— the state's deliberately segregated job structure and compensation system, the state's job evaluation studies, and the statistical evidence correlating wages and sex. By showing intent to discriminate the plaintiffs aimed to establish a prima facie case of disparate treatment, one of the two theories available to a plaintiff in a Title VII case.

They also sought to make a prima facie case of sex-based wage discrimination under the disparate impact theory—that "some facially neutral employment practice has a substantially disproportionate impact upon a group protected by Title VII."[5] The state's "facially neutral employment practice," which had the effect of discriminating, they said, was its biennial salary survey, which it used to relate its benchmark wage rates to prevailing market rates.

"The state's salary setting system clearly has a disparate impact on employees in predominantly female jobs," the plaintiffs' brief said.

In 1982 100 percent of the predominantly female benchmarks were paid less than their comparable worth minimum salary. 96.49 percent of all employees in predominantly female jobs are paid less than the comparable worth salary for their job. . . . The average annual loss in salary due to discrimination to employees in predominantly female jobs at DOP compared to *all* other classifications is $2,297, nearly double the disparity in 1976. The average annual loss at HEPB is $1,604. The cost of being in a predominantly female job has almost doubled since 1976.[6]

"What did you say about the market?" I asked Winn Newman. "That's the defense I hear the employers making," I added. "That they're simply paying market wages and what's wrong with that?"

"We hit the market issue head on," he answered.

The state in this case had the strongest case the market people could come up with. In that sense, this was a bad case to bring. Here was a law that required a biennial survey. It spelled out how they would do it, with a very formalized procedure for conducting and reviewing and adjusting to the survey. The union was instrumental in getting the law passed. And then here comes somebody that says that by complying with this law you are discriminating.

The facially neutral practice was the survey, and we had to walk a tightrope because the union had supported the survey. We couldn't say the survey itself was discriminatory. We didn't. The survey wasn't discriminatory. What we said was that to the extent you are surveying employers who discriminate, that data cannot validly be considered.

Since no effort was made, and couldn't be made, to learn which employers were discriminating, you are incorporating their discrimination into your wage structure when you do the survey. If the survey had been restricted to male jobs, that would have been fine, so long as you paid female jobs of equal skill, effort, and responsibility the same amount. And, indeed, the relief that the judge has indicated he is going to order brings the women's jobs up to the survey rates of the men's jobs.

I guess I should say that another basic finding here is that it's the first case that may have really met the issue head on. Now there are other cases that hit market, for example, the *Norris* v. *Arizona* pension case. The defense there was that all insurance companies have different rates for pensions for women and for men. So in a sense that was a market defense case.

The plaintiffs' brief cited the ninth circuit court ruling in *Norris* v. *Arizona Governing Committee* that "Title VII has never been construed to allow an employer to maintain a discriminatory practice merely because it reflects the marketplace. . . ."[7]

"The federal government defended its practice of discriminatory treatment of women at the Government Printing Office," Newman continued, "on the ground that it was industry practice. But the court of appeals was not impressed with perpetuating discriminatory industry practice."

The plaintiffs' lawyers buttressed their disparate impact argument with testimony from expert witnesses, one of them the state's, that the market discriminates—that "the market has traditionally paid women's jobs less because they are women."[8] They pointed out that the defendant's defense "that an ideal market would not tolerate such discrimination" is no defense to "concrete evidence of discrimination" in the real world of imperfectly competitive markets. The state, they said, "made no effort to show that the labor market covered in the state salary survey was in fact perfectly competitive."[9]

They also asserted that, even if the market were a defense to a Title VII claim, the state deviates from its survey rates. The recommendations stemming from the salary survey are advisory only. The legislature has fully funded the salary survey's recommended increases only once. And it has used various formulas for making salary adjustments, each of which distorts market relationships.

Furthermore, as the brief points out, the salaries for about 98 percent of all state jobs are not determined by the market survey but are set by an indexing process linking them to the surveyed, benchmark jobs. "The state admits that indexing is designed to preserve historical relationships, not to reflect market relationships."[10] And the preservation of historical relationships, the brief argues, "preserves historical discrimination resulting from the state's segregated job structure, segregated recruiting policies and discriminatory wage practices. Predominantly female jobs are generally indexed to predominantly female benchmarks even if there is no logical relationship between the jobs."[11]

The brief gives examples. The campus police assistant, a security officer position and a female job, is indexed to the female clerical benchmark rather than to the male security guard benchmark. The female positions of drug room clerk, stock clerk, and stores clerk are indexed to the average of the clericals benchmarks, rather than to the male warehouse worker benchmark.

A final point that the plaintiffs' lawyers made was that cost is not a defense to a Title VII violation. "Congress did not put a price tag on the cost of correcting discrimination," their brief said, "nor did Congress authorize an employer to perpetuate discrimination if the elimination thereof would be disruptive."

The Defendants' Defense

The defendants in this case—the state of Washington—are the governor; the director of financial management; the directors and members of the state boards, institutions, and agencies who hire employees or determine employment policies; and the members and leaders of the state legislature. Lawyers from the attorney general's office defend them. What was their defense before Judge Tanner in the district court?

The defense lawyers moved for summary judgment, that is, for dismissal of the Title VII claim. "We argued at the beginning," Christine Gregoire, deputy attorney general, told me, "that the disparate impact theory used in discrimination law was not available to the plaintiffs because they could not establish what is required—namely, an objective, facially neutral practice. Which, in the case law, typically means a requirement for height or weight or that you have graduated from high school, or whatever.

"We said that they were first going to have to identify what the practice was. But if, in fact, it was the Washington practice of setting salaries based on the market, then that did not fall within the concept because inherent in that are subjective employer criteria. And therefore it was inappropriate. That's basically what the ninth circuit court of appeals said in the decision that just came out in the case of *Margaret Spaulding et. al.* v. *University of Washington,*" she added. "That's why the *Spaulding* case is so significant."

"The survey of prevailing market price is not a facially neutral practice because it's not objective?" I asked.

"Setting salaries based on the market is inherently a subjective employer practice," she said. "You may have a study, as Washington does, where we study 3,000 employers in the state bienially, and then base our salaries on those studies—which is an objective practice. Nonetheless, those salaries themselves are based on subjective criteria; union negotiations, supply and demand, individual employer preferences, biases, and so on. And therefore that theory of law cannot be used in sex-discrimination cases. But the trial court rejected that argument and used disparate impact theory throughout the decision in finding Washington State liable in this discrimination case.

"The second thing we argued," Gregoire said, "was a legal argument, namely that comparable worth *alone,* and I emphasize *alone,* is insufficient to establish a prima facie case under Title VII. That's consistent with the case law that predated *Gunther,* that postdated *Gunther,* and the ninth circuit decision in the *Gunther* case. That's also what *Spaulding* v. *University of Washington* says.

"What we said," she explained, "is that if you are limited to disparate treatment, i.e., the plaintiff has to prove discrimination based on intent— the employer's intent to discriminate—then the proof cannot be based simply on a study of comparable worth. That alone doesn't show intent. You're going to have to show some other employer practices, some individual acts of discrimination.

"In this particular case," she said, "they attempted to show channeling of people into particular jobs by various employer practices as a basis to substantiate intent. They said that the state used an advertising practice of soliciting prospective employees in classified want ads entitled female wanted, or male wanted. That practice was discontinued by the state in 1972 when the Civil Rights Act became applicable to the states. We argued that, in order for that evidence to even merit attention by the court, they had to tie that practice to a current state practice.

"The plaintiffs failed to show that we had done anything inadvertently or subtly to continue the practice," Gregoire said. "And, in fact, we *attempted* to show not only that we advertised in a nondiscriminatory manner, but that we used affirmative action programs to integrate women into nontraditional work. I keep emphasizing to you that we *attempted* to introduce the evidence, because all of it was excluded by the trial court."

"Why was it excluded?" I asked. "On what grounds?"

"Let me just give you a brief glimpse of what happened," she answered. "We attempted to introduce 13 witnesses at trial and the judge excluded 11 of them. We attempted to introduce more than 50 documents, most of which were not objected to by the plaintiffs, and he excluded all but 2 documents. That sort of thing occurred again at the back pay trial, when he excluded all of our documents and 6 of our 7 witnesses. That's why, on appeal to the ninth circuit, the decision there could be limited to the procedural error and never address the issue of comparable worth.

"Our contention is," she said, "that we are entitled to put on a case. We submitted that we were putting on the case not only to show appropriate employer practice—use of the market as the basis for setting salary—but also to rebut the judge's prima facie finding of discrimination. To which he said, 'I found discrimination. I'm not going to let you rebut it.'

"I guess we figure that that's flat wrong," she said, "that we're entitled to put on a rebuttal. And we're entitled to put on a case."

"I don't think one should automatically assume that when a court excludes evidence that means you weren't allowed to make a case," Winn Newman said, when I asked him about Christine Gregoire's complaint. "Courts exclude evidence all the time," he explained. "The court excluded a lot of evidence we wanted to put in."

"Judge Tanner refused to take some evidence because he had already ruled that there was discrimination," Pat Thibaudeau, lobbyist for Washington Women United, told me. "And the evidence was repetitive. He said that they had already demonstrated these points, and the evidence they wanted to offer would not add to nor alter their previous testimony." She said that a lot of people feel, however, that the court of appeals may remand the case to the district court for a hearing on some of this evidence.

"Another argument which is probably more appropriate for back pay," Christine Gregoire said, "but is, nonetheless, one that we attempted to make throughout the trial, is a Tenth Amendment argument which says that the federal government is limited in how much it can interfere with integral state operations, in this case, setting salaries. That is bolstered by a couple of Supreme Court cases, particularly in the area of back pay, where the Supreme Court denied back pay because it would be such a tremendous interference with the practice of the individual employer and could have such a big rippling effect throughout the country. So we argued," she said, "that in this case the setting of salaries based on the market was an acceptable, nondiscriminatory employer practice with which the federal government should not interfere.

"We, of course, used the market defense, which I have just alluded to," she added. "And we attempted to introduce two economists at the trial. . . ."

"You had June O'Neill of the Urban Institute as an economics expert, didn't you?" I asked.

"She was not allowed to testify at the liability trial," Gregoire said. "She testified at the remedy stage."

"Could you go back for a minute and explain to me what the difference is between these three different trials?" I asked. "Liability is whether you are guilty?"

"Whether you did it, right," she said. "And the second stage is prospective, or injunctive, relief; what are you going to give them? Are you going to totally change the compensation system of the state? And the third is on back pay. That has to do with what formula you're going to use for determining back pay."

The plaintiffs' brief on remedy for the claimed discrimination said that injunctive relief is needed "to prevent perpetuation of the state's discriminatory compensation system." And, it said, back pay is necessary to achieve "the goal of a Title VII remedy [which] is to 'make whole' the victims of discrimination."[12]

The last argument of the defense that Christine Gregoire discussed was their claim that the comparable worth methodology developed by Willis and used by the state was, as she put it, "inherently subjective." It was all right for the legislature to adopt such a methodology as an individual employer practice. "But," she argued, "in terms of basing a case in a trial court statistically on it, it did not have the necessary certainty within it on which a court can rely."

Judge Tanner did not allow the state's expert witness, Richard Jeanneret, to testify on what was wrong with the Willis system. "The testimony is irrelevant," Dorothy Remick quoted the judge as saying. "The system is already in place. The legislature has already passed a bill saying that's what the state is going to do. It has a ten-year history of using this system. It's a little out of place," Judge Tanner said, "for the state to be attacking the way the state pays wages."

"The irony was," Remick added, "that the deputy attorney general who was heading up the case has her salary set by the method that she was then attacking. It was fairly bizarre."

The Judge's Decision, Declaratory Judgment, and Decree

"The threshold question presented to this court," Judge Jack Tanner wrote in his December 1983 decision,

> is whether Defendant's failure to pay the Plaintiffs their evaluated worth, under the provisions of Defendant's comparable worth studies, constitutes discrimination in violation of the provisions of Title VII. The central focus of the inquiry, in a case such as this, is always whether the employer is treating ". . . some people less favorably than others because of their race, color, religion, sex or national origin."[13]

The judge stated that "the record in this case shows, by a preponderance of the evidence," that the state of Washington not only "historically engaged in employment discrimination on the basis of sex," but also that these "discriminatory practices are continuing at the present time."[14] "The court's finding of discrimination based on the theories of disparate impact, and disparate treatment, requires formulation of a remedy," Judge Tanner concluded. He pointed out that under Title VII a remedy for unlawful discrimination is not "automatic" but is left up to the discretion and judgment of the district court. The remedy may include enjoining the discrimination, ordering appropriate affirmative action, back pay, "or any other equitable relief as the court deems appropriate."[15]

He listed the state's reasons for objecting to injunctive relief—tremendous costs, lack of revenue due to a depressed state and national economy with particular emphasis on the depressed condition of the forest industry, prior state revenue commitments to other projects, a state constitutional mandate of a balanced budget, disruption of the state's salary setup and work force, the state's already initiated remedy for eliminating sex-based wage discrimination by 1993, and, finally, the Tenth Amendment to the U.S. Constitution. He then responded to these arguments.

Cost is not a defense under Title VII, he said. "Neither Congress nor the Courts have recognized such a defense." As for lack of revenue, he pointed out that the state had a surplus in its budget in the 1976–77 biennium. It recognized the sex-based wage disparity, it had the money available, but then it chose to do nothing about it. "The bad faith of Defendant's action is patent," he wrote. He argued that any disruption caused by equitable relief "is a direct result of the discrimination Defendant created and has maintained."[16]

"Title VII remedies are *now*," he wrote, in response to the argument that the legislature planned to remedy discrimination by 1993. "It is time, *right now* for a remedy," he emphasized. "Defendant's preoccupation with its budget constraints pales when compared with the invidiousness of the impact ongoing discrimination has upon the plaintiffs herein," he added. He pointed out that the legislature's "belated," token appropriation in May 1983 did not claim to eliminate discrimination.[17]

As far as the Tenth Amendment argument was concerned, he said that the Supreme Court had found that Congress acted constitutionally under Section 5 of the Fourteenth Amendment when it applied Title VII to state governments as employers. And nothing in Title VII's legislative history, he said "would indicate that the Federal Courts, after finding sex discrimination in employment, could not then fashion a remedy to eliminate the discrimination."[18]

Finally, he looked at the state's arguments against assessing back pay. He cited the Supreme Court's opinion that "it is also the purpose of Title VII to make persons whole for injuries suffered on account of unlawful employment discrimination. . . . The general rule is, that when a wrong has been done, and the law gives a remedy, the compensation shall be equal to the injury."[19] The Supreme Court held that the courts may find exceptions to this rule in cases where the employers have not acted in bad faith. Then the cost of a remedy may become relevant. But, Judge Tanner pointed out, it ruled in *Albemarle* that "where an employer *has* shown bad faith—by maintaining a practice which he knew to be illegal or of highly questionable legality—he can make no claims whatsoever on the Chancellor's conscience."[20] Judge Tanner found that "the persistent and intransigent conduct of Defendant in refusing to pay Plaintiffs indicates 'bad faith.' " Therefore he ruled that "plaintiffs are entitled to declaratory judgment, injunctive relief, and back pay. . . ."[21]

The judge then ordered the state to cease its "sex discriminatory practices" and to "forthwith" pay each plaintiff the compensation due them according to the state's May 1983 comparable worth plan. He defined the class entitled to relief as "all female and male employees of all job classifications . . . which were 70 percent or more female as of November 20, 1980 or anytime thereafter." He ordered DOP and the HEP boards to evaluate additional classes so that all the female-dominated classes are evaluated and to furnish the court with a list of employees entitled to relief. Finally, he ordered that the plaintiffs are entitled to back pay and all fringe benefits, starting from September 16, 1979. He appointed a special master to help implement the court's decision.

The Sequel

"I do want to tell you, it's nicer to win than to lose," Winn Newman told the National Committee on Pay Equity at a reception they held for him in early December 1983, shortly after Judge Tanner gave his oral decision in the *Washington State* case. "But you know," he said, "lawsuits are not tried in a vacuum. The efforts made by the National Committee and the organizations you are all affiliated with have created the climate which permitted this kind of decision to come about.

"Hopefully, what all of us have now done is to catapult pay equity into the national picture. It is the litmus test, along with ERA, of where people are on women's rights and where they are on rights in the working place.

"In terms of substance, we do know," he said, "that this decision will affect *all* employers who hire women. . . . A clear holding that market is not a defense, that is, the fact that everybody else discriminates and that all you're doing is paying what everybody else does is not a defense. And that cost is not a defense. . . . I would hope," Newman concluded, "that with a combined effort through collective bargaining routes, carefully selected legislation, as well as the threat of lawsuits, that we can and will break the back of sex-based wage discrimination."

Newman was right. Pay equity hit the national scene. The *Wall Street Journal* for December 6, 1983, came out with a scare headline for an alarm-ringing article: "Washington State Fears Sex-Bias Award to Have 'Devastating' Effect on Economy." The state might have to pay nearly a billion dollars in the next 18 months, according to the *Journal*. It quoted the state as saying that the taxes needed to meet this charge "would invite political and economic crises of the highest magnitude." Soon after this *The New York Times* featured the issue but decided to inform rather than frighten. It published a lengthy article detailing the various economic and political arguments for and against pay equity in its Sunday Business Section on January 1, 1984.

The San Jose strike was the first pay equity event to get widespread national attention. But the *Washington State* decision stirred up pay equity opponents more thoroughly than San Jose or *Gunther* or anything else had done before. The Reagan administration's reaction was a striking example of this concern. "U.S. May Challenge Equal-Pay Decision Made in Case Against Washington State," the *Wall Street Journal* wrote on January 23, 1984. The article reported that the Justice Department was considering challenging Judge Tanner's order by entering the case, either with an *amicus* brief or more actively as an intervenor. It quoted the assertion of Assistant Attorney General for civil rights William Bradford Reynolds that "the comparable worth theory suggests that we will change to have the government set salaries for every job in the marketplace . . . a dramatic and revolutionary change."[22] But despite their anxiety the administration had not filed an *amicus* brief in the appeals court by the due date in mid-September. The news media reported that political considerations, especially worry about the "gender gap," led them to decide to postpone help to *Washington State* until after the November elections.

The Washington state attorney general responded to Judge Tanner's decision by filing an appeal with the ninth circuit court of appeals and requesting a stay of the district court decision. The appeals court granted a stay on that part of the order requiring the state to use a new comparable worth pay scale. But the rest of the order stands.

So the special master set to work on how to implement the order. The DOP and HEP boards started developing the list of employees entitled to relief under the order. And they began doing the required additional job evaluations, some 96 every two weeks, with evaluation committees trained by Willis Associates. The committees are made up of representatives of the personnel agency, the employing agencies, and the employees' organizations. The personnel boards route the completed evaluations through Larry Goodman at the Washington Federation of State Employees for review. Then they go to the special master.

The state legislature, meanwhile, has reacted in two ways. It set up a joint committee to study the issues involved in implementing its 1983 comparable worth legislation. This is the Joint Select Committee for Comparable Worth Legislation, headed by legislator Jennifer Belcher. And after the district court decision it created a committee to look into the possibility of negotiating a settlement of the suit. After much debate the legislature gave the attorney general's office rather than the committee the power to negotiate a settlement.

"The state's attorneys are convinced the state will win its appeal in the ninth circuit court of appeals," Carroll Boone told me, implying that therefore they are not much interested in settling now. "Apparently," she added, "some legislators do not share the state's attorney's conviction."[23]

"Do you have any comments on the cost of implementing comparable worth?" I asked Helen Remick. Cost has been a major issue in both the state's failure to remedy sex-based wage discrimination and in the state's defense of the court suit.

"Cost is very interesting," she said. "During the trial the cost estimates of the state, which were based on something other than numbers, went up and up. On one of the last days of the trial I was sitting behind two reporters. One turned to the other and said, 'Every time they talk about cost the numbers go up.'

"Shortly afterward, the state's attorney said, 'It's going to cost a billion dollars in the next two years.' And then four sentences later he said, 'It's going to cost a billion dollars in the next 18 months.'

" 'See,' the reporter said, 'There it goes again.' "

"They were making estimates, somehow," Remick said. "But those estimates don't reflect the actual cost. The cost to bring *all* salaries below the average salary line up to the line were calculated for the 1983 legislature by the Department of Personnel and the Higher Education Personnel Board. And that included male-dominated, mixed male and female, and female-dominated jobs. The cost for the female-dominated jobs is about $62 or $63 million. The cost to bring the mixed and the male-dominated jobs to that line is another $62 or $63 million. So to bring *all* jobs up to that line would cost a little over $120 million a year."

According to the staff of the legislative Committee on Comparable Worth Implementation, the $120.5 million implementation cost estimate presented by the state's Office of Financial Management is 1.5 percent of the $8.1 billion "general fund state operating budget" for the 1983–85 period. For the biennium, the cost would come to 3 percent of that operating budget.

"But the court case includes only the part for the female-dominated jobs," Helen Remick continued, "because the court case only deals with discrimination against women. So we're talking about $62 million to bring the female-dominated jobs up to that line. And then we're talking about another $310 million, which is the cost of back wages and back contributions to pension plans."

"$310 million?" I said. "The cost of back wages and pension contributions? Where is the $1 billion or $2 billion that I saw in the papers?"

"They made them up," Helen Remick answered. "That happens sometimes. What can we say?"

"Part of those figures were a result of our budget office being very adamantly opposed to comparable worth," Jennifer Belcher told me when I asked her the same thing. "So they put anything and everything in to make it as big as possible because it scared people to death."

"Well, it certainly did scare the employers," I said.

"You bet," she said. "It scared everybody. The billion dollar figure included fully funding the pension rights for those employees," she explained. "And they would be the only state employees with fully funded pension rights, because our pension system is not fully funded. So that, to me, was really stretching your imagination—to include that kind of figure and say this is part of comparable worth implementation. But it ballooned the figure and made for great headlines all over the place."

Helen Remick pointed out that the union asked for more than it appears that Judge Tanner gave, and this, too, caused higher cost estimates. The union asked that the female-dominated jobs be raised to the male salary practice line, which lies 10 to 11 percent above the average salary practice line and is some 31 percent above the female salary practice line.

"Over the last ten years we've been using the average salary line in our effort to resolve discrimination," Larry Goodman explained. "But we had to go to court and sue under Title VII, saying that women are discriminated against compared to men. In order to comply with legal precedents and with the standard interpretation of what constitutes discrimination and how to eliminate it, we are using the men's salary line."

"Is that the line the special master will use?" I asked.

"That hasn't been resolved yet," Goodman answered. "We feel the judge mandated the men's line. The state feels he told them to implement their idea of comparable worth and they're using the average line. But at some point we're going to have to go to the master and say, 'Now that you've got the data and everybody agrees on it where are you going to draw the line, here or there?'

"Keep in mind," Goodman said, "that throughout these ten years we never wanted back pay. Up until the time we got into the litigation we were telling everyone—especially the governor's office, but also the legislative leaders—that we'll drop this. We are not intending to bankrupt the state. But we want some meaningful, legitimate, concrete, enforceable steps toward the elimination of this discrimination. They didn't want to start talking to us till all of a sudden it looked like they were going to lose the case. And then it was, in fact, almost token."

"The present administration doesn't want to negotiate a settlement?" I asked.

"It doesn't want to do anything," Goodman said. "As far as the governor's office is concerned we've had virtually no communication of any sort. We had a very good relationship with the governor's predecessor, now U.S. Senator, Dan Evans. So it isn't partisan. They're both Republicans. And the person that cut out the original implementation was not only a Democrat but a woman."

"There are real problems involved in settlement, at this point," Christine Gregoire told me. "We attempted to settle the case in November, before the back pay trial. We had very serious settlement negotiations then. Following the back pay trial, but prior to the entry of the decision, I called counsel and made it very clear that if a settlement was to be reached it virtually had to be done prior to the entry of the decision. But they never began negotiations again with us."

She explained some of the problems the state saw in settling now. The state is not willing to pay back pay. Since it is a class action case, ex-employees, who are eligible for back pay, can choose to "opt out" of the settlement. And these former employees could then sue the state for the back pay. Secondly, she said, the state wants to implement its own comparable worth pay system in its own way. It doesn't want the supervision of a federal judge. But that decision would be up to the judge. Therefore the state is subject to the possibility of continued judicial "interference" in its pay system. Finally, she said, the plaintiffs' attorneys' fees will be large. But they can't be discussed in a settlement in a sex-discrimination Title VII case. So she believes the plaintiffs would go to the trial court with an "astronomical" request for attorneys' fees.

"I've gotten the impression that the state hasn't really wanted to settle," I said. "And that they may be looking forward to several conservative Reagan appointees to the United States Supreme Court who would look favorably on the state's case on appeal."

"Well," she replied, "we were the last ones to put the foot forward. And in the negotiations we had with the local counsel and the local union, before the decision, we were making real progress. And the negotiations cut off when a several-hour telephone call was placed to Winn Newman. He just took us back to square one.

"I'll be candid with you," she said. "If all I had to do was negotiate with the local union and local counsel, I think a settlement would be within the realm of possibility. But when you're dealing with outside counsel with a different agenda—I mean it doesn't take an Einstein to figure out what happened as soon as this decision was entered. Lawsuits were filed. The national union organization put out a pamphlet on how to sue your employer. And so on. Theirs is a different agenda from the local union's or the state's. It makes it very, very difficult to settle."

"Do you think the union is interested in settling the case?" I later asked Winn Nerman.

"I would be happy to talk about something that would be constructive and would send the message to the rest of the country as soon as possible," he replied. "We won't sell out. But we'd be happy to settle."

I asked deputy attorney general Gregoire about the committee set up by the legislature to see what could be done about a settlement. She agreed that the legislature might have thought that settling would be less expensive than going on with the appeals process. But she said that there was less emphasis on settling since the attorney general's office presented the problems involved. She added that the ninth circuit's July 3, 1984, decision in the case of *Margaret Spaulding et al. and James Bush et al.* v. *University of Washington* "will have dampened any thought of the state pushing settlement."

"You might want to take a look at the *Spaulding* case," Christine Gregoire said. "And you might want to talk to Elsa Cole, the assistant attorney general who was primarily responsible for it. She'll be here tomorrow."

The plaintiffs and the intervenors in the *Spaulding* case were members of the nursing faculty at the University of Washington. In 1972 they filed complaints with the Washington State Human Rights Commission and, later, with the EEOC. In 1974 they filed suit against the university under both the Equal Pay Act and Title VII of the Civil Rights Act, claiming that the university discriminated against them in compensation. In 1979, the district court dismissed their suit on the recommendation of a United States magistrate sitting as special master.

The nursing faculty appealed the decision to the ninth circuit court. They argued, among other things, that the university had violated the Equal Pay Act, and that they had made "a prima facie showing of discrimination prohibited by Title VII under both the disparate treatment and disparate impact models [and] that the University cannot rely on the 'competitive marketplace' defense. . . ." They contended that the district court had erred in dismissing their action.[24]

"The important part of the case," Assistant Attorney General Elsa Cole told me, "is in the disparate impact analysis done by the court. The court said that to make an allegation that the defendants are basing their salaries on the market place and that the market place is inherently discriminatory is not sufficient for you to have established a prima facie case under the disparate impact theory. Here, on page 39," she continued, "the court said, 'Relying on competitive market prices does not qualify as a facially neutral policy or practice for the purposes of the disparate impact analysis that was first articulated in *Griggs*.' This is a departure from the decision in the *AFSCME* v. *State of Washington* case, in which the district court held that it was sufficient. That is why Chris Gregoire feels that this is such an important case. And I do too."

Elsa Cole said that the *Spaulding* opinion was also significant because it discussed two pre-*Gunther* cases—*Lemons* v. *City and County of Denver* and *Christensen* v. *State of Iowa*—and upheld these decisions, although many people thought the law established in these cases was no longer valid.

"We agree with *Lemons* and *Christensen*," the two judges who wrote the majority *Spaulding* decision said, "and join those courts in refusing to accept a construction of Title VII allowing the nursing faculty to establish a prima facie violation of that Act 'whenever employees of different sexes receive disparate compensation for work of differing skills that may, subjectively, be of equal value to the employer but does not command an equal price in the labor market.'"[25]

The decision brought up these two cases because it defined the nursing faculty's claim as a comparable worth claim. It said, "The nursing faculty has only the 'comparable worth' theory upon which to rely. Its case essentially becomes a claim that the nursing faculty received unequal pay for comparable work of equal value to its employer."[26]

In a special concurring opinion, Mary Schroeder, the third circuit court judge in the case, objected to "the majority's analysis of the adverse impact issue. It confusingly meshes adverse impact with varying concepts of comparable worth," she wrote. "The majority fails even to define what it means by 'comparable worth,'" she asserted. "The plaintiffs repeatedly disclaim having presented any comparable worth theory," she added. She pointed out that the case predated the *Gunther* decision, which was the first to recognize that sex-based wage discrimination could be proved in some way other than showing unequal pay for substantially equal work. She concluded: "It is thus not possible for this court in this case to render any definitive ruling on the validity of comparable worth as a tool in employment discrimination cases."

Judge Schroeder did agree with the other two judges that the plaintiffs failed to prove any violation of the Equal Pay Act. And she agreed that they failed to prove a violation of Title VII on grounds of either disparate treatment or disparate impact. So the nursing faculty lost their appeal.

Prospects for Pay Equity in Washington State

How does the *Spaulding* decision affect the outlook for the state's appeal of *AFSCME* v. *State of Washington* to the ninth circuit? Deputy Attorney General Gregoire is clearly hopeful. She interprets *AFSCME* as being primarily a comparable worth case. She thinks that the *Spaulding* holdings on comparable worth would, therefore, be relevant on appeal. Winn Newman insists that the issue in *AFSCME* is not comparable worth. He says it is a straight Title VII sex-based wage discrimination case. "We're undaunted," he said to a *Wall Street Journal* reporter when asked about the impact of the *Spaulding* case.

In his decision, Judge Tanner seems to agree with Newman, saying that rather than being a comparable worth case, "It is more accurately characterized as a straightforward 'failure to pay' case, remarkably analogous to the recently decided *County of Washington* v. *Gunther* case. The Plaintiffs herein are challenging the State of Washington's failure to rectify an acknowledged disparity in pay between predominately female and predominately male job classifications by compensating the predominately female job employees in accordance with their evaluated worth, as determined by the State."[27]

The *Spaulding* decision also says that a survey of market prices is not a facially neutral practice that can be used to establish a prima facie case under the theory of disparate impact. This appears to contradict Judge Tanner's finding of discrimination based on disparate impact in the *Washington State* case.

The *AFSCME* case does differ from *Spaulding,* however, in several ways. *Spaulding* lacked convincing evidence of intent to discriminate. But the plaintiffs in *AFSCME* provided substantial evidence of intent that Judge Tanner found persuasive. Furthermore, the state of Washington admitted, following the 1974 pay equity study, that it discriminated in pay by sex. It hired a consultant to develop a job evaluation system for measuring the amount of sex-based wage discrimination in its compensation system. It continued to make these measurements as part of its biennial salary setting procedure. Governor Evans did, in fact, put money into his 1977 budget to rectify sex-based wage discrimination only to have the legislature take it out. After the union filed suit the legislature belatedly passed legislation moving toward correcting pay inequity.

"What do you feel the effect of the *Spaulding* decision will be on the *Washington State* appeal?" I asked Winn Newman shortly after he and his associates had filed their appeals brief with the ninth circuit court. "Christine Gregoire felt it would be very helpful to the state," I added.

"Well," he said, "we've had disagreements before on the meaning of things. So far we seem to have been right and they seem to have been wrong. And if we run true to form it will apply in *Spaulding* also. I don't think *Spaulding* has any real significance for *Washington State* in the area of disparate treatment. It may well have in the area of disparate impact, which we don't really have to reach. And I suspect that if the court agrees with us on treatment they won't reach disparate impact to begin with. We can distinguish the case on disparate impact as well, but I don't think we're going to have to.

"In *Spaulding,* you will recall," he continued, "the court noted the fact that the comparisons were made by the plaintiffs. And that the plaintiffs selected only male jobs to compare with, as distinguished from *Washington State,* where the employer selected the comparisons. Where the employer selected male *and* female jobs to compare. Where there was a *pattern* of discrimination—a *pattern* of distinction between female jobs and male jobs, not just a comparison of one job with another job. Statistically the pattern provides the basis for inferring discrimination.

"Our brief doesn't really treat with the impact issue, because we had strategy decisions to make, having devoted nearly 40 of our 60 pages to facts and to showing both the treatment violation and why the state did not follow the market—so you don't even reach the legal issue of whether a market defense is an appropriate one. That's about the best answer I can give you on that," he said.

"Do you think the appeals court is apt to remand the case to the district court for the hearing of further evidence?" I asked. "Several people did comment to me that it seemed a likely possibility."

"As I see it," Newman answered, "I would not expect to be reversed. It is possible we would get a remand. But I am satisfied that if we get a remand we will come back stronger than we were before. Because every defense witness that testified strengthened our case."

Meanwhile, it is also possible that the state may negotiate a settlement of the case. Governor-elect Booth Gardner, who beat incumbent governor Spellman in the recent elections, favors a settlement.

"Comparable worth was the first woman's issue he came out with in his campaign," Pat Thibaudeau told me in a recent phone conversation. "And he said over and over again that he was going to negotiate that settlement. But," she added, "the attorney general, who has a fair amount to say about the legal situation in this state, is the same man that defended the suit in the first place. And my understanding of this is that the attorney general is the one who makes that determination."

"The attorney general was just reelected?" I asked.

"Yes," she said. "The governor-elect, however, feels very strongly that he has the right to decide whether or not to negotiate and settle the suit. The situation is quite cloudy and I think it will remain so.

"But," she added, "we have two areas of interest here. One is the court suit. The other is the statute. And there are a lot of people working diligently on the implementation of that statute. Because our revenue picture is somewhat uncertain it's important that we begin to think about actual monies for implementation of the statute rather than just what's going to happen to the court suit. I've just made an appointment with our Ways and Means Chairman this afternoon to talk about that."

"Will the implementation of the state's comparable worth legislation make judicial action irrelevant?" I asked Deputy Attorney General Gregoire when I talked with her some months ago.

"Sure," she said. "That's my ultimate prediction, to be perfectly candid with you." She explained the length of time involved in getting a decision on the present appeal, with a possible retrial at the district court level, another appeal to the ninth circuit, and then an appeal to the Supreme Court.

"By the time all that occurs," she said, "it's not hard to believe that the legislation will have been implemented and the issue will be mooted. Now it will never be mooted as to back pay," she added. "And it may not be mooted as to the formula the state chooses to implement comparable worth. But what the federal judiciary would have to be saying is, 'We're going to tell you, you have to do it this way.' And that is a course that the Supreme Court has been very hesitant to take."

"The state is now moving in the direction of doing everything that the court ordered," Winn Newman said. "So I think this case has been won. We're prepared to declare victory now. The legislation would never have been passed. It was sitting around for ten years. It was passed on the eve of trial and it's being implemented posttrial. So I don't think there's much question that the lawsuit has caused the legislation to occur. And now all we're really talking about is how many years will it be before there is full implementation."

"I think it's a victory, no matter what," Carroll Boone said when I asked what she saw as the outlook for the *Washington State* case. "I think that if we lose, we have won, because we get more direction about where we should go with the next case and how we should go about proving it. But I also think we have a very good chance of winning. Because the evidence is there."

"What do you think the outlook for pay equity generally is?" I asked her.

"Oh, I think that there's no doubt about it, it's coming," she said. "And, in fact, much has already been done throughout the nation. People aren't waiting for the court cases to come down. In Washington State, for example, the city of Spokane has implemented comparable worth. The city of Seattle, the city of Olympia, the city of Lacey, the city of Bellevue—all of these people are at various stages in the process of looking at comparable worth. And people are looking at it all over the country. I think there is *no way* it can be stopped."

In its recent September 1985 ruling the ninth circuit appeals court overturned Judge Tanner's *AFSCME* decision. The union plans to appeal to the U.S. Supreme Court or to ask the appeals court for an *en banc* review by at least half of the more than twenty appeals court justices.

"We'll take a shot at it," Chris Owens, Winn Newman's associate told me. She explained that the appeals court had categorized the plaintiffs' case as a comparable worth argument and a disparate impact argument although the plaintiffs had never presented it as a comparable worth case and had not used the disparate impact argument at the appeals court level. The court, she said, substituted its analysis for that of the plaintiffs and of the trial court.

"We don't think the ball game is over," she added. "Clearly a lot has happened because of the District Court decision. A lot of momentum has been gained and it would be difficult for all of that to be stopped right in its tracks. At worst," she concluded, "what this decision says is that on this set of facts there is not a legal violation established. That dictates trying to put together a different kind of suit the next time around."

In August 1985, shortly before the appeals court ruling, Governor Gardner and the union agreed to begin negotiations for a settlement of the suit. At the governor's request, the legislature, in July, earmarked $42 million in its budget to use for correcting sex-based pay inequities if the negotiations proved successful. The state and the union are continuing to work on a settlement despite the appeals court decision. It seems likely that Gregoire's prediction that pay equity will be implemented in Washington State well before the appeals process is finished will prove correct.

Notes

1. Decision of U.S. District Court for Western Washington in *American Federation of State, County, and Municipal Employees* v. *State of Washington, Daily Labor Report,* Bureau of National Affairs, December 15, 1983, p. D-9.

2. Ibid., p. D-7.

3. Ibid.

4. Ruth G. Blumrosen, "Wage Discrimination, Job Segregation, and Title VII of the Civil Rights Act of 1964," *University of Michigan Journal of Law Reform* 12 (1979): 402–15.

5. Plaintiffs' Proposed Findings of Fact and Conclusions of Law, *AFSCME et al.* v. *State of Washington et al.,* p. 52.

6. Ibid., p. 32.

7. Ibid., pp. 54–55.

8. Ibid., p. 46.

9. Ibid., p. 47.

10. Ibid., p. 42.

11. Ibid.

12. Plaintiffs' Supplemental Findings of Fact and Conclusions of Law as to Injunctive Relief *AFSCME et al.* v. *State of Washington et al.,* p. 6.

13. *International Brotherhood of Teamsters* v. *U.S.,* 431 U.S. at 335, note 15.

14. Decision of U.S. District Court, p. D-9.

15. Ibid.

16. Ibid., p. D-10.

17. Ibid.

18. Ibid.

19. *Albemarle Paper Company* v. *Moody* 422 U.S. at 418-419, 95 S.CT. at 2372.

20. Ibid. at 2374.

21. Decision of U.S. District Court, p. D-12.

22. Jeanne Saddler, "U.S. May Challenge Equal-Pay Decision Made in Case Against Washington State," The *Wall Street Journal,* January 23, 1984, p. 16.

23. Carroll Boone, "The Washington State Comparable Worth Trial," *Comparable Worth Project Newsletter* 3, 4 (Fall 1983, Winter 1984): 12.

24. *Spaulding* v. *University of Washington,* Opinion, United States Court of Appeals for the Ninth Circuit, No. 82-3038, D.C. No. CV 74–91, p. 2.

25. Ibid., p. 37; The opinion quotes from *Christensen* v. *State of Iowa,* 563 F.2d at 356.

26. Ibid., pp. 34–35.

27. Decision of U.S. District Court, pp. 8–9.

10

PAY EQUITY UPDATE:
Progress and Prospects

The growing vehemence of the opposition to comparable worth is a good measure of the policy's progress. The civil rights commissioner recently ridiculed it as "the looniest of Looney Tunes." Nevertheless, the commission has taken pay equity seriously enough to study it extensively. The assistant attorney general for civil rights belittled the policy but has taken the trouble to consider legal action against it. During the 1984 presidential campaign a member of the president's Council of Economic Advisers called comparable worth "truly crazy" but spent time analyzing it. Undoubtedly, the advocates of comparable worth would prefer support rather than opposition. But when the administration's name-calling indicates the policy's growing strength it should, in a perverse way, be music to the ears of supporters. A decade ago most people had never heard of pay equity.

Court decisions set the legal parameters for sex-based wage discrimination. Litigation is, therefore, important in determining what is or is not deemed discrimination according to the courts' interpretations of the civil rights laws. Given the legal framework—and the courts are still filling out that framework—the development of compensation systems free of bias based on sex, race, religion, or national origin is carried out by individual public and private employers working with their employees as part of their wage-setting process. Contrary to the arguments of its opponents, effecting comparable worth policy does not mean that the courts will start setting wages for every business in the country. Two recent and important examples of private sector initiatives in freeing wage systems of bias are the strike for pay equity at Yale University and the cooperative development of a bias-free occupational job evaluation system by American Telephone and Telegraph Company's management and three unions.

189

What's Happening in the Private Sector: Yale Workers Strike for Pay Equity

On September 26, 1984, 1,600 clerical and technical workers at Yale University "made history," the National Committee on Pay Equity reported, "by initiating the first major private sector strike over the issue of pay equity."[1] The strike of workers in Local 34 of the Federation of University Employees went on for ten weeks, seriously disrupting the academic and social life of the university. To avoid having to cross picket lines, many professors moved classes to rooms off campus in church basements, movie theaters, nursery schools—wherever rooms could be found. Maintenance and dining room workers, in Local 35, most of them male, honored the picket lines, so the residential college dining rooms, centers of student social life, were effectively closed. Many university functions were canceled. Disagreements among the faculty, the students, and between both groups and the Yale administration about settling the strike divided the campus.

"The business of education is going on only with difficulty," Cyrus Hamlin, professor of German literature, said. "The whole routine of the university is in difficulty because of this situation."[2]

Local 34 of the Federation of University Employees won the right to represent the 2,650 clerical and technical employees at Yale in 1983, after three years of organizing work by its parent union, the International Union of Hotel and Restaurant Employees. Women make up 82 percent of the group, 83 percent are white, 14 percent are black, and 3 percent belong to other minority groups. The "C and T's," as they are called at Yale, work at 257 varied jobs—secretaries, computer programmers, departmental administrative assistants, psychiatric aides, laboratory technicians, editorial assistants, telephone operators, and athletic trainers, to name a few.

Efforts to organize these workers had been going on since the 1960s and had been vigorously and, until 1983, successfully opposed by Yale. Conventional wisdom says that female clerical workers are harder to organize than female or male blue-collar workers. Experience indicates that this should be particularly true in the all-in-the-family, company town atmosphere of a college town. Furthermore, institutions of higher learning can be as tough as private business in opposing affirmative action policies for themselves, however quick their "university families" may be to urge them on others. They will certainly not welcome the organization of a union of nonacademic staff, mainly women and minorities, which has a goal of increasing its members' relative pay and benefits. How did this union grow in such a sterile field?

"Although we did not use the term comparable worth," John Wilhelm, chief negotiator for Local 34 and vice president for the New England District of the parent union, the International Union of Hotel and Restaurant Employees, AFL-CIO, told me, "that concept has always underlain the whole organizing effort. People thought intuitively," he said, "and it turned out to be true statistically, that the principal mechanism the university used to hold down salaries was essentially to stop giving you any noticeable increase after you'd been here for two or three years. New Haven is very much a company town, you know, and Yale is the company. Although they didn't put it this way," he said, "they operated on the theory that once you were here for two or three years they sort of had you. The statistical reflection of that is that the majority of the people in every salary grade were clustered in the bottom 15 percent of the range for that grade. If, for example, a grade ran from $10,000 to $15,000 you'd find most of the people between $10,000 and $11,500. Campuswide, only 61 people, less than 3 percent of the group, were at the maximum in their particular grades."

So although the environment was hostile, the issues around which to organize the Yale C and T's were there. And so was John Wilhelm, a Yale graduate of 1967, described by William Serrin of *The New York Times* as the "chief architect" of the organizing campaign. Wilhelm went to work for the Hotel and Restaurant Employees Union in 1969.

I asked John Wilhelm to what extent he felt that comparable worth was an issue in the strike and how it was reflected in the settlement. He replied that it was "very much a comparable worth situation" although the university didn't agree. He explained that there were two reasons why the union didn't suggest a comparable worth study. First, it was so obvious that the C and T workers were underpaid by "any set of comparisons you might want to make here at Yale, that one didn't need a study. And the amounts by which salaries ought to be increased were so great that we didn't run any risk of overpaying people in the first contract in the absence of a study.

"Secondly, it seemed to us inevitable that if we proposed a study the university would quite logically say that, pending the results of a study, we shouldn't try to negotiate more than the conventional increases people are settling for these days. And we didn't want to settle for a two- or three-year contract with only the usual increases."

The statistics provided by the university to the union showed that women workers in the C and T group earned $13,290 on average and had worked at Yale an average 6 years. Male workers earned $14,056 and had averaged 5.6 years. Black workers had worked 6.8 years and earned an average $12,644. White workers had averaged 5.8 years and earned $13,563.

A concerned group of Yale faculty and graduate students with diverse views on the dispute made a lengthy study titled "Facts on the Current Dispute." They hoped that agreement on the basic facts might help to resolve the disagreements. For evidence on wage differences at Yale they cited the study of sex and race differences in wages between job classes within the C and T group done by Yale economics professor Ray Fair. They reported:

> In a calculation similar to those done by the National Research Council, Yale Economics Professor Ray Fair found that after adjusting for age, time at Yale, time in grade, and education, women are on average paid approximately $700 per year less than men, and minorities approximately $1,000 less than whites within the C and T workforce. His statistics were significant at the 5 percent level.

They pointed out that the C and T group is mainly female. Therefore, they suggested that a complete study of sex-based wage discrimination in the university as a whole would probably show even greater wage discrimination than the Fair statistics found. Fair commented on his analysis, "The results of the regression are disturbing. . . . The results show that the charge of discrimination should be taken seriously by Yale and a careful study should be made of what is going on."

In April 1984, after many months without progress in bargaining, the union and the university agreed on a group of noneconomic issues in an effort to avert a strike. They continued to negotiate on the issues of pay increases, pay structure, pension increases, health care benefits, and job security, but without progress. Students, faculty, and local and state leaders urged both sides to submit the disputed issues to binding arbitration. The union agreed. The administration did not, saying that these matters were too vital to Yale to be decided by an outsider.

The university argued that the union demands were too costly. Furthermore, they said, Yale did not discriminate so pay equity was not an issue. They pointed out that they paid equal pay for the same work. They claimed the dispute was just a typical union struggle for higher wages.

The strike began in September. During the winter break in December the strikers went back to work, seeing no sense in picketing empty buildings. In late January Yale and the union reached an agreement on the disputed issues, signing a three-and-a-half-year agreement that was retroactive to July 1984.

The union's principal salary objective and its way of achieving pay equity for women and minorities, most of whom were at the bottom of the salary structure, was "to establish a system of step progression based on years of service, with significant pay increments for each year of service," Wilhelm explained to me. "And then," he continued, "having established that structure, to put the current employees on it where they belonged, according to their years of service."

"We think we were very successful in that," he said. "The average increase for people who were here at the time the contract was signed is about 35 percent over the three and a half years."

The settlement increases pensions and health care benefits. Both of these were prime concerns of the women workers. The contract also provides for a joint union-administration committee to study job descriptions and classifications and make recommendations on revisions. The committee will hear employee appeals from personnel department decisions on the correctness of the worker's job classification. This mechanism can lead to a reduction in discrimination in the salary structure.

Even without the usual technique of a job evaluation study that compares the point values of jobs, the union, the media, and the public have typed the Yale dispute as a "test for comparable worth" and the outcome a victory for pay equity. The successful organization of a strong union of largely female white-collar workers in a university community is in itself a notable accomplishment.

What's Happening in the Private Sector: Comparable Worth in the Telephone Companies

AT&T and the Bell group of operating companies are among the largest employers of women in the country outside of the government. So it was good news for working women when, in 1980, the "old," predivestiture AT&T and its three unions agreed to cooperate in developing and testing a job evaluation system for the whole company that would be as free of sex bias as they could make it. Frank Garon, of the Telecommunications International Union (TIU) and chair of the unions' committee on the plan, told me that their objective was to simplify the system's job structure with a single bias-free plan—the Bell system had some 1,400 titles, many of which probably were duplications. Furthermore, the company wanted to be able to update changes in job descriptions continuously during the three-year life of the contract as new technology changed job content.

"It was not simply a comparable worth objective," Garon said, "although we recognized that the by-product of a single job evaluation system that evaluated all jobs would be comparable worth. If a job received the same points it was going to receive the same money."

"My opinion is that what we have is a fairly leading edge," Dr. Wilfredo Manese, district manager for occupational job evaluation, Bell Communications Research (Bellcore), said as he described to me the occupational job evaluation system (OJE) that the joint union-management group developed. "I believe it is the way to go. Our problem," he said, "is that with the break-up of the Bell system we've had to scramble."

"Your position as I understand it from what you've written," I said, "is that it's technically feasible to develop an occupational job evaluation plan which is free of sex bias, and you think that your OJE plan has done that, but the Bell system's problem now lies in implementing it." Manese agreed.

"The union also feels it is a very good plan, for a number of reasons," Lorel Foged, economist/statistician with the Communications Workers of America, AFL-CIO, told me. Foged is the union staff person working with Manese on the development and implementation of the plan. "One reason is that we put a lot of time and effort into it. We looked at existing plans and took the best from them. But the main reasons are that we developed it jointly," she said, "and we tested it out for a year in one company, Chesapeake and Potomac Telephone Company in Maryland. That test was meant to be the prototype for how we would implement the plan in the entire Bell system."

"Will Manese and I were the project managers," she explained. "We trained two workers and two first line supervisors to write job descriptions for 25 titles. We verified the job descriptions by going back to the jobholders and their supervisors. And then we trained 10 to 12 people to work as a joint group of evaluators. This group was a mix of management and workers and also of race, sex, and geographical location. They evaluated the 25 job descriptions." Both union and management were satisfied that the resulting job rankings were approximately right. "That meant to us that the system worked," she said.

"What happened then," she continued, "was a three-week strike in August 1983 when national bargaining took place. The strike was really over wages but this was part of it as well. The bargainers did not agree to a job evaluation plan because of a hang-up over who was going to run it— the implementation. The union wanted to do it jointly as we had done it in the pilot study, and the company wanted pretty much to run it themselves. At least they wanted to keep control over job descriptions, which would give them ultimate control over the system even though we might have a joint job evaluation team.

"Our problem with that is that we've had something similar to that at Western Electric for years. What happens is that if the company downgrades a job and changes the job description there is nothing the joint evaluation committee can do about it. That is our big problem now with the way technology is being implemented. It is deskilling the jobs. We feel we need to actually have real input—effective involvement, it's called—in both the job description and the job evaluation. So we did not agree to a national plan.

"What they said in that 1983 bargaining," she explained, "was that each of the Bell operating companies—of which there are about 22—plus AT&T could set up their own joint committees to study a plan. The intent was that they would take the technical aspects of the plan we had developed and each company and union would decide in bargaining how they wanted to implement it. And then of course the turmoil of divestiture came along to aggravate the problem.

"What's been happening since," she said, "is that the companies organize their committees and then they turn to Will Manese at Bellcore, or to me at CWA and have one or both of us come to teach them what we did. We've done that now in four or five of the companies. Then, if they agree on how the system is to be run, we train them in writing the job descriptions and then we train the evaluators.

"The 22 companies are grouped into seven regions," she said. "So some of the companies are working now as a region. And some of the companies are not interested in this at all," she added.

I had already heard this from Douglas Wiegand, the union person handling job evaluation for the International Brotherhood of Electrical Workers (IBEW) and from Frank Garon of TIU. They agreed that Illinois Bell was probably ahead of the other companies on implementation. Connecticut, Garon's area, is also doing job analysis training and developing job descriptions, using the national plan. "The only area we haven't agreed on yet," Garon said, "is implementation." He said that New York "was getting started."

Lorel Foged thought that North West Bell, Mountain Bell, Pacific Telephone, Pacific Northwest Bell, Bell South, and Chesapeake and Potomac were all interested in doing something. "Some of the committees like the one at New Jersey Bell have met several times," she said, "and they couldn't agree on anything. I think they have pretty well agreed not to do anything, though I'm not real sure," she said.

"Southwestern Bell doesn't want any part of it," Douglas Wiegand told me.

"Why is that?" I asked.

"I imagine they want to continue to discriminate on the basis of sex," he said. "I don't know. They have a very poor relationship with the union, CWA," he added. "Neither party trusts the other, so codetermination on wage setting would never work. There are a couple of others that have some problems too," he added, "like Ohio Bell. But that's not one of our properties either. Fortunately for IBEW, in most of our properties we are able to sit down jointly and work this thing out.

"The original concept was great," Wiegand said. "One job evaluation system for the entire Bell system. So that there was no discrimination across the system. It would have been beautiful, if we could have done that on a national basis, or even on a regional basis and then have an oversight committee on a national basis to keep an eye on it to make sure that it was uniformly applied. Now we don't have that because of divestiture. The best we can do is say, 'Here are the ground rules that you should adopt,' and hope they'll continue on that path. But they can change the whole thing around, if they want."

"Do you think the system that was developed was nondiscriminatory?" I asked.

"I think it's as nondiscriminatory as we can make it," Douglas Wiegand said. "We had females represented on the committee and we did our best to recognize and deal with the biases that have been built in. I think that it's a pretty decent system all in all because it can measure both clerical and nonclerical types of jobs with a single measuring device. It doesn't give the traditional job evaluation categories of lifting and so on high values because they are male jobs. It doesn't discriminate against the predominantly female classifications.

"Discrimination all starts with the employer anyway," Wiegand said. "They hire women for the job with no future where they can pay them least. And the unions have nothing to say—we can't even represent them during the normal 30- or 60-day probationary period. So job evaluation doesn't cure all the ills," he concluded. "And it is still a subjective system. There is no plan that is not subjective.

"We have companies all over," Wiegand said. "GE, Westinghouse, Western Electric. We have job evaluation plans in most of those plants. And they seem to work. Some of them may discriminate against females because of the way they weight the plan. That's easy to do. They ought to have a clause at the end of the plan," he suggested, "that says, 'This plan shall self-destruct in five years.' And then you develop a new one. Because they become management tools that can be manipulated. And by unions, too."

The individual Bell companies are currently covered by the 1983 national contract. But in 1986 they will be bargaining for themselves on new contracts, which, for some at least, will include provisions for the new OJE plan. The good news for pay equity supporters is that both management and unions agree that the AT&T occupational job evaluation plan is free of sex bias and that it does work. The problems arise in implementation. They stem from the politics of control—who runs the plan—and from the indications that some companies or regions may not be interested in the bias-free OJE system.

There are, of course, other private employers who have adopted nonbiased pay structures. The electrical industry, for example, has been involved in settlements of sex-based wage discrimination claims since the mid-1970s. The 1981 decision in the *IUE* v. *Westinghouse* case spurred the industry to continue moving ahead on pay equity in settlements of claims and in collective bargaining agreements. A comparable worth study funded by the Ford Foundation and done by the National Committee on Pay Equity reports that 64 private sector companies have implemented pay equity. The study found that most of this activity resulted from collective bargaining rather than from litigation.

Progress in the Public Sector: The Pace Quickens

"It's hard to keep up with pay equity in the states and localities," I said to June Inuzuka, research fellow at the National Committee on Pay Equity, "because things keep happening every week."

"Oh yes," she said, "every day."

Putting the states into what she termed "mutually exclusive categories" representing their progress on the way toward implementation of pay equity, she told me that by her most recent count 6 states have programs in place and are spending money to implement them—Idaho, Iowa, Minnesota, New Mexico, South Dakota, and Washington. Job evaluation studies addressing pay equity have been undertaken in 19 states. Pay equity task forces or commissions that have not yet undertaken job evaluation studies are in place in 12 states. Another 9 states are still in the preliminary research stage. And only 4 states—Arizona, Arkansas, Georgia, and Oklahoma—have not taken some sort of specific action on pay equity.

This activity began at a rather slow pace a little over a decade ago when, in 1974, Washington State made the first formal comparable worth study. A number of states already had laws enacted in the 1950s and 1960s requiring equal pay for comparable worth. In fact, Alaska's law, which appears to be the earliest, dates back to 1949. California, Idaho, Maine, Maryland, Massachusetts, and Nebraska also passed early comparable worth laws.[3]

Idaho, however, was apparently the first state actually to implement pay equity for state employees. In 1969, the Idaho legislature passed a comparable worth law titled Discriminatory Payment of Wages Based upon Sex Prohibited. This law forbade "an employer to pay 'any employee in any occupation in this state at a rate less than the rate at which he pays an employee of the opposite sex *for comparable work* on jobs which have comparable requirements relating to skill, effort and responsibility. . . .' "[4] In 1975, the Idaho legislature followed this up by requiring the state civil service commission to study the "internal equity" of the state's compensation system using the methods developed by Hay Associates. Hay Associates conducted the study. In 1977, Idaho implemented an "internal equity compensation system" based on the Hay method with some modifications designed principally to meet market competition. The system covered 8,000 classified state employees in 1,100 job classes. It applied to both men and women employees. Market modifications to the system affected job classifications covering about 1 percent of the employees.

Idaho implemented the system in one year. When pay equity went into effect women's salaries went up an average 16.2 percent and men's rose an average 6.8 percent. The salaries of secretaries rose by 20 to 30 percent.[5] The estimated cost was 4 percent of the total state budget for the year or about 10 percent of the classified employee payroll.[6] Other states and localities that have adopted pay equity programs have found their overall costs are less than Idaho's, running around 4 percent of total payroll for a year. They have typically lessened the immediate financial impact by spreading the equity increases over several years. Minnesota, for example, is making adjustments of 1 percent a year for four years.

Minnesota is frequently cited as the "pay equity model for the nation."[7] It is, according to the *National NOW Times,* "the country's best example of a cooperative model being effectively used to achieve parity in salaries for comparable jobs."[8] After seeing the results of a study of the state's pay system, the Minnesota legislature voted, in 1982, to set up a system for reaching pay equity over a four-year period. It allocated $21.7 million in 1983 for the first two years of adjustments. Salary increases will cost about 1 percent of the state payroll for each of the four years. The *NOW Times* terms it "a cooperative model" because the "State Office of Employee Relations works in cooperation with state government officials, unions and women's groups to ensure full and fair implementation of pay equity."[9] Minnesota's enthusiasm for getting rid of sex-based wage discrimination led the legislature in May 1984 to require local governments to do job evaluation studies and to set up nondiscriminatory pay systems.

New York is currently working on one of the largest comparable worth efforts that any state has yet made. It has funded two studies—one on pay equity by the New York State Center for Women in Government and a second on the state's system of classification and compensation by the consulting firm of Arthur Young. The pay equity study covers 175,000 workers in 5,000 jobs. In late March 1985 the state and its largest employee union agreed on a three-year labor contract providing $16 million in the first year to start correcting pay inequities that the study may find.

"Both parties recognize," James Roemer, counsel to the employees union, said to a *New York Times* reporter, "that this is going to cost 1 percent of the settlement for at least the next four or five years."[10]

"This Governor and this administration are in favor of pay equity," the *Times* quoted Nancy Hodes, executive deputy director of the Office of Employee Relations, as saying. The *Times* contrasted the positive attitude of New York State officials with the recent assertion of the U.S. Commission on Civil Rights that "federal agencies should 'reject comparable worth and rely instead on the principle of equal pay for equal work.' "

"They said comparable worth is not a valid theory—we disagree," Nancy Hodes said in the interview.

"We're going to go full speed ahead," James Roemer told the *Times.*

Meanwhile, in Ohio, Governor Richard Celeste has asked the legislature to fund $9 million for pay equity adjustments in 1986–87. This amounts to 1.5 percent of the general revenue fund's state payroll. The Ohio study documented an overall 13 percent female-male wage gap.[11]

In Oregon, Governor Victor Atiyeh has included $25 million in his 1986–87 proposed budget for pay equity adjustments. This is 1.1 percent of the state payroll. The Oregon pay study found a 20 percent female-male overall wage differential with a 32 percent gap for predominantly female classes.[12]

In Maryland, Governor Harry Hughes requested an 11 percent pay increase for 10,000 state clerical workers. This amounts to 7 percent more than the 4 percent raise he requested for all state workers. The clerical classification is 96 percent female.[13]

No one seems to have counted all of the local jurisdictions carrying on pay equity activities. But if school districts as well as towns, cities, and counties are included there are undoubtedly 100 or more. In 1984 the staff for the Washington State legislature's Joint Committee on Comparable Worth listed ten cities and counties in Washington State alone that were undertaking pay equity activity. Four of these had already mandated implementation of comparable worth programs.

California has produced the most notable pay equity activity at the local level of any state. In 1981 the successful San Jose strike for comparable worth brought the issue to national attention. In April 1985, Los Angeles and the American Federation of State, County and Municipal Employees, in what Mayor Tom Bradley described as "a historic step," negotiated a three-year contract providing for equal pay for comparable worth.

"Without a legal battle or costly study," Mayor Bradley told a news conference, "we will achieve pay equity among men and women who work for this city. We will send a message to all cities across this country."[14]

The pay equity raises will cost Los Angeles an estimated $12 million. This amounts to about .5 percent of its $2.1 billion budget. The union membership overwhelmingly approved the agreement and the union withdrew its complaint to the EEOC charging sex-based wage discrimination.

Localities in other states have been active as well—in New York, Virginia, Pennsylvania, Maine, Maryland, and Colorado, to name only a few. The list is long and constantly growing.

Litigation: Some Recent Developments

"The largest ever sex-based wage discrimination suit was filed on November 21st [1984] in Federal district court by the California State Employees Association, a Service Employees International Union local," the National Committee on Pay Equity reports.[15] The suit charged that the state has failed to correct pay discrimination against 37,000 women and men in predominantly female jobs.

The history of the union's complaint resembles the *Washington State* case. The state of California did a pay equity study in 1982 and found an overall female-male wage gap of 20 percent, which the state senate Office of Research attributed to discrimination. The study had concluded that "the large wage gap could not be explained by any relevant or equitable factors, but instead was the result of the discriminatory belief that 'men's work is worth more than women's work.' "[16] In 1984 the Democratic legislature voted $80 million to begin a five-year, $400 million program to close the gap. But Republican governor George Deukmejian vetoed the bill, although the state budget had a surplus. He argued that collective bargaining should be used to settle the issue. The union's president, Leo Mayer, pointed out that the governor's veto of funds left nothing to bargain with. The union seeks an end to the discriminatory pay practices and the award of back pay. Mayer estimates that as many as 100,000 workers, past, present, and future, may be affected.[17]

Nurses have also been active. They lost *Lemons,* a pre-*Gunther* case, but they have continued to attack the pay equity issue. In December 1983, Cynthia Dittmar, a lobbyist in the government relations office of the American Nurses' Association (ANA) in Washington, D.C., told me that the current major project of the ANA was to find an appropriate place to file a suit against sex-based wage discrimination.

"It is really the major issue for nurses," she explained. "Nurses see themselves as the prime example of pay inequity, which they certainly are."

In May 1984 the ANA, the Illinois Nurses' Association (INA), which is a member of the ANA, and 21 individual employees of the state of Illinois filed a class action suit against the state of Illinois charging that the state and its agencies and officials intentionally discriminated against female employees "in the terms and conditions of their employment because of their sex and because of their employment in historically female-dominated, sex-segregated job classifications." The complaint also alleged that the defendants have "intentionally discriminated and continue to discriminate against male state employees because of their employment in historically female-dominated sex-segregated job classifications."[18] The complaint charged that the state discriminated against employees in female-dominated occupations by using a sex-biased system of pay and classification. As a result these employees get a lower rate of pay for job classes that are evaluated "as being of comparable, equal, or greater worth than historically male-dominated sex-segregated job classifications which receive higher rates of pay."[19]

The background of the case follows a familiar pattern—concern about discrimination in state employment dating back to the early 1970s, growing emphasis on the problem of sex-based wage discrimination leading to the commissioning of a formal pay equity study by Hay Associates in 1982, findings of substantial female-male pay inequities, and no action by the state to correct the inequities. The study analyzed 12 large employee classes in which 80 percent or more of the workers were female and 12 large classes in which 80 percent or more of the employees were male. Hay Associates directed the job evaluations of these classes. They found a female-male wage gap ranging from 29 to 56 percent for work with the same evaluated worth. They found that women held most of the jobs in the lower pay grades and men held most of the top-paying jobs. They also found substantial occupational segregation by sex, with nearly 70 percent of the 1,281 classifications dominated by one sex or the other.

The Hay study found substantial sex-based wage discrimination even though the state agency directing the study said that "the majority of the Job Evaluation Committee members felt that certain management and sex biases are extant in the Hay method." For example, they said that the Hay system valued "people" skills, like those required of nurses and secretaries, lower than "mechanical" skills, required in many male occupations. They asserted that Hay measures "accountability," one of its four evaluation categories, only in terms of money and does not include accountability for human life, an important kind of accountability in such female work as nursing. And in rating working conditions Hay considers that "lifting on male-dominated jobs (i.e., unloading a truck or stocking shelves) is . . . more strenuous and rates a higher value . . . than lifting in female-dominated jobs (i.e., lifting patients)." They pointed out that the Hay system also lists the working conditions of an office as a "normal" environment while working outdoors is rated "disagreeable."

The state of Illinois and the other defendants asked the district court for dismissal of the case or, alternatively, for summary judgment. The plaintiffs presented a memorandum opposing dismissal or summary judgment.

"The Mountain States Legal Foundation is trying to intervene on behalf of various people who are in the male-dominated classes, on the side of the defendants," Edith Barnett, counsel for the plaintiffs, told me, in December 1984. "We are in the process of trying to oppose that as well. So we have a lot of skirmishes going on, even before we get to the main event," she said.

The district court added another skirmish when it recently ruled in favor of the defendants and dismissed the case. I asked Edith Barnett what the judge's grounds were for dismissal.

"Basically he bought all the ideological arguments by the defendants—that this is a terrible comparable worth case and so on," she said. "He just dismissed on the basis of the complaint, which we think is premature at best. Dismissal is a technical issue of whether the complaint states a cause of action," she explained. "We think it does. He said it didn't."

"We're planning to appeal," she said. "But I have no crystal ball as to what the appellate court is going to do. And we haven't formulated all of our arguments yet. But you can say we thought it was premature."

In August 1985 the Reagan administration moved to implement its opposition to pay equity for women by siding with the state of Illinois against the nurses at the appeals court level. Eunice Cole, president of the ANA, said of this action, "It culminates many months of ridicule of the principle of pay equity for working women by this Administration."[20]

In 1978 public health nurses in Alaska filed a complaint against the state claiming that they were being paid less than physician's assistants for doing work requiring comparable skill, effort, and responsibility. This is one of the few comparable worth complaints brought under state law. The Alaska fair employment practices law requires equal pay for work of "comparable character," but the courts have not interpreted the meaning of comparable character.

The Alaska Human Rights Commission tried to settle the case with a conciliation agreement that included back pay for the nurses, but the state refused to settle. Instead, in 1980 the state did a study of the pay differences between the two classes. It then raised the entry-level salary range of the physician's assistants from a grade 17 to grade 18 and lowered the educational requirements for the nurses from a B.A. to a two- to three-year nursing degree. The nurses' entry-level salary range is grade 14. They work in clinics and outreach programs around the state. The physician's assistants have to complete a one- to two-year training program. They provide "primary care" to state prison inmates.

In late 1984, after public hearings on the case, a hearing officer for the Human Rights Commission advised the commission to turn down the complaint of the public health nurses. The officer interpreted the Alaska law as requiring equal pay for equal work. The case now goes to the Human Rights Commission and its decision may be appealed to the state supreme court.[21]

"Hospital Nightmare: Cuts in Staff Demoralize Nurses as Care Suffers," a headline in the *Wall Street Journal* for March 27, 1985, reads. "Nursing is in turmoil," the article says. "Cost pressures brought on by a new Medicare payment system are causing hospitals to reduce nursing and support staffs." The article details the effects on nurses and patients of the heavy workloads that result from the staff cuts.

These cost pressures are creating a difficult climate for nurses' efforts to improve their status in the health care system. But they seem to be making nurses more, not less, militant. Last summer, for example, in what *The New York Times* termed "the largest nurses' strike in the nation's history," over 6,000 nurses in Minneapolis, Minnesota, struck 16 hospitals. The issues were improved benefits and job security. The strike lasted a month before it was settled with an agreement satisfactory to both the nurses and the hospitals. There have been other nurses' strikes around the country over control of job assignments, seniority, wages, and benefits. Striking is not something that nurses take to naturally. But, like the clerical workers, they have to work and therefore they are becoming increasingly aware of the need to improve their economic situation and to have greater control over their jobs and their working environment.

At the local level, the American Federation of State, County and Municipal Employees filed a suit in April 1984 charging Nassau County, New York, with sex-based wage discrimination. The suit received a good deal of publicity in part because it was filed by a big union with a record of bringing well-prepared, often successful cases and also because it can be an important model for other localities. It is a class action suit filed on behalf of 5,500 people working for Nassau County in predominantly female jobs. Winn Newman, the lawyer for AFSCME in the *Washington State* case and for the IUE in the successful *Westinghouse* case, is handling the Nassau County suit.

"For more than a year," Gerald F. McEntee, president of Nassau Local 830 said, "we've been trying to work responsibly through collective bargaining to remedy pay disparities that exist between male-dominated jobs and jobs of comparable value and worth which are filled mainly by women."[22] The union filed a complaint with the EEOC after failing to get pay equity through bargaining. When the EEOC refused to act the union sued, claiming sex-based wage discrimination under both Title VII of the Civil Rights Act and the Equal Pay Act. Nassau County has made a motion to dismiss. The judge has not yet ruled on that motion.

Pay Equity in the European Economic Community: "Female Cook Wins Pay of Craftsman"

"A woman cook in a work canteen must be paid the same wage as a skilled shipyard craftsman, an industrial tribunal has ruled in the first case brought under amended [English] equal pay legislation," the British *Financial Times* reported on October 31, 1984. In the early 1970s, the European Economic Community required all of its member countries to enact and enforce laws requiring equal pay for work of equivalent, or comparable, value. But Britain, like some of the other community members, dragged its feet on compliance with the EEC requirement. In 1982 the European Court of Justice ruled that the existing British equal pay act did not satisfy EEC law. Finally, by January 1984, the English had put an amended law into effect.

In this first case, Julie Hayward, a cook at the Cammell Laird shipyard in Liverpool, "found herself"—after a four-year apprenticeship program—"serving meals to men at the yard, including former schoolmates, who had a comparable level of training, easier jobs and higher salaries."[23] Her union "agreed with her that it was a raw deal."[24] With advice from a consultant retained by the union and the British Equal Opportunities Commission, Julie Hayward went through the long process of hearings before an industrial tribunal that British law requires. The tribunal ruled that she should be paid "on the same scale as Cammell Laird painters, joiners and insulation installers."[25] Her wages went up from $125 to $164 a week.

Making a sex-based wage discrimination claim in Britain is not easy. Britain does not allow class action suits, so each aggrieved worker must go through the lengthy process of negotiations and hearings herself. "In practice," *New York Times* reporter Feder writes, "that has meant that almost all the 20 cases now in progress, involving some 60 women, are complaints backed by trade unions. Even with support, claimants can find the complicated process daunting."[26]

There has been less activity in the other community countries than in England. *Wall Street Journal* reporter Paul Hemp attributes this to the lack of publicity about the law in these countries as well as the lack of support for women workers from government agencies.[27]

Nevertheless, companies both in England and on the Continent are concerned about the ripple effect of these cases. "Some firms are vulnerable," a representative of the Confederation of British Industry said, according to reporter Hemp. "The cases so far haven't opened the floodgates, but there is the potential for serious harm."[28]

"Once the pay is upgraded for one person for one occupation, the pay structure within that organization could be blown open," another British consultant worried.[29]

"A lot of companies hope the issue will go away," an advisor to the British Equal Opportunity Commission said, "But if we take the law seriously, there are incredible implications for companies' pay structures."[30]

The unions apparently look at sex-based wage discrimination from a different point of view. Male workers in the Hull, England, Transport and General Workers Union, for example, agreed to take lower pay increases in order to get larger raises for their women workers. But even with the men's efforts a female-male pay gap of 7 percent remained.

"We've been trying for four years to get justice for the lasses in the factory," said Peter Allen, an organizer for the Hull union. Paul Hemp points out that support like this from the male-dominated unions is critical to the effectiveness of the British pay equity law.[31] But even with the essential support of the unions it seems doubtful that the European equal pay for work of equivalent value laws will make rapid progress in getting rid of sex-based wage discrimination in the community countries.

Notes

1. Committee on Pay Equity, "Pay Equity Newsnotes," December 1984.

2. Edward A. Gargan, "Yale, As Strikers Return, Weighs the Damage to an Intellectual Community," *The New York Times,* December 1, 1984, pp. 25–26.

3. Alice H. Cook, *Comparable Worth: The Problem and States' Approaches to Wage Equity.* Occasional Publication no. 145 (Honolulu: Industrial Relations Center, University of Hawaii at Manoa, 1983), pp. 39, 42, 47, 70–71, 77.

4. Ibid., p. 73.

5. Ibid.

6. Ibid.; Mary Tuominen, "Comparable Worth—Evaluation and Implementation in Other States," Washington State Joint Select Committee on Comparable Worth Implementation, March 19, 1984, p. 9.

7. Liz Nicholson, "Pay Equity: State Roundup," *National NOW Times* (January/February 1985): 7.

8. Ibid.

9. Ibid.

10. Maurice Carroll, "Albany to Study State Jobs for Pay Inequities," *The New York Times,* April 14, 1985, p. 43.

11. Nicholson, "Pay Equity," p. 8.

12. Ibid.

13. Ibid.

14. Pauline Yoshihashi, "Los Angeles Backing Equal Pay for Jobs of 'Comparable Worth,' " *The New York Times,* May 9, 1985, pp. A1, A27.

15. National Committee on Pay Equity, "Pay Equity News Notes," December 1984, p. 3.

16. Nicholson, "Pay Equity," pp. 6–7.

17. "Union Sues California on Sex Discrimination," *The New York Times,* November 22, 1984, Sec. I, p. 21.

18. *American Nurses' Association et al.* v. *State of Illinois et al.,* Case No. 84 C 4451, U.S. District Court for the Northern District of Illinois, Eastern Division, p. 6.

19. Ibid., p. 7.

20. Robert Pear, "Court Cases Reveal New Inequalities in Women's Pay," *The New York Times,* August 21, 1985, pp. C1, C10.

21. This information on the Alaska nurses' case comes largely from the issues of the *Comparable Worth Project Newsletter* for December 1981, Spring 1982, and Winter 1985.

22. John T. McQuiston, "Nassau County Charged in Suit on Wage Bias," *The New York Times,* April 24, 1984, Sec. II, p. 2.

23. Barnaby J. Feder, "Key British Ruling on Wages," *The New York Times,* November 19, 1984, Sec. IV, p. 10.

24. Ibid.

25. Ibid.

26. Ibid.

27. Paul Hemp, "Flurry of Lawsuits by European Women Seeking Equal Pay for Equal Jobs Worries Corporations," *Wall Street Journal,* March 28, 1985, p. 36.

28. Ibid.

29. Ibid.

30. Ibid.

31. Ibid.

EPILOGUE

Support for pay equity is growing steadily. More and more people are interested in eliminating sex-based wage discrimination. In February 1985 almost 47 million women over 20 years old in this country were in the civilian labor force. This amounted to a labor force participation rate of 54.5 percent for women 20 and over in the "civilian noninstitutional population." The female labor force participation rate has increased continuously in the post–World War II decades from 31.6 percent in 1948 to 37.5 percent in 1960, 43.3 percent in 1970, and 51.3 percent in 1980. The total number of women over age 20 who were working in 1948 was 15.5 million, less than a third of the 1985 figure.

In the last three decades, as a result of this influx of women workers, six out of every ten of the new workers coming into the labor force have been female. And the Bureau of Labor Statistics predicts continued growth in the numbers of working women, with the female participation rate reaching 60.3 percent by 1995. With this substantial growth in both the number of women working and in the proportion of women relative to men in the labor force, it is inevitable that the pressures against sex-based wage discrimination should strengthen.

Furthermore, as more and more women have gone to work outside the home the number of two-income families has risen. In 1981 more than three fifths of all married couples reported to the census bureau that both husband and wife worked. This means that many men who might formerly have been expected to question pay equity now support it.

It is clear, therefore, that the issue of equal pay for comparable worth is not going to go quietly away. What is the outlook for its future? What are the obstacles to achieving pay equity? What are the grounds for optimism?

A major obstacle is employers' concern over the cost of eliminating sex-based wage discrimination. They assert that implementing comparable worth policy in this country would cost hundreds of billions of dollars. Like Judge Winner in the *Lemons* case, they predict that economic chaos would result. This cost fear is particularly strong in businesses with many low-paid female workers, like banks and insurance companies with their large clerical staffs. It is a fear both of the absolute size of the pay remedy and of the ripple effect on the rest of the pay structure of raising wages in female-dominated occupations. The stake of business in inequity is high and their opposition to this perceived threat to their economic interests is formidable. Their concern, however, indicates how extensive pay inequity is.

Because of this concern, employers who oppose comparable worth have mounted a strong campaign against it. The conservative press frequently denounces it, trotting out the by now familiar arguments to show that it is a foolish concept with dangerous implications for government control of the economy. Organizations representing business have filed friend of the court briefs opposing pay equity in legal cases at every opportunity. They have funded books and articles and speakers and conferences on the issue. And they have put strong pressure on the government, particularly at the federal level, to fight it.

The Reagan administration has obliged. Every federal agency responsible for enforcing Title VII's prohibition against sex-based wage discrimination—the Equal Employment Opportunity Commission, the Office of Federal Contract Compliance, the Justice Department, the Civil Rights Commission—has backed off from enforcing the law. The Justice Department has, in fact, taken a stand actively opposing implementation of comparable worth policy. And Chairman Clarence Pendleton expressed the majority attitude of the Civil Rights Commission when he said that comparable worth is "the looniest of Looney Tunes."

Another obstacle to achieving pay equity may be the legal one. The courts are still developing the law on this issue. The 1981 Supreme Court decisions in the *Gunther* and *IUE* cases opened the door to claims of sex-based wage discrimination when women work in jobs that are not the same as men's. And the 1983 district court decision in *Washington State* was a big victory for pay equity. But that decision is under appeal and it will undoubtedly be several years before it gets through the whole appeals process.

The ninth circuit court of appeals came down against comparable worth in *Spaulding* v. *University of Washington* in the summer of 1984. In September 1985 the ninth circuit court again ruled against pay equity by reversing the district court decision in *AFSCME et al.* v. *State of Washington et al.* Also in 1985, the judge in a U.S. district court in the northern district of Illinois dismissed what seemed to be a strong pay equity case brought by the American Nurses' Association and the Illinois Nurses Association against the state of Illinois. The judge claimed the nurses did not have sufficient grounds for their complaint. The nurses appealed the judge's dismissal of their case. The federal government has entered the case on the side of the state.

In the meantime the federal courts are taking on a more conservative hue as the Reagan administration appoints new judges. The situation on the Supreme Court is particularly worrisome to civil rights advocates. Most of the judges are elderly. If they retire, Reagan's replacements would certainly make the Court less sympathetic to issues like equal pay for comparable worth. It is obvious, therefore, that the path of litigating comparable worth successfully still faces some substantial hurdles.

Unions have been responsible for some of the most significant pay equity successes achieved so far. But only 14 percent of women workers are union members. And they are concentrated in two categories—government, where there are many women teachers who are unionized; and manufacturing, in industries like electrical equipment and textiles with numerous female blue-collar operatives. About a third of the women workers in the transportation, communication, and public utilities sector also belong to unions, but although the percentage of organized women workers is about as high there as it is for government, the absolute number is small. On the other hand, in the finance, insurance, and real estate area only 2.2 percent of the female employees are organized. In the service category only 6.3 percent of the women workers belong to unions. And of the women working in the wholesale and retail trade sector, only 6.4 percent are union members.

The service-producing sector, however, has produced the big job gains as the economy has moved into the postindustrial era. There was, for example, an increase of five million jobs in service occupations between 1980 and 1984 alone, while employment in manufacturing industries fell during the same period. And the majority of women work in the service-producing areas. The largest percentage—about 35 percent—are clerical workers. The next largest group—around 20 percent—are service workers. About 18 percent are professional and technical workers. But not only are most of these women workers unorganized, the common perception is that they are difficult to organize. So the continuing influx of women into these occupations appears to be another obstacle to achieving pay equity.

Nevertheless there are grounds for optimism about the outlook for equal pay for comparable worth. Faced with severe declines in union membership in the traditional union strongholds of heavy industry, mining, and transportation, some unions have mounted vigorous campaigns to organize workers in the service sector. In the process, they have discovered that eliminating sex-based wage discrimination is an issue of primary concern to women workers. Consequently they have made it a key organizing issue.

The American Federation of State, County and Municipal Employees (AFSCME) has a big and growing membership with many clerical workers as members. Pay equity is an important issue with AFSCME both in organizing and in sex discrimination litigation. The Service Employees International Union (SEIU) and the Communications Workers of America (CWA) are among the other large unions actively organizing and representing clerical and service workers. After struggling with bitter employer opposition, District 925 of SEIU recently won the right to represent service employees at a branch of Equitable Life Assurance Society, one of the nation's largest insurance companies. The number of workers involved is small, but getting even a toehold in this industry, with its large numbers of female workers, is significant. One of the interesting aspects of SEIU's strategy was the tactic it used, apparently successfully, of putting pressure on Equitable by asking unions nationwide to remove their pension funds from the company.

The recent experience of the Hotel Employees and Restaurant Employees International Union at Yale University provides further encouraging evidence that women clerical workers in the private sector will join unions. John Wilhelm, who directed the organization of the clerical and technical workers there, told me that he believes that women are "highly organizable." Wilhelm's method was to get the women thoroughly involved as leaders in the organizing effort and in the union after it became a certified bargaining agent.

"I don't agree with the proposition that's widespread within the labor movement and elsewhere, that both women in general and these kinds of women in particular are more difficult to organize than anyone else," he said. "I think they're easier to organize. I think that one of the results of the whole change in women's consciousness over the last 10 or 15 years is that women are both more receptive to organization and are also more effective when they get involved."

Pay equity advocates may also glean comfort from the fact that some 150 of the country's largest companies support an organization like the NOW Legal Defense and Education Fund. This fund works on a variety of projects benefiting women, among them equal pay for comparable worth. This is not the primary nor the only issue that NOW LDEF is concerned with. But it is encouraging that they can pursue pay equity, as well as other women's issues, with the support of prestigious businesses.

As pay equity has become a visibly important women's issue, Democratic politicians have been eager to show support for it. They have promoted studies of sex-based wage discrimination in federal government agencies. They have made it a campaign issue. Democrats worked for equal pay for comparable worth in the decades leading up to the civil rights legislation of the 1960s, so their interest is not new. But the current resurgence of concern is evidence that the issue is alive and flourishing.

The economic issues that stir the passions are those that deal with equity in income distribution. The question "Are women being paid what they are worth?" translates into "Are women receiving their fair share of the economic pie? Is the value of what women contribute greater than what they get?"

As more and more women work for wages the question grows more important to them and to their employers. The stakes increase and the conflict heightens. The economic issue turns into a political one, a question of control over who gets what and how much.

What will be the outcome of this political struggle over women's share in the nation's output? Perhaps the best judges are the women who have lived a long time with the conflict. They know better than anyone else what it is about, what it was like when they started on it, and how far the issue has come. The comments they made in their interviews with me summarize their views on the future of equal pay for comparable worth.

"I think we *have* won whether we make it past this stage or not," Peggy Holmes, a plaintiff in *AFSCME* v. *State of Washington,* told me in her assessment of Judge Tanner's decision in the case. "I think it's a huge victory for women. It's given women a lot of hope that they didn't have before. And that's really important."

"I think there's no doubt about it," Carroll Boone said when I asked her about the outlook for pay equity. "People are looking at it all over the country. I think there is *no way* it can be stopped."

"There will be efforts to water down women's anger and to find ways to circumvent them," Dorothy Haener, who has worked on this issue since the 1940s, told me. "But I think women are getting smart enough now that they do understand and that they aren't going to let that happen to them. You know," she concluded, "it *is* a nice time to be alive, for me. In terms of what women are accomplishing, it is a beautiful time."

BIBLIOGRAPHY

Ashenfelter, Orley, and Albert Rees, eds. *Discrimination in Labor Markets.* Princeton: Princeton University Press, 1973.

Beatty, Richard W., and James R. Beatty. "Job Evaluation and Discrimination: Legal, Economic, and Measurement Perspectives on Comparable Worth and Women's Pay." Prepared for a symposium on Women and the Work Force, sponsored by Virginia Polytechnic Institute, 1983.

Becker, Gary S. *The Economics of Discrimination,* 2nd ed. Chicago: University of Chicago Press, 1971.

_____. *Human Capital.* New York: Columbia University Press, for the National Bureau of Economic Research, 1st ed., 1964, 2nd ed., 1975.

Blaxall, Martha, and Barbara Reagan, eds. *Women and the Workplace: The Implications of Occupational Segregation.* Chicago: University of Chicago Press, 1976.

Blumrosen, Ruth G. "Wage Discrimination, Job Segregation, and Title VII of the Civil Rights Act of 1964." *University of Michigan Journal of Law Reform* 12 (Spring 1979): 402–15.

Boone, Carroll. "The Washington State Comparable Worth Trial." *Comparable Worth Project Newsletter* 3, 4 (Fall 1983, Winter 1984): 3–13.

Bureau of National Affairs. *The Comparable Worth Issue: A BNA Special Report.* Washington, D.C., 1981.

Bureau of National Affairs. *Pay Equity and Comparable Worth.* Washington, D.C., 1984.

Cadieux, Rita. *Equal Pay for Work of Equal Value—The Canadian Experience.* Ottawa: Canadian Human Rights Commission, 1982.

Cain, Glen. "The Challenge of Segmented Labor Market Theories to Orthodox Theory: A Survey." *Journal of Economic Literature* 14 (1976): 1215–57.

_____. "The Economic Analysis of Labor Market Discrimination: A Survey." IRP Special Report no. 37, Madison, Wis.: Institute for Research on Poverty, University of Wisconsin.

Cairns, Scott S. "Wage Discrimination Under Title VII After *IUE* v. *Westinghouse Electric Corp." Virginia Law Review* 67 (April 1981): 589–613.

Canadian Human Rights Commission. "The Canadian Human Rights Act, Employer Guide." Ottawa, Ontario, Canada, 1981.

_____. "Methodology and Principles for Applying S. 11." Working Paper, Ottawa, Ontario, Canada.

_____. "Summary of Decisions." May 1982.

Chafe, William H. *The American Woman: Her Changing Social, Economic, and Political Role, 1920–1970.* New York: Oxford University Press, 1972.

Chertos, Cynthia, Lois Haignere, and Ronnie Steinberg. "Occupational Segregation and its Impact on Working Women." Report of a conference held at the Ford Foundation, June 9, 1982. Center for Women in Government, State University of New York, November 1982.

Chiplin, Brian, and Peter J. Sloane. *Tackling Discrimination at the Workplace: An Analysis of Sex Discrimination in Britain.* Cambridge: Cambridge University Press, 1982.

Commission des Droits de la Personne du Québec. "À Travail Équivalent, Salaire Égal, sans Discrimination." Montreal, Canada, 1980.

Comparable Worth Project. *Newsletter* Oakland, Cal.: Comparable Worth Project, published quarterly.

Comparable Worth Project, National Committee on Pay Equity and National Women's Political Caucus. *Who's Working for Working Women? A Survey of State and Local Government Pay Equity Initiatives.* Washington, D.C., 1984.

Congressional Research Service. "Summary of Pay Equity/Comparable Worth Activities by State Governments." Prepared for Congresswoman Patricia Schroeder. Washington, D.C., 1985.

Cook, Alice H. "Collective Bargaining as a Strategy for Achieving Equal Opportunity and Equal Pay: Sweden and Germany." Paper prepared for the Wellesley Conference on Equal Pay and Equal Opportunity Policy for Women, Wellesley College Center for Research on Women, 1978.

_____. *Comparable Worth: The Problem and States' Approaches to Wage Equity.* Occasional Publication No. 145. Honolulu: Industrial Relations Center, University of Hawaii at Manoa, 1983.

_____. *The Working Mother,* rev. ed. New York: New York State School of Industrial and Labor Relations, Cornell University, 1978.

Dertien, Marvin G. "The Accuracy of Job Evaluation Plans." *Personnel Journal* (July 1981): 566–70.

Eagle Forum Education and Legal Defense Fund. "Equal Pay for Unequal Work." Conference Proceedings. Washington, D.C., 1984.

Equal Employment Advisory Council. "Comparable Worth: A Symposium on the Issues and Alternatives." Proceedings of November 21, 1980. Washington, D.C.: Equal Employment Advisory Council, 1981.

Friss, Lois O'Brien. Testimony at the Pay Inequity Hearings held by the State Department of Industrial Relations, the Department of Fair Employment and Housing, the Fair Employment and Housing Commission and the Commission on the Status of Women. Los Angeles, February 25–27, 1981.

_____. "Work Force Policy Perspectives: Registered Nurses." *Journal of Health Politics, Policy and Law* 5 (1981): 696–719.

Gasaway, Laura N. "Comparable Worth: A Post-*Gunther* Overview." *Georgetown Law Journal* 69 (1981): 1123–69.

Gold, Michael. *A Dialogue on Comparable Worth.* Ithaca, NY: Cornell University, ILR Press, 1983.

Gordon, David M., Richard Edwards, and Michael Reich. *Segmented Work, Divided Workers: The Historical Transformation of Labor in the United States.* Cambridge: Cambridge University Press, 1982.

Gregory, R.G., and R.C. Duncan. "Segmented Labor Market Theories and the Australian Experience of Equal Pay for Women." *Journal of Post-Keynesian Economics* 3 (Spring 1981): 403–28.

Grune, Joy Ann, ed. *Manual on Pay Equity.* Washington, D.C.: Committee on Pay Equity and the Conference on Alternative State and Local Policy, 1980.

Hubbard, Givens & Revo-Cohen, Inc. *Pay Equity Trends.* A newsletter published every six weeks. Reston, Virginia.

International Labour Office. "Declaration on Equality of Opportunity and Treatment of Women Workers." *Women Workers and Society: International Perspectives* 202 (1976).

_____. *Standards and Policy Statements of Special Interest to Women Workers.* Geneva: International Labour Organisation, 1980.

_____. *Women at Work.* A semiannual news bulletin published by the Office for Women Workers' Questions of the International Labour Organisation.

Jain, Harish C. "Canadian Legal Approaches to Sex Equality in the Workplace." *Monthly Labor Review* (October 1982): 38–41.

Lindsay, Cotton Mather. *Equal Pay for Comparable Work: An Economic Analysis of a New Antidiscrimination Doctrine.* An LEC Occasional Paper. Coral Gables, Fla.: the Law and Economics Center of the University of Miami, 1980.

Livernash, E. Robert, ed. *Comparable Worth: Issues and Alternatives.* Washington, D.C.: Equal Employment Advisory Council, 1st ed., 1980, 2d ed., 1984.

Lloyd, Cynthia B., ed. *Sex, Discrimination, and the Division of Labor.* New York: Columbia University Press, 1975.

Madden, Janice Fanning. *The Economics of Sex Discrimination.* Lexington, Ky.: D.C. Heath and Co., Lexington Books, 1973.

Manese, Wilfredo R. "Comparable Worth—One Manager's Perspective." Paper on the Occupational Job Evaluation plan developed by AT&T and its three unions. Presented at the University of Maryland Workshop on Comparable Worth, College Park, Md. April 10, 1984.

McDermott, F. Arnold. *"Lemons versus the City and County of Denver:* An Account of the Proceedings in a Title VII Pay Discrimination Case." *The Personnel Administrator* (October 1980): 95–106.

Meeker, Suzanne E. "Equal Pay, Comparable Work, and Job Evaluation." *Yale Law Journal* 90 (1981): 657.

National Committee on Pay Equity. *The Cost of Pay Equity in Public and Private Employment.* Ford Research Project. Washington, D.C., 1985.

_____. *Pay Equity Newsnotes.* Washington, D.C.

National Organization for Women. *National NOW Times.* Published eight times a year. Each issue has a section entitled "Pay Equity—State Updates," and also news articles on current pay equity events. Washington, D.C.

National Organization for Women Legal Defense and Education Fund. "Pay Equity; State by State." Washington, D.C.: NOW Legal Defense and Education Fund, Media Office, 1985.

Nelson, Bruce, Edward M. Opton, Jr., and Thomas E. Wilson. "Wage Discrimination and the 'Comparable Worth' Theory in Perspective." *University of Michigan Journal of Law Reform* 13:2 (Winter 1980): 231–301.

Newman, Winn. "Affirmative Action in the United States—Its Strengths and Weaknesses from a Union Perspective." Paper presented to the National Council for Civil Liberties: Positive Action for Women at Work Conference. London, April 6, 1981.

_____. "Does AFSCME Know the Way to San Jose?" Paper presented to the EEO in the Public Sector Conference. Washington, D.C.: Government Employees Relations Report, Labor Relations Reporter and BNA Conferences, February 8, 1982.

_____. "Policy Issues." *Signs: Journal of Women in Culture and Society* 1 (1976): 265–277.

Newman, Winn, and Jeanne M. Vonhof. " 'Separate but Equal'—Job Segregation and Pay Equity in the Wake of *Gunther." University of Illinois Law Review* 2 (1981): 269–331.

Organisation for Economic Cooperation and Development. *Women and Employment: Policies for Equal Opportunities.* Paris: OECD, 1980.

Perlman, Nancy, ed. *Preliminary Memorandum on Pay Equity.* Albany: Center for Women in Government, 1980.

Power, Margaret. "Women's Work Is Never Done—by Men: A Socio-Economic Model of Sex-typing in Occupations." *Journal of Industrial Relations* (September 1975): 225–39.

Ratner, Jonathan B. "The Employment Effects of Comparable Worth Policy." Working Paper 4. Center for Women in Government, State University of New York at Albany, November 1980.

Ratner, Ronnie Steinberg, ed. *Equal Employment Policy for Women: Strategies for Implementation in the United States, Canada, and Western Europe.* Philadelphia: Temple University Press, 1980.

Remick, Helen, ed. "The Comparable Worth Controversy." *IPMA Public Personnel Management Journal* 10 (December 1981): 7.

_____, ed. *Comparable Worth and Wage Discrimination: Technical Possibilities and Political Realities.* Philadelphia: Temple University Press, 1984.

_____. *Comparable Worth and Wages: Economic Equity for Women.* Honolulu: Industrial Relations Center, University of Hawaii at Manoa, 1984.

_____. "Strategies for Creating Sound, Bias-Free Job Evaluation Plans." In *Job Evaluation and EEO: The Emerging Issues.* IRC Colloquium, Atlanta, Georgia, Sept. 14–15, 1978.

Reynolds, Lloyd G. *Labor Economics and Labor Relations,* 7th ed. Englewood Cliffs, N.J.: Prentice-Hall, 1978.

Selden, Catherine, Ellen Mutari, Mary Rubin, and Karen Sacks. Business and Professional Women's Foundation. *Equal Pay for Work of Comparable Worth: An Annotated Bibliography.* Chicago: American Library Association, 1982.

Sexton, Patricia Cayo. *The New Nightingales: Hospital Workers, Unions, New Women's Issues.* New York: Enquiry Press, 1982.

Sharpe, Ivan. "Is the Future Female?" *Working Woman* (January 1983): 73–77.

Spelfogel, Evan J. "Equal Pay for Work of Comparable Value: A New Concept." *Labor Law Journal* (January 1981): 30–39.

Steinberg, Ronnie. "Labor Market Inequality and Equal Employment Policy for Women." Working Paper 5. Center for Women in Government, State University of New York at Albany, September 1979.

Straw, Ronnie J., and Lorel Foged. "The Limits of Job Evaluation to Achieve Comparable Worth." Paper on the Occupational Job Evaluation plan developed jointly by AT&T and its three unions. Presented to the Atlantic Economic Conference, Montreal, Canada, October 11–14, 1984.

Stromberg, Ann H., and Shirley Harkess, eds. *Women Working.* Palo Alto, Cal.: Mayfield Publishing Co., 1978.

Taber, Gisela, and Helen Remick. "Beyond Equal Pay for Equal Work: Comparable Worth in the State of Washington." Paper prepared for Conference on Equal Pay and Equal Opportunity Policy for Women in Europe, Canada, and the United States, Wellesley College, May 1–4, 1978.

Thomsen, David J. *Nondiscriminatory Salary Report: Survey and Model.* Los Angeles: Compensation Institute, 1979.

Thurow, Lester. *Generating Inequality: Mechanisms of Distribution in the U.S. Economy.* New York: Basic Books, 1975.

Treiman, Donald J. *Job Evaluation: An Analytic Review.* Washington, D.C.: National Research Council, National Academy of Sciences, 1979.

Treiman, Donald J., and Heidi I. Hartmann, eds. *Women, Work, and Wages: Equal Pay for Jobs of Equal Value.* Washington, D.C.: National Academy Press, 1981.

U.S., Commission on Civil Rights. *Comparable Worth: Issue for the 80's.* Washington, D.C., 1984.

U.S., Comptroller General. *Options for Conducting a Pay Equity Study of Federal Pay and Classification Systems.* Washington, D.C.: U.S. General Accounting Office, March 1, 1985.

U.S., Congress, House. Committee on Post Office and Civil Service. *Pay Equity: Equal Pay for Work of Comparable Value,* Joint Hearings, Subcommittees on Human Resources, Civil Service, Compensation and Employee Benefits. Parts I and II. 87th Cong., 2d sess., 1982.

U.S., Dept. of Health and Human Services. *Report to the President and Congress on the Status of Health Personnel in the United States,* May 1984.

U.S., Equal Employment Opportunity Commission, *Hearings on Job Segregation and Wage Discrimination,* Washington, D.C., April 28–30, 1980.

Wetzel, Frances L. "The Bennett Amendment—Title VII and Gender-Based Discrimination." *Georgetown Law Journal* 68: 1169–90.

Wilkinson, Frank, ed. *The Dynamics of Labor Market Segmentation.* New York: Academic Press, 1981.

Williams, Robert E., and Lorence L. Kessler. *A Close Look at Comparable Worth: A Study of the Basic Questions to Be Addressed in Approaching Pay Equity.* Washington, D.C.: National Foundation for the Study of Equal Employment Policy, 1984.

Women's Equity Action League. *WEAL Washington Report.* Published bimonthly. Washington, D.C.

Women's Rights Law Reporter, "Special Issue: Comparable Worth" 8 (Winter 1984).

INDEX

ABOUT THE AUTHOR

Dr. Frances Hutner is a labor economist with a special interest in women's issues. An invited speaker at Yale University during the clerical workers' strike in 1984-85, she has made numerous presentations on comparable worth to business and professional associations. In 1980 she testified before the Equal Employment Opportunity Commission as an expert on the economics of job segregation and wage discrimination.

In addition to her involvement with women's economic issues, Dr. Hutner is president of the Princeton Research Forum and an active director of two public utilities in New England. In recent years she has taught economics at Stevens Institute of Technology, Rider College, and Rutgers University.

Dr. Hutner received her B.A. from Middlebury College, and an M.A. and Ph.D. in economics from Columbia University.